KANT AS PHILOSOPHICAL THEOLOGIAN

Kant as Philosophical Theologian

Bernard M. G. Reardon
*formerly Head, Department of Religious Studies
University of Newcastle upon Tyne*

BARNES & NOBLE BOOKS
TOTOWA, NEW JERSEY

© Bernard M. G. Reardon 1988

First published in the USA 1988 by
BARNES & NOBLE BOOKS
81 ADAMS DRIVE
TOTOWA, NEW JERSEY, 07512

ISBN: 0-389-20759-4

Printed in Hong Kong

Library of Congress Cataloging-in-Publication Data
Reardon, Bernard M. G.
Kant as philosophical theologian.
1. Kant, Immanuel, 1724–1804—Contribution in philosophical theology. 2. Philosophical theology.
I. Title.
B2799.R4.R38 1988   200'.1   87-15503
ISBN 0-389-20759-4

Contents

Preface ix

Introduction: The Young Kant – Pietism and Rationalism 1
    The Age of Enlightenment 1
    The Pietist Movement 4
    Rationalism and Deism 8
    Kant's Upbringing and Education 19

PART ONE: THE TRUE BASIS OF THEISM

1 The Pre-Critical Period 27
    The Early Writings 27
    A Question-Mark over Metaphysics 33

2 The So-Called Proofs of Divine Existence 40
    'A Critical Inquiry into the Faculty of Reason' 40
    The Case against Rational Theology 41

3 The Moral Argument 49
    Kant's Ethical Teaching 49
    God as a Postulate of the Practical Reason 54
    A Metaphysic of Faith 60
    Immortality 65

4 Teleology 68
    'The Critique of Judgment' 68
    'Purpose' in Nature 70

Contents

5	**Rational Theology Reviewed, and the Question of Theodicy**	76
	Kant's Lectures on Philosophical Theology	76
	Where Reason Falters	79

PART TWO: INTERPRETING CHRISTIANITY

6	**The Radical Evil in Human Nature**	87
	'Religion within the Limits of Reason Alone'	87
	The Evil in Man is Willed	93
	Conversion	101
7	**Good and Evil in Conflict**	110
	The Opposing Principles	110
	The Good Principle Personified	111
	The Devil's Claim to Lordship over Man	116
	Miracles	120
8	**The Victory of Good over Evil**	123
	The Ethical 'State of Nature'	123
	The Ethical Commonwealth as a Church	125
	Revelation, Church Doctrine and Scripture	128
	What the Coming of the Kingdom of God Means	134
	Historical Religion	137
	Religious Mysteries: the Trinity	140
9	**Institutionalism in Religion**	145
	What Is the True Service of God?	145
	'Afterdienst'	149
	Conscience and Belief	151
	The Means of Grace	153

	Contents	vii
10	Last Thoughts on Philosophy of Religion	157
	The 'Opus Postumum'	157
	The Idea of God Once More	158
11	Conclusion	167
	Retrospect	167
	Kant and Modern Theology	177

References and Notes   188
Select Bibliography   210
Index   211

Preface

My aim in this book has been to provide some account of Kant's philosophy in so far as it treats of belief in God and the nature and obligations of religion, which for Kant himself of course meant the Christian religion and more especially that particular form of it – Lutheran Pietism – in which he had been nurtured as a child. Kant's later views on religion had much in common with those very generally held by 'enlightened' opinion in his century but he never, I think, cast off the Pietist influence of his early years. His philosophical treatment of religious problems was, however, of such scope and importance that he may fairly be described as the founder of the study now known as Philosophy of Religion. I have sought to present his thinking in this field from his *Allgemeine Naturgeschichte* of 1755 to the *Opus Postumum*, of which latter we now have, since its publication by the Berlin Academy, the complete text. But most attention has been paid to *Die Religion innerhalb der Grenzen der blossen Vernunft*, for which purpose I have used the English translation by Theodore M. Greene and Hoyt H. Hudson, first published in 1934 but currently available in the Harper Torchbook edition of 1960. I have to thank the Open Court Publishing Co., Inc. for their kind permission to quote from it as freely as I have done.

Introduction: The Young Kant – Pietism and Rationalism

THE AGE OF ENLIGHTENMENT

In the year 1784 Immanuel Kant wrote an essay the title of which posed the question *Was ist Aufklärung?* – 'What is Enlightenment?' No one at that date was in a better position than he either to ask or to answer it, for the author himself was both a product and a highly typical representative of the age to which the epithet 'enlightened' has become attached; as he also, through his own critical philosophy, was among the most potent forces by which its characteristic tendencies were eventually checked or at least diverted into new channels. The reply he gave to his question was, briefly, that 'Enlightenment' – although the translation of *Aufklärung* is not as easy as might appear – signifies the advance of man beyond a state of voluntary immaturity: of unwillingness, that is, to use his own intelligence except under the guidance of another. What the modern epoch required of him was to release himself from this self-incurred tutelage and to trust instead to his own understanding. Not that this new liberty had already been attained; by no means. 'But', says Kant, 'we live, if not in an enlightened age altogether, then surely in one of enlightenment in which the free-ranging intelligence is now active and abroad.' And a liberated intelligence would eventually lead to liberty of action. To that extent Kant was an optimist in outlook, but the essay, a work of his own ripest years, reveals that his confidence was not untempered. The brash self-assurance of all too many who extolled the name of Reason, in Germany as well as in France, was misplaced. A right use of the understanding would be gained only by 'a genuine reform in habits of thought' such as was the responsibility of contemporary philosophers and men of letters to initiate and pursue. One must attain to a knowledge of what *reason* really is, alike in its reach and in its limitations. To have attempted this prime task, systematically and thoroughly, was

1

Kant's own signal achievement and distinction. And in no area, he believed, was a sound rationality more important than that of religion, the subject to which the last of his principal writings, *Religion within the Limits of Reason Alone*, is wholly devoted. Kant's personal upbringing had been strictly religious, according to the standards of evangelical piety, and in his own moralistic way a religious man he certainly could be said to have remained: it behoves us, he insisted, to believe in God, even though divine existence be incapable of proof. But as an upholder of the right of free-thinking, and responsive as he was to the demands of the critical intellect, he was convinced that Christian doctrine could and should be re-stated in terms which the moral reason will endorse. Modern man has to learn to be autonomous – to see that the needs of faith, like the imperatives of duty, are in essence the fulfilment of his own nature as a rational being.

The principles of the Enlightenment were already at work in the later decades of the seventeenth century, and in their origin may be traced back to the Renaissance. But it was in the eighteenth century that they received explicit statement, thus conferring upon the age its most clearly identifiable tone. For the eighteenth century was an age of critical questioning of a kind hitherto without precedent in the Christian era. In the political and social orders this critical spirit culminated in the French Revolution and the collapse of the *ancien régime*. In that of religion and philosophy its effects were more widely diffused and of more fundamental import. It challenged the immemorial supernaturalism of Christian belief, whether Catholic or Protestant, and with it the authority of ecclesiastical institutions either as privileged organs of society or as claiming control of the intellectual and moral freedom of the individual. Rather did it seek an explanation of the world and the life of man through principles of knowledge seen as universally valid. Nothing therefore lay beyond the pale of critical analysis or utilitarian reformism. In matters of religion the Enlightenment denigrated tradition, which it readily equated with superstition and priestcraft, and extolled the right and the capacity of the individual judgment not merely in its personal and subjective aspect but as the vehicle of that universal Reason of which each individual consciousness was the repository. True religion would consist in the affirmation of truths approving themselves to the intelligence and conscience of any 'reasonable' man.

This of itself implied a corresponding view of human nature. Here again the basic conception was abstract. What above all was stressed was man's intrinsic rationality and hence his intrinsic capability of good. In so far as he had failed to demonstrate that capability under historic conditions it was because he had always been thwarted by social institutions, political and ecclesiastical, that rested upon a corrupt disposal of power but which in themselves were essentially contingent and removable, however long established they might have been. And nature, in man as in the physical world at large, is inherently beneficent, despite so many adventitious appearances to the contrary. Progress towards perfection might be slow. 'It took centuries', wrote d'Alembert, 'to make a beginning; it will take centuries to bring it to an end.' Yet, in the words of Gibbon, 'the experience of four thousand years should enlarge our hopes and diminish our apprehensions'. In retrospect the fanaticism and cruelty which marred the Reformation and the period of religious wars would be superseded by good will and tolerance. For too long man had walked in cultural darkness, but the light of a new day was upon him to show how fair was the world which the benevolent Author of Nature had given him as the sphere of his potential felicity. Knowledge might be almost indefinitely extended, but it was not necessary to know all things, and the spirit of the Enlightenment was pragmatic. 'If', said Locke, 'we can find out those measures whereby a rational creature, put in that state which man is in this world, may and ought to govern his opinions, and actions depending thereon, we need not be troubled that other things escape our knowledge.' Humanity's real good consists in virtue and happiness.

The Enlightenment view of man was thus a priori and static, based upon a conception of his nature purely as a rational and moral being whose essential character time and circumstance do not alter. The portrait of him drawn from his historical existence may be dismissed as false because in the long run composed only of accidents and irrelevancies. The mental outlook of the age of reason, even though it was the same eighteenth century that witnessed the actual birth of the historical method, was for the most part deficient in historical sense. The genetic approach to the study of human affairs – an interest in growth as such, in evolution and in continuity – was not considered instructive. Unsurprisingly, any understanding of religion as a historical phenomenon was almost wholly lacking. Even orthodoxy chose to defend its positions by abstract reasoning. The truth of religion was not to be discovered by investigating its origin and development, since whatever was of value in it was by definition eternal and immutable. Mankind, that is to say, had always possessed the truth, even though the conditions of life here on earth may have forced it into obscurity. Christianity might hence be deemed to be in fact 'as old as the Creation', provided its content is stated in a manner universally intelligible. For religious truth, in this restricted meaning of the idea, is incompatible with the confusing diversity of the beliefs and practices which actually exist. That truth might be found in the diversity itself, that it might assume, according to time and place, a variety of forms or manifest itself in differing degrees, was not appreciated and in any case would have been thought inconsistent with the criteria of right judgment. In themselves historical events were to be looked on only as contingencies unable to ground the permanently necessary principles on which genuine religion must rest. This defect of historical sympathy and insight is to be discerned even in Hume, skilled historiographer though he was. And the same assuredly goes for Kant. Yet the critical, questioning, erosive spirit of the age served an end by no means purely negative. The slogan, *Ecrasez l'infâme!*, although its use might turn out to be crassly undiscriminating, could not be ignored. The result was an exhilarating feeling of freedom, above all in France, where, with Voltaire as its most eloquent spokesman, the new secular drive in society was especially evident. But in Germany also rationalism was an indigenous growth, and it was natural enough – indeed inevitable – that the young Kant himself should soon register its effects in his own mind.

THE PIETIST MOVEMENT

His upbringing, however, had been pietistic, pietism being a phase in German Protestantism which may well be regarded as the very antithesis of rationalism, but which some would consider as having itself nurtured the *Aufklärung*. Either view is in fact exaggerative. That pietism and rationalism were opposed on a number of basic theological issues, in particular the place of revelation and the authority of the Bible, is incontestable, but they also had something in common, chiefly their antagonism to Lutheran orthodoxy, which by the middle of the seventeenth century had on its doctrinal side hardened into scholasticism, and on its institutional into a formalistic churchiness. Justification by faith alone had come virtually to mean an intellectually binding dogma, while the Bible was used less as a source of spiritual inspiration than an armoury to be drawn on *ad libitum* by ecclesiastical polemicists. Lutheran theology appeared, in truth, to be little more than a dry intellectualism, tinder for the always smouldering fires of controversy. Hence between a highly professionalized clergy and the laity at large a widening gap had opened. Pietism, one cannot but conclude, was a fitting protest at this. Yet to argue that Enlightenment thinking actually sprang from pietism is a mistake. The influences determining the former were many and complex, and in the main antecedent to the latter's appearance. More satisfactory is it to regard the two movements as in a sense parallel, alike hostile to the prevailing ecclesiasticism and theologism.

The founder of German pietism, as is generally agreed, was Philipp Jakob Spener (1735–1705), a man of deep religious feeling who in early life had been much affected by Johann Arndt's *Von wahren Christenthums* ('Of True Christianity').[1] In 1666 he was appointed senior pastor at Frankfurt-am-Main, where in pursuance of an idea that had occurred to him when a preacher at Strassburg cathedral he inaugurated his *collegia pietatis* – twice-weekly private gatherings for devotional fellowship and Bible study. His intentions were of the best and his catechetical discourses were highly considered, but the dangers of freelance religiosity soon became obvious, although Spener himself was no separatist. He is best remembered for his little book *Pia Desideria*, published at Frankfurt in 1675, which attracted wide attention. Whilst deploring the religious condition of the times he expressed his confidence in a brighter future, provided a proper spiritual discipline were embraced. This would include, besides assiduous Bible reading under pastoral guidance – 'the Word', he declared, 'must penetrate to our heart' – a genuine resort to the principle of the priesthood of all believers by according laymen their due place in church government. Spener taught that religion involves action more than theory and that unbelievers and heretics should be treated with charity and pastoral concern rather than pharisaical censure. He also pointed to the need for improved theological training, again emphasising its practical aspect, and for a simpler and more direct mode of preaching aimed at the needs of ordinary folk and offering them a religion of the 'inner or new man', with personal faith – *fides qua creditur*, a disposition of the believer himself – as its very 'soul'. But Spener's methods did not satisfy the sticklers for orthodoxy and he left Frankfurt to assume a new post as court chaplain at Dresden, where he was at first well received. For here too he ran into trouble before long, and in 1691 he was glad to accept a call to the pastorate of the Nikolaikirche in Berlin, with the sympathetic favour of the monarch, Elector Frederick III of Brandenburg, afterwards Frederick I of Prussia.

In this more congenial atmosphere Spener's teaching became increasingly influential, and he was to witness the establishment of a theological school after his own heart in the newly-founded (1694) University of Halle, which for long was to be a main centre of pietist activity. Among his supporters there was one Christian Thomasius (1655–1720), a man of progressive opinions and a vigorous campaigner for toleration, even of atheists and witches. Yet Spener himself was again not spared the *odium theologicum*, chiefly on the part of the theological faculties of Wittenberg and Leipzig, the former of which charged him with no fewer than two hundred and sixty five errors. Nevertheless he managed to weather the storm, tenaciously upholding his well-known views, in his *Theologische Bedenken* (1700–2) and other writings, until his death. Throughout his whole career he showed himself to be a man not only of strong convictions but of sound judgment and practical resource.

Spener's principal disciple was August Hermann Francke (1663–1727), who came under pietist influence while still a student at Halle. Its attraction for him grew when he moved to Leipzig and devoted himself to Bible study along pietist lines. Here, with two companions, he founded a 'Collegium Philobiblicum' in order to promote such study among university graduates, with the purpose of directing their interests towards a serious religious end. This venture, which had Spener's warm commendation, proved very popular and Francke's own biblical lectures drew large audiences. Like Spener, however, he encountered opposition that resulted in the eventual closure of the college and the termination of his public discourses. He then took up a pastorate at Erfurt, only to meet with renewed antagonism leading to his abrupt dismissal from office in 1691. Happily Spener was able to secure for him the chair – albeit without salary – of Greek and Oriental languages at Halle, along with a new pastorate at nearby Glaucha. Here at last he was to find the right environment and he made the place his home for the rest of his life. Revered both as an inspiring teacher and as a dedicated pastor, Francke was a man of indubitable charisma – energetic, learned, eloquent and saintly. He certainly left his own impress on the movement, although as a writer he was less effective than Spener and his personal influence was more localized.[2]

The strength of pietism lay in its stress on religion not only as inwardness but as a way of life whose dynamic was prayer and the study of the scriptures. Theology was valued much less as an intellectual quest than as a means to spiritual enrichment, as a matter of the heart to be tested in experience. Thus the cardinal Lutheran doctrine of justification *sola fide* signified above all the individual's inner re-birth, its formal definition being something wholly subordinate. Similarly the Bible was to be read as the source of the believer's personal knowledge of divine revelation. But pietism also had its weaknesses. It encouraged an excessive subjectivism and individualism, especially later, under the influence of Zinzendorf,[3] and although it had theological implications of its own it carried its neglect of intellectual values too far. The Bible study groups tended to be self-absorbed and disregardful of the wider fellowship of the church. Again, it came too readily to be assumed that every believer, as evidence of his vocation, should have undergone a certain type of conversion-experience, following a specific pattern. A particular style of language also developed, unfamiliar and sometimes distasteful to such as did not share it; while most serious of all perhaps, religious emotion came for many to be looked on as the express mark of their acceptance before God. The movement might have been saved from these growing defects by more central control, but this it lacked. What emerges, however, as its most positive features were its ethical and philanthropic concern, and its belief that the real value of Christian doctrine is to be assessed in moral terms. It was this side of pietism, one may fairly judge, which left a permanent impression on Kant's own outlook, despite his later reaction against what he came to see as the rather mawkish religiosity forced upon him in his youth.

RATIONALISM AND DEISM

But if pietism represents one aspect of the German Enlightenment, the other, the rationalistic, is certainly the more typical. Indeed rationalism could be said to relate to pietism by filling the intellectual vacuum which the latter, with its want of constructive theological or philosophical interest, had created; a deficiency to which the learned New Testament commentary of Johannes Albrecht Bengel (1687–1752), *Gnomon Novi Testamenti* (1742),[4] a work well thought of and used by John Wesley, would appear to be the sole really notable exception. Yet there is an unquestionable affinity between seventeenth-century Lutheran orthodoxy itself and its rationalist aftermath.[5] In fact there was a conscious element of continuity between the two, as is indicated by the earlier rationalists' evident determination to stay within the bounds of received doctrine. Like its counterpart in England, as instanced at any rate by Chillingworth and Tillotson,[6] 'orthodox' rationalism looked to the Bible as the one authoritative fount of doctrine and was generally content to follow the usual Protestant exegesis, as orthodoxy itself was confident not only that the biblical teaching was acceptable to all reasonable minds but that the essentials of Christian belief were capable of rational demonstration. Thus it was frequently argued that the true meaning of scripture must be apparent to the intelligent and attentive reader irrespective of any antecedent 'change of heart' on his part. Or in the jargon of the day, a *theologia irregenitorum* is quite feasible. This was the view upheld by scholars like Johann August Ernesti (1707–81), professor of theology at Leipzig, who maintained that to read the New Testament as one would any other book, treating it historically and philologically, would suffice to uncover its meaning, and Johann David Michaelis (1717–91), professor of philosophy and Oriental languages at Göttingen, who employed all the resources available to him to prove the rational credibility of scripture, even though, like Ernesti, he believed in verbal inspiration and taught a supernaturalistic Christianity. For neither of these authors did rational religion imply mere reductionism.

However, more characteristic of the *Aufklärung* was the kind of rationalism presented by the Leibnizian–Wolffian philosophy, for which clarity and 'reasonableness' were the immediate criteria of truth: what involved contradiction was manifestly impossible and what was affirmed as actual had to be shown to have sufficient grounds. Furthermore, the influence of English deism was already being felt in Germany by the close of the seventeenth century and became increasingly pervasive over the ensuing fifty years or so. The writings of the 'father' of deism, Lord Herbert of Cherbury (1581–1648), brother of the priest-poet George Herbert, were introduced to German readers not later than 1680,[7] while John Toland's *Christianity not Mysterious*, published in 1696 – a year after Locke's *Reasonableness of Christianity*, to which it was clearly indebted – was appreciatively discussed by Leibniz.[8] (Toland himself had resided in Germany for some months.) The deist controversy in England, which attained its height by 1720, was eagerly reported by sympathetic German commentators, and by 1743 the chief deistical publications had found German translators.[9] Indeed by the mid-eighteenth century *Freidenken – A Discourse of Free-thinking* (1713) was the title of one of Anthony Collins's most popular works – had become part of the spectrum of public opinion and in theological circles the entire English intellectual 'war' of treatise and pamphlet, attack and riposte, was the focus of keen attention. Wolff's disciple, the theologian Siegmund Jakob Baumgarten (1706–57), had discussed it publicly in all its aspects. Kant's own early acquaintance with its ideas, whether direct or indirect, is therefore fairly to be assumed.[10]

Leibniz (1646–1716) himself was much influenced by Lutheran scholasticism, through the works in particular of Jakob Thomasius and Abraham Calov. This is evident in his *Theodicée*, in which he considers the problem of evil and why the Almighty allows it to exist. His own answer is that the scheme of the created world, being in the nature of things the best possible, must nevertheless afford a place for sin, so that actual moral evil constitutes no real objection either to God's omnipotence or to his benevolence. For the possibility of sin is a condition of human freedom. Whether Leibniz succeeded in his aim of reconciling the Christian revelation with his own rationalist principles may well be questioned. Voltaire satirized him in *Candide* as Dr Pangloss. But his follower and popularizer Christian Wolff (1679–1754) had no doubt that divine revelation and human reason were fully consonant. He professed indeed to uphold the autonomy of theology, urging the danger of confusing it with philosophy and insisting that if each after its own fashion contains the truth the two cannot conflict. Scripture, as authoritatively revealed, is one thing, philosophy, with its methods of rational demonstration, another, but supernatural and natural truth are complementary not competitive. Yet the very error he warned others of he fell into himself, and his system is now remembered only as a thoroughgoing effort to fuse natural and supernatural in the crucible of a formalistic rationalism.

A native of Breslau – now Wraclaw, in Poland – Wolff was educated at the city's gymnasium and subsequently at the university of Jena, where in addition to his philosophical studies he embarked on a course in mathematics, which discipline greatly attracted him as paradigmatic of scientific method generally. In 1707 he assumed a post at Halle, lecturing on mathematics and physics as well as philosophy. Here he very soon made a name for himself as a gifted teacher, and his reputation was further enhanced by his early publications, which appeared in German instead of the usual scholarly medium of Latin,[11] although he returned to the dead language for literary purposes later in his career. His ascent to fame was altogether remarkable. King and government honoured him, and scholars throughout Germany paid tribute to his abilities. In some religious circles, on the other hand, he was less well thought of, the pietists, whose beliefs had by now acquired the status of orthodoxy, considering his teachings to be subversive of faith. A lecture of his, *De sinasmi philosophia practica*, in which he ranked Confucius along with Jesus among the great prophets, brought hostilities to a head.[12] His critics denounced it as sub-Christian. The upshot was that in 1723 Wolff was deposed from office and banished from the kingdom. Thereafter he resided at Marburg, where the university gave him a professorship. These years, in fact, turned out to be the high summer of his lifetime, when he attracted students from far and wide, gaining adherents to his doctrine and reaping a second harvest of public honours. Meanwhile attitudes towards him in Prussia were undergoing change. By 1733 the king decided on his recall and issued instructions that his works were to be expressly prescribed in university teaching. The monarch's death delayed Wolff's restoration, but his successor, Frederick the Great, who had decided opinions of his own on such matters, proclaimed him to be the greatest philosopher of the age, and appointed him both privy councillor and vice-chancellor of Halle university, to which he triumphantly returned in 1740. His position as the foremost philosophical thinker and teacher in Germany was now unassailed, and so it continued until he ceded place to the new master at Königsberg, whose own distinction, after Wolff's death, gained increasing recognition.

At the root of Wolff's system lay his conviction that the aim of philosophy is to promote human well-being by a reasoned understanding of the nature of things. An admirable teacher himself, nothing seemed to him more desirable than clear instruction, and the first requirement of any philosophy had to be order, balance and lucidity. The danger is that even these qualities can be bought too highly if they also mean loss of contact with reality. Thus Wolff defined philosophy as 'the science of everything that is possible, showing why and how it is so'. But the possible he saw only as the non-contradictory. At any rate, the principle complementary to that of non-contradiction, namely sufficient reason, which for his mentor Leibniz was the necessary test of factual truth, Wolff either disregarded or else equated with non-contradiction. Kant esteemed Wolff as an 'excellent analyst', and analysis no doubt was his *forte*, but his actual procedure betrayed him into a superficial schematism. His most considerable philosophical work dealt with ontology, which he judged to be of fundamental importance as treating of propositions valid for all possible forms of being.[13] He held indeed that discoveries in mathematics or in physics – even experimental physics – are capable, given the right method, of being deduced from ontological principles. Ontology, that is, will not only specify an entity's predicates, it will demonstrate them. Thence Wolff passes to cosmology, which he sees as the a priori science of any possible material world; in a word, its *necessary* characteristics. Physics, contrastingly, is the empirical study of the contingent characteristics of the actual world, even though ultimately it can be shown to be a mechanism determined in all its parts.

Wolff, however, places great emphasis on the human consciousness. Rational psychology, which posits the existence of the soul as a power capable of representing the world, is concerned with the problem of knowledge; and although initially its representations may be unclear the soul nevertheless is impelled towards perfection and away from imperfection. In consciousness this impulse becomes desire and purpose. But Wolff follows Leibniz in not envisaging any direct interaction between soul and body, preferring to see the two as coexisting in a pre-restablished relation of harmony. He also attempts to provide rational demonstration of the soul's simplicity and immortality.

Although Wolff conceives the world and man mechanistically he does not regard them as self-explanatory. They require a pre-existent and transcendent ground or cause, namely God, whose being Wolff purports to prove by means of the well-worn scholastic arguments, so that his system is rounded off with a natural or rational theology. Here again he follows Leibniz by re-habilitating the aprioristic ontological argument, but he buttresses it with the cosmological, of the effectiveness of which he is particularly persuaded. All the same, natural theology is to be clearly distinguished from revealed, and Wolff is careful to avoid the sphere of church dogma while accepting the essential rationality of the basic principles of religious belief. The omnipotence of God, he contends, makes revelation a conceptual possibility and his goodness renders it probable. Yet Wolff does not deny that the actual content of revelation is such as in principle to be discoverable by human reason, even if only tardily and painfully. Nor does he think that revelation is above critical judgment. To begin with, there must be an evident want of it. The world having been created as an orderly system there would seem, *prima facie*, to be no need of special divine intervention. But man's condition demanded it. Further, revelation must not appear to contradict what the human understanding is already able to infer as to God's nature; nor of course can it be such as to negate the primary truths of reason itself. Wolff does not discount miracles; they are not impossible events, though they have no evident natural cause. At least, the knowledge they contradict is not, according to Wolff, that of 'necessary' truths but only of 'contingent', by which he presumably means the knowledge of nature as stated in terms of natural law. Finally, Wolff is assured that a revelation claiming to be divine must be plain and unambiguous, couched in language not only intelligible but fitting.[14]

Historians of philosophy now afford Christian Wolff small enough room, but in the setting of his own time he was a conspicuous figure. His talents were on any showing by no means negligible, and he expressed the thinking and aspiration of his age with a degree of success no contemporary of his in western Europe seriously rivalled. His skill lay in popularizing ideas that otherwise might have remained opaque to ordinary educated opinion in Germany. He professed to have expounded Leibniz, and the claim has a measure of justification. Leibniz's was a highly original and creative mind which our own century has learned how to appreciate, but his thought was fragmentary in its presentation and without overall unity. This Wolff himself sought to give it, but the disciple, as often happens, lacked the perceptiveness and understanding which a genuine development of the master's doctrine would have needed. Thus he achieves comprehensiveness but not depth, and what finally emerges has lost the sparkle of the original. That Wolffianism should have gained its prestige on the very eve of the appearance of such a philosophical genius as Kant meant that in the perspective of time it became completely overshadowed.[15] Wolff had his followers, however – men like Gottshed and Alexander Gottlieb Baumgarten (1714–62) – who added this or that point to the system, if to no lasting purpose. Opposition to Wolff came from orthodox Lutheran churchmen, of whom Valentin Ernst Löscher (1673–1749) of Dresden was typical, but mainly from pietists like Joachim Lange (1670–1744) of Halle. The former objected to his subordination of theology to philosophy, the latter to his intellectualism generally. In their eyes Wolffianism destroyed the true character of faith.

Better known today, perhaps, than Wolff is one who, among those to be counted as his followers, was certainly the most radical, Hermann Samuel Reimarus (1694–1768), the greater part of whose career was spent as professor of Oriental languages at the university of his native Hamburg. He perpetuated Wolff's theological rationalism in two works on natural religion published in 1754 and 1756 respectively. But Reimarus was also markedly influenced by the English deists, by whom he may have been deflected from the traditional biblical religion of the day, towards which he adopted the decidedly critical attitude that became known to the educated world with G. E. Lessing's publication in 1774 and later of the notorious *Wolfenbüttel Fragments*, written by Reimarus when in charge of the Duke of Brunswick's library at Wolfenbüttel. These extracts from an unpublished larger work having the title 'Apology or Defence of the Rational Worshipper of God', were widely regarded as an open attack on the authenticity of the biblical tradition and the authority of historic Christianity.[16] Their appearance precipitated controversy immediately. They were assailed not only by conservatives but by liberal theologians like Johann Salomo Semler (1725–91), who issued his own reply to the *Fragments* in 1779. It was the seventh extract, dealing with the aims of Jesus and his disciples, which caused most trouble. Jesus was here depicted as a purely human figure with messianic illusions who preached a simple and practical morality in anticipation of the imminent arrival of the kingdom of God on earth. It was further contended that after his death Jesus' followers made away with his body, declared that he had risen to life again, and founded a religious community in his name dedicated to preaching his divinity. Reimarus in these writings was obviously going a long way beyond the rationalism of Wolff, which he otherwise shared. Wolff believed in Christianity as a divine revelation and was concerned to defend it as such by reasoned argument. Reimarus rejected all idea of revelation in a supernatural sense and dismissed miracle as irreconcilable with natural law. Testimony of the biblical miracles, including of course Jesus' resurrection, was therefore an imposture. The only religion he could envisage as acceptable to a rational man was one based wholly on the principles of reason and morality, which alone offered a true way of salvation. For salvation had to be a universal possibility and only natural religion, uncommitted to the falsities, witting or unwitting, of so-called revelation, has universal standing. Indeed Reimarus was not merely prepared, like some of the English deists, to dispense with Christianity as otiose, he was frankly opposed to it. Its eventual disappearance he thought not only inevitable but desirable.

Semler, a professor at Halle, combined rationalism in theology with deep personal piety. But he could not accept the orthodox doctrine of biblical inspiration and felt bound to recognize, from his study of the history of the canons of both the Old and the New Testament, that the scriptures are, in their form, human documents, however divine their essential content. His own theory was that although the biblical writings are inspired the Holy Spirit did not disdain to use human means capable, as impartial investigation shows, of error in matters of scientific and historical fact.[17]

Lessing himself, poet and critic and the fountain-head of classical German literature, could be said to be the very embodiment of the *Aufklärung*.[18] His theological writings belong in the main to the last period of his life. The only religion he could seriously contemplate was the religion of reason,[19] although with the rationalistic theologians of the day he had little sympathy – *Halbphilosophen*, as he called them. If in certain respects critical of Reimarus, he believed that the latter had raised a problem of fundamental importance, and in his personal contribution to the dispute over the *Fragments*, he pointed out the futility of any attempt to reach demonstrative certainty from data which, like the scriptural prophecies and miracles, are themselves among the contingencies of history and depend on the vagaries of human testimony.[20] 'Prophecies fulfilled', he wrote, 'which I myself experience, are one thing: prophecies fulfilled of which I only know from history that others declare themselves to have experienced then, are another. Miracles, which I see with my own eyes, and have opportunity to test for myself, are one thing: miracles, of which I only know from history that others declare themselves to have seen and tested them, are another.' The conclusion is thus inevitable: 'If no historical truth can be demonstrated, then nothing can be demonstrated by historical truths. That is to say: *accidental truths of history can never become the proof of necessary truths of reason.*' And Lessing's inference would not have been denied by Kant. But although the former distinguishes sharply between truths that are capable of universal demonstration, and those the knowledge of which depends on evidence always less than totally verifiable, he does not dismiss history as scientifically irrelevant. Rather does he see it as a living force which discloses the fact of the gradual development of man's spiritual nature, intellectual and religious. It is indeed the revelatory process by which the human race is nurtured and educated. His famous essay, *Die Erziehung des Menschengeschlechts* ('The Education of the Human Race') (1780),[21] opens with the statement that what 'education is to the individual, revelation is to the race'. The implication here is that revelation is not something *ab extra* and heteronomous, but is substantial with man's own historic experience. 'Education gives to man nothing which he might not educe out of himself; it gives him that which he might educe out of himself, only quicker and more easily. In the same way, too, revelation gives nothing to the human species, which the human reason left to itself might not attain; only it has given, and still gives to it, the most important of these things earlier.' A particular people was chosen to receive it for that special purpose. But the Old Testament was only a primer, so to speak; a better way was to come in the person of Christ. He it was who first taught practically the immortality of the soul. The learning process does not end there, however. Just as, regarding the divine unity, we can dispense with the Old Testament, although that was the lesson it clearly taught, so, regarding the doctrine of immortality, we now can dispense with the New. Likewise will it be with other biblical truths, and Lessing himself attempts to offer moral explanations of the doctrines of the trinity, original sin and the satisfaction of Christ. Providence, he says, may be inscrutable, but man has always the moral law, apart from which there can be no spiritual blessedness.

In his posthumous essays and fragments Lessing distinguishes between the Christian religion, which makes of Christ an object of worship – though as to the precise nature of Christ, he thinks, no two persons will agree – and the religion which he 'as a man recognized and practised' and which therefore is antecedent to the gospels. Finally, the view set forth in Lessing's well-known drama, *Nathan der Weise*, which Nathan the Jew voices in dialogue with a Christian at the time of the Crusades, is that creeds are not of importance, but rather charity and tolerance. Divine truth is a goal towards which, over the ages and by divers paths, mankind is slowly advancing – a belief which brings Lessing to the verge of Romantic historicism.

What pietism and rationalism had in common, then, was the conviction that the meaning and value of Christianity lie in its practical ethic. This they sought to emphasise either by reducing the actual content of Christian doctrine to the principle of 'natural' religion, or by virtually denying to such doctrine any speculative interest whatever. But rationalism proved much the more potent force intellectually, and although the influence of pietism was by no means eclipsed – as witness not only the Moravian Brethren among whom Schleiermacher was reared but the early nineteenth-century neo-pietism of Gottfried Mencken (1768–1831) and the Berlin circle of Baron von Kottwitz – the effect of rationalism was to present a challenge to orthodoxy such as very largely determined the nature and direction of theological developments in Germany throughout the nineteenth century. And the headwater of these developments was Kant, in whom an Enlightenment religion of 'reason' drew nevertheless on a tributary pietism.

By the time of Kant's birth at Königsberg in 1724 the old East Prussian city had for many years been a centre of pietism, although at the university – the Albertina, as it was called[22] – the Wolffian philosophy was also fairly well established, with the result that tension between the two, given their disparity in temper and outlook, could not for long be contained, and in the ensuing struggle for predominance it was the former which had to cede place. However, the ascendancy of Wolffianism was not fully attained until well into the fifth decade of the century and throughout the years of Kant's childhood and youth a certain balance, even a kind of partnership, was maintained. This was achieved mainly by the strong personal influence of Franz Albert Schultz (1692–1762), a man to whom Kant always acknowledged a deep sense of gratitude. Schultz had imbibed his pietism at Halle, but he was scarcely less affected by Wolff's philosophy; indeed it was said that Wolff signalled Schultz out for special praise because of his unusually thorough understanding of his teaching. In 1730, when at the age of thirty-nine, Schultz was appointed pastor of the Altstädtische Kirche of Königsberg and soon became an important figure not only in ecclesiastical and civic life – he was also a school superintendant and a government official – but at the university too, where his instruction seemed able to combine evangelical fervour with philosophic rigour. His reputation stood high also in the Prussian capital, where he enjoyed the royal esteem.

Schultz was not the only teacher at the university to advocate Wolffianism, and by 1730 it counted a fair number of adherents among the academic staff, at any rate at the more junior level, for at that date pietism was still so firmly rooted in the city that the profession of rationalist principles, even in the service of orthodox faith, had to be made with some caution. But a change in the intellectual climate gradually became evident, not least because of its penetration by deist ideas from England which had all the appeal of *avant-garde* novelty. Among those who had studied the English writers was Martin Knutzen (1713–51), like Kant a native of and life-long resident in Königsberg and a pupil of Schultz's at the university.[23] Although his own pietism was wholly sincere and he never went back on its principles, his bent was to philosophy, which inevitably meant Wolffian rationalism. In fact he was too closely identified with it for him ever to gain the academic preferment to which his abilities entitled him, but his influence in the university was potent and generations of students succumbed to it, the youthful Kant among them.[24]

If Knutzen's first love was philosophy, his second unquestionably was theology. Notable among his works was a treatise with an overtly apologetic aim entitled 'A Philosophical Demonstration of the Truth of the Christian Religion' (*Philosophische Beweis von der Wahrheit der christlichen Religion*), published in 1740. The author's purpose was to offer a systematic account of Christian belief with all the characteristic pietist emphases, underlining the fundamental importance of faith and the practical needs of the spirit, but seeking also to show that Christianity can be justified at the bar of philosophical reason and so to defend it against the inroads of doubt. The work is remarkably free from the exaggerations and emotional excesses which all too often marred pietist writing, as it certainly gave no encouragement to the kind of morbid asceticism to which religious zealots were sometimes prone. It is a volume which merits the attention of any student of Kant desirous of understanding the latter's own stance on religious matters. A brief survey of its content here is, then, in order.

Knutzen is firmly committed to the Christian belief that a divine revelation is necessary in view of man's impotence to discover for himself a way of salvation and atone for the guilt of his sin. For the measure of his guilt is that his disobedience is an offence against God's infinite righteousness, which of its very nature demands a satisfaction not in man's power to render, try as he might. Human incapacity can only be made good by God's own act, in which he declares not only his righteousness but his mercy. This redeeming act is the incarnation of his Son, the preaching of which makes Christianity unique among religions. For Christ's self-sacrifice is the supreme manifestation alike of the holiness and the loving condescension of God's will, and its example is far more effective in securing man's regeneration than the exaction of punishment could ever have been. The truth of a historical revelation such as this of course requires attestation, and it is provided by the miracle of Christ's resurrection, itself sufficiently well authenticated, Knutzen thinks, by the historical evidence of the gospels. Christian doctrine purports to demonstrate the meaning of Christ's atoning work as dependent on his divine status. The dogma of the trinity therefore is seen to have its due place, albeit as a mystery which reason alone could never have discovered. Similarly the Christian life, illuminated and empowered by scripture and the Spirit, is the appropriation on man's part, after repentance, of the grace of forgiveness and spiritual renewal. Its moral fruit is love for one's fellow-men and growth in personal holiness.

Here certainly is Lutheran pietism, but advanced in reasoned theological shape.

Introduction

KANT'S UPBRINGING AND EDUCATION

Immanuel Kant was baptized, according to custom, on the day following that of his birth, 22 April 1724. His parents were Lutheran pietists of the simple, old-fashioned kind, and this child, their fourth, was, like the others, conscientiously brought up in the ways of religion. His mother's influence was especially strong. As in later life Kant himself declared to a friend: 'I shall never forget my mother, for she implanted and nurtured the first seed of good in me; she opened my heart to the influence of Nature; she awakened and broadened my ideas, and her teachings have had an enduring, beneficent effect on my life.' He mentions in particular how it was she who, little education though she had, would take him outside the city and 'direct [his] attention to the works of God, express herself with pious rapture over His omnipotence, wisdom, and goodness, and impress on [his] heart a deep reverence for the Creator of all things'. Of his home life he says that he never once knew his parents to utter an unbecoming word or do an unworthy act, and that no misunderstanding ever disturbed the harmony of the household. The family's social position was humble – his father was a saddler – and their income was meagre to the point of poverty. It was in these early days that Kant acquired the simple tastes and habits, along with a spirit of self-reliance, which he exhibited throughout life.[25]

In the autumn of 1732, at the age of eight, Kant entered the city's Collegium Fridericianum, a school run on the strictest pietist lines. Academically it was narrow, with a very restricted range of teaching; Latin grammar occupied the chief place, but mathematics and logic were included, although the actual instruction therein seems to have been no more than sketchy. It is said that some history and geography was also taught, the Fridericianum being the first school in Königsberg to do so, but Kant's later interest in the natural sciences was most probably of subsequent growth. Schultz, however, who succeeded J. H. Lysius as the school's director a year after Kant entered it as a pupil, did impress him, as we have seen. Otherwise he had no great opinion of the pedagogic skills of his teachers. The religious regime the boy found oppressive. Not only did religious instruction and devotional exercizes take up a considerable proportion of the time, it was formalistic and apparently more concerned with the techniques of spiritual discipline than with its real aim and substance.

The pupil became increasingly disillusioned and impatient with it. 'He was quite unable', says his biographer Borowski, 'to acquire a taste for that form of piety – or rather affected piety – to which many of his school-fellows seemed able to adapt themselves, even if with low motives.' Afterwards Kant remembered this religious servitude with abhorrence and when he left the school he abandoned religious practices for ever, avoiding church attendance even on official university occasions. Yet he by no means despised the inwardness of pietism; on the contrary, he retained a deep respect for it. What he disliked were its outward observances, which all too easily degenerated into conventionalism. As he wrote to his friend F. T. Rink, a Danzig pastor:[26]

> Even if the religious consciousness of that time, and the conceptions of what is called virtue and piety were by no means clear and satisfactory, it yet contained the root of the matter. One may say of pietism what one will; it suffices that the people to whom it was a serious matter were distinguished in a manner deserving of all respect. They possessed the highest good which man can enjoy – that repose, that cheerfulness, that inner peace which is disturbed by no passions. No want or persecutions rendered them discontent; no controversy was able to stir them to anger or enmity.[27]

Kant matriculated at the university of Königsberg on 24 September 1740, but it is very doubtful whether the tradition that he enrolled in the theological faculty is correct. In fact we know little about his university studies, an ignorance shared even by his friends of after years. His financial situation at the time was straightened enough – of that we do have some record – but he quite evidently declined to equip himself technically for a professional career of any sort. He certainly attended Schultz's lectures on dogmatic theology, but for no other reason, it seems, than intellectual curiosity, as he told Schultz himself. This however is indicative of the attitude of mind he had already developed. His intention was to range over as many fields of human knowledge as possible, for the sheer pleasure of knowing. Actually he much enjoyed these lectures, although they did not have the effect of inducing him to advance his theological learning – apart from reading the occasional book on church history – even in a desultory way, and throughout his career as a university teacher he evinced little or no interest in contemporary theological writing or even the then emerging science of biblical criticism. His intellectual pursuits during his student years were, evidently, the humanities generally, since at this stage he had no wish to confine himself to a single course. On the face of it might look as if he were merely a dilettante. But intellectual frivolity, like any other, did not accord with the young man's serious turn of mind. Whether consciously or not, he was preparing himself to assume that 'synoptic' view of the whole domain of the human understanding which was eventually to unfold the grand perspectives of his own philosophy. Nor was it simply a matter of acquiring theoretical knowledge, however diverse. Kant already was imbued with a sense of the need for intellectual and moral discipline, a temper of mind and spirit, necessary for the kind of life he envisaged ahead of him, a life without worldly ambitions or desire of any material advantages that distinguished achievement might bring him. In this respect his student days truly were a vocational training, if not in accordance with any conventional pattern. The way of life he was to choose was the academic, and even as such it was to prove to be an unusually narrow one: the university in which he studied, in the city in which he was born and schooled, was to be that also in which he taught, year in and year out, first as *Privatdozent* and then as professor, until the failing powers of old age obliged him to retire. To all showing the university lecture-room and his own study provided but a very limited sphere, but they sufficed for the purposes of his life's work.

What precisely were Kant's religious views at the time of his leaving the university is uncertain, but there is no doubt that he had given up the evangelicalism of his childhood, or that he had embraced the Wolffianism of Knutzen. For occupation there was little alternative to service as a private tutor, his first post of the sort being in the family of a Reformed pastor at Juschen, some sixty miles east of Königsberg, and then in the household of a landowner named von Hülsen at Gross-Arnsdorf. That he also acted in the same capacity for Count Keyserling at Rautenburg, near Tilsit, has not been established and is unlikely. In any case, although his social status was only modest and his pecuniary reward still less so, the work involved was such as to afford him ample leisure for study and meditation, for the enrichment of his mind and the working-out of his own ideas. Long afterwards he recalled these days spent in the East Prussian countryside with pleasure.

The year 1749 saw the publication of his first work, *Gedanken von der wahren Schützing der lebendigen Kräfte* ('Thoughts on the True Estimation of Living Forces'), which he had begun three years previously, while still a *studiosus*. This, which dealt with a question of mechanical theory much controverted between Leibnizians and Cartesians, is of interest now solely as showing the direction in which his intellectual concern had moved. Yet although its subject-matter is physics, its orientation is metaphysical and speculative. In regard to former the content is thin in comparison with other treatises in this field that had lately appeared – one by d'Alembert was published only three years before Kant wrote; but as Ernst Cassirer observes, 'even today, when almost all its conclusions are obsolete, the work radiates a charm, a charm that lies not in what it explicitly contains and offers us, but in what it aspires to and promises us'.[28] As its young author himself stated in the preface: 'I imagine that it is sometimes useful to place a certain magnanimous reliance on one's own powers. Confidence of this sort quickens all our efforts and imparts to them a certain buoyancy which greatly assists the search for truth.' One passage, however, is significant in view of his future attainment:

> Our metaphysics is really like many other sciences – only on the threshold of genuine knowledge; God knows if it will ever get farther. It is not hard to see its weakness in much that it undertakes. Prejudice is often found to be the mainstay of its proofs. For this nothing is to blame but the ruling passion of those who would fain extend human knowledge. They are anxious to have a grand philosophy; but the desirable thing is, that it should also be a sound one.

A scheme to encompass all human understanding is a fine idea, but it must be firmly based.

In 1755 Kant secured a post as *Privatdozent* in the university, and for the ensuing fifteen years lectured on a variety of subjects covering not only logic and metaphysics but mathematics and the natural sciences, including physical geography, then a novelty. The interest and sparkle of his discourses attracted numerous and eager audiences; but he had to work long hours – at times up to twenty a week – for a remuneration barely enough to maintain him above the level of poverty. His application, first, in 1756, for the extraordinary (*extraordinarius*) professorship of philosophy, and then, two years later, for the ordinary professorship, which had remained vacant since Knutzen's death, were both unsuccessful.

Part One
The True Basis of Theism

1
The Pre-Critical Period

THE EARLY WRITINGS

Promotion for Kant did not materialize until 1770, when in March of that year he was appointed professor *ordinarius* of logic and metaphysics in his university.[1] His elevation was not only a landmark in his professional career, it may also be seen as the turning-point in his development as a philosophical thinker. Hitherto his interests had to a large extent been scientific, but after 1770, the period of gestation of his 'critical' doctrine, he dedicated himself more or less exclusively to the philosophical pursuits for which his name was to become world-famous. Not that his scientific concern faded, nor that he stood less firmly by the Newtonian physics, the general validity of which he fully accepted. But his efforts henceforth were concentrated on the immense philosophical enterprise which culminated in the publication, over the space of some ten years, of the three great *Critiques* and his attempt therein to reconcile the world of Newtonian science with that of moral experience and religious faith. His inaugural dissertation, 'On the Form and Principles of the Sensible and Intelligible World', was the significant pointer to the new paths his thought was to follow.

But what is usually termed the 'pre-critical' period – roughly the fifteen years or so after 1755 – is not, from our standpoint in this book, simply to be passed over as having little or nothing of relevance to offer. Kant's *Allgemeine Naturgeschichte und Theorie des Himmels* ('General Natural History and Theory of the Heavens'), which appeared in that year, although through lack of advance publicity it received virtually no attention, is to be reckoned among the most notable of his works composed during the period.[2] Dealing with the overall problem of cosmology, it to some degree anticipated Laplace's 'nebular' theory in that author's celebrated *Exposition du système du monde* (1796). The first part, beginning with an account of Newton's planetary system, advances the hypothesis of a similar system for the stellar universe, since the stars are to be regarded as suns like our own – which in fact is one of them – and as forming the aggregate we call the Milky Way. We need not here go along with Kant in his cosmological speculations – for example, his idea of a central star, or 'super-sun', pivotal to our galaxy, as still less that of a super-sun regulating the movements of all the star-systems in space, a notion which modern astronomy would of course dismiss. Nor need we dwell on the second, more strictly cosmogonic part treating of the first state of nature, the formation of the celestial bodies and the causes of their movement and systematic connection, not only in the planetary sphere but in 'creation as a whole'. Here Kant envisages a time when all the matter now condensed in the sun, the planets and the comets existed simply in a gaseous state throughout the space now occupied by these bodies in their revolutions. But the tendency of his thinking, towards boldly constructive synthesis rather than critical anlysis, does call for remark. What impressed Kant was the consistent unity of the cosmos:

> The universe [he says], by its immeasurable greatness and the infinite variety and beauty that shine from it on all sides, fills us with wonder. If the presentation of all this perfection moves the imagination, the understanding is seized by another kind of rapture when, from another point of view, it considers how such magnificence and such greatness can flow from a single law, with an eternal and perfect order.[3]

Yet to discover the system by which the entire order of nature is thus unified, and to derive the formation and movements of the heavenly bodies themselves from their primal state purely by way of mechanical laws, as in the Newtonian physics, would seem, he surmises, to go far beyond the powers of human reason; while on the other hand he is aware that 'religion threatens to bring a solemn accusation against the audacity which would presume to ascribe to nature by itself results in which the immediate hand of the Supreme Being is rightly recognized', the very ingenuity of such a view appearing as 'an apology for atheism'. Kant admits the difficulty fully, but does not despair of reaching a satisfactory solution. He concedes the great value of the proofs to be drawn from the beauty and perfect arrangement of the universe in establishing the existence of 'a Supremely Wise Creator', but fears that the defenders of religion, by using such proofs badly, perpetuate the conflict with the advocates of naturalism by presenting only the weak side of their position. For the trouble is that the advocates of the doctrine of divine creation invariably seem to imply that adaptation is something foreign to nature, which if left to its own general laws would produce nothing but disorder. 'These harmonies show an alien hand which has known how to subdue to a wise plan a matter that is wanting in all order or regularity' although this 'alien hand', by their account, need in fact be no more than a great but not infinite power.[4] The objection of the religious believer, that if the universe can be sufficiently explained by natural causation then recourse to a 'higher government' is needless, is obviated; and with this the naturalist agrees, since the laws of matter and motion are enough 'to satisfy without compulsion the rules of harmony'.

The question then is: How is it possible to reconcile a theory of the universe as a mechanism with one which sees the whole order of creation as an expression of design? And is not the allusion to design itself an admission that the cosmos has not been produced by the general laws of matter? Kant's answer states that such means may very appropriately subserve the end planned by the divine wisdom, to which the order detectable throughout the entire universe bears striking testimony. The more we learn of nature, he contends, the better we shall perceive that in their general constitution things are not separate or alien from one another. And he goes on:

> I accept the matter of the whole world at the beginning as in a state of general dispersion, and make of it a complete chaos. I see this matter forming itself in accordance with the established laws of attraction, and modifying its movement by repulsion. I enjoy the pleasure, without having recourse to arbitrary hypotheses, of seeing a well-ordered whole produced under the regulation of the established laws of motion, and this whole looks so like the system of the world which we have before our eyes, that I cannot refuse to identify it with it.

This may at first be disconcerting, nevertheless 'such a development of nature is not a thing unheard of in it'. Rather is it that 'its inherent essential striving brings such a result necessarily with it, and that this is the most splendid evidence of its dependence on that pre-existing Being who contains in himself not only the source of these beings themselves but their primary laws of action'.[5] A general conclusion therefore can be reached with assurance: the laws of nature are themselves the instruments of God, who is a God of order:

> Matter, which is the primitive constituent of all things, is bound to certain laws, and when it is freely abandoned to these laws it must necessarily bring forth beautiful combinations. It has no freedom to deviate from this perfect plan. Since it is thus subject to a supremely wise purpose, it must necessarily have been put into such harmonious relationships by a First Cause ruling over it; and there is a God, just because nature even in chaos cannot proceed otherwise than regularly and according to order.[6]

But although Kant does not see the mechanistic theory as at all incompatible with belief in God as the creator and sustainer of the material universe – 'Give me matter, and I will build a world out of it', he quotes – he encounters doubt when the step has to be taken from the inorganic to the organic. Could one equally well say, 'Give me matter, and I will show you how a caterpillar can be generated'?[7] His own view appears to be that the structure of living things exhibits an adaptation for which the universal and necessary laws of nature are insufficient. However, the principle of the design argument is here expressly asserted, and with an eloquence, moreover, which Kant rarely permitted himself in writing.

But the principle only; for when the design argument, as usually stated, is examined its deficiency becomes obvious. Not that Kant regards defect of logical proof as in itself a valid objection to religious belief, for as he says at the close of an essay published towards the end of 1762, *Der einzig mögliche Beweisgrund zu einer Demonstration des Daseins Gottes* ('On the only possible Ground for a Demonstration of God's Existence'),[8] 'although it is unquestionably necessary to be convinced of God's existence, it is not quite so necessary that one should demonstrate it'.[9] To have faith, that is, is more important than to be able fully to substantiate it by rational inquiry. Nevertheless the cogency of rational demonstration is so frequently urged in this matter that the claim, Kant thinks, is one which the philosopher must take with due seriousness. There are, as he sees it, four ways which an attempted demonstration may follow, two of them *a priori*, two *a posteriori*. The former, in other words, are abstract, having resort to a concept only, the latter empirical, starting from the fact, or facts, of existence. In the one case we may seek to argue either from the concept of possibility as ground to the existence of God as consequent – i.e. the so-called *ontological* proof set out in rather differing forms by St Anselm and Descartes (as too by Leibniz); or, alternatively, from possibility as a consequence to divine existence as the ground of such possibility. In the other case – which to most people is much the more interesting – we may start to reason from what actually exists. Specifically, the existence of things may be said to be explained only by that of a prime and independent cause of their so existing – i.e. the *cosmological* argument, stemming from Aristotle and used repeatedly since, being especially favoured by the Wolffian school, even though it falls short of demonstrating the nature or characteristics of such a cause. An alternative and preferable option would be to prove not only God's existence but his attributes as well, on the basis of visible evidences.

The first of these four arguments Kant rejects on the ground that it treats existence as a predicate; for as he points out, simply to say that a thing exists is in no way to identify its character. In other words, to conceive of a thing with its determinate qualities is to assume its existence already; whether it does exist or not is another matter. The third of the four arguments, that to a first cause, although seemingly of much logical force, fails to show the equivalence of this entity to what we understand when we speak of God. To render the argument effective we should have to add something else to it; as it stands it is inadequate. The fourth argument, which of course is that from design, or the *teleological* proof as it is sometimes called, Kant finds, as we have seen, appealing, and if successful would yield not only design – giving a *telos* or purpose to nature – but a wise designer also, whom we may presume to be God. Yet as a demonstration it likewise fails. Immanent teleology we need not doubt, and from it we may infer a purposive intelligence at work. But again this is not enough to prove the existence of God as *creator*, which theism requires:

> The contingent order in the parts of the world, so far as it indicates as its source an act of will, can be of no use towards proving that God created the matter of the universe. . . .

Whether this matter is eternal and self-subsisting, or has been produced by the Author, remains doubtful.[10]

Thus what is wanted is, once more, not provided.

The remaining argument, the second form of the *a priori* mode, is the only one that Kant will allow as having cogency. It is, that if human thought can admit possibility – and we are unable in fact to deny it without *thinking*, and to think is implicitly to affirm possibility – then it must also admit the ground of possibility, i.e. an actual being antecedent to any merely possible being. It involves no logical contradiction to deny all existence whatsoever, but to deny the possibility of it does do so:

> That some sort of possibility exists, yet nothing actual, is self-contradictory, because if nothing exists nothing is presented which is thinkable, and we are at odds with ourselves if we continue to want something to be possible.[11]

However, once this necessary Being is affirmed we further see that 'it' must be one, simple, immutable and eternal, and possessed of intelligence and volition: in a word, that it is *God*. Thus although Kant has rejected the ontological argument in its more familiar shape, he does grant the final inseparability of thought from reality; as likewise the truth that ultimately necessary Being must comprise all perfections. Evidently Kant has not yet awakened from his 'dogmatic slumbers'. The whole tone of his thinking in this essay remains 'Leibnizian–Wolffian', its language being consistently Leibnizian; but the reader will also sense that Kant's thought is developing, becoming more critically self-conscious, and that 'rational theology' has raised a dubiety in his mind which will lead him, before long, to challenge its entire basis. We need no longer dwell on Kant's argumentation, therefore, since he himself subsequently dropped it.

In 1763 the Berlin Academy offered a prize for a competition essay having for subject 'the Distinction of the Principles of Natural Theology and Ethics'. Although a very close runner-up, Kant did not win the prize, the successful candidate being Moses Mendelssohn,[12] but in the following year he published his work under the title *Untersuchung über die Deutlichkeit der Grundsätze der natürlichen Theologie und der Moral* ('Inquiry into the Distinction of the Principles of Natural Theology and Ethics').[13] The question under consideration, namely whether or not metaphysical truths in general, and more particularly those of natural theology and morals, can be regarded as having the same degree of certainty as the truths of mathematics, drew from him the answer that mathematics and metaphysics differ in some fundamental respects. Mathematics frames its definitions with exactitude but arbitrarily, and then uses them as the fundamental of its systematic constructions; its method is essentially synthetic. Philosophy, on the other hand, has to arrive at its definitions – if and as it does so – only by analysis; it begins with ideas more or less confused and inadequate, which, after careful scrutiny, it endeavours to express in more precise, albeit abstract, terms. This analytic procedure is thus the reverse of that adopted in mathematics. The 'genuine method' in metaphysics, Kant thinks, is at bottom the same as that which Newton introduced into natural science 'and which had so many fruitful consequences': namely, to discover what one knows immediately and with certainty in a given subject-matter and then to use this to form proximate judgments of like certainty. In the case of metaphysics, says Kant, 'seek out by secure inner experience – that is, immediately evident consciousness – those properties which undoubtedly lie in the concept of any sort of universal condition, and if you do not know the entire essence of the matter, you can still safely make use of them to infer a good deal about the thing'.[14] Nevertheless he gives his own opinion on the limitation of metaphysics – 'the most difficult of human studies'; it is, he states, 'nothing else but philosophizing about the ultimate principles of our knowledge'.[15] It is not a source of new knowledge; by itself it can discover nothing, but only clarify the basic connections within experience. On the particular question of natural theology and morals, however, Kant adheres to his already declared view that the fundamental principle of the former, the existence of God, is certain, a matter of *knowledge*; whereas in respect of the latter we have to do with *feeling*, and the two ought not to be confused,[16] an idea which contrasts sharply with his later doctrine of the 'categorical imperative'.

A QUESTION-MARK OVER METAPHYSICS

It was in the early 1760s that Kant became interested in the strange psychic experiences of the theosophist Immanuel Swedenborg, then much talked about, and he made a careful study of the latter's chief work, the *Arcana coelestia*, dating from 1749–56.[17] His impressions he set down in a curious little book published in 1766, *Träume eines Geistersehers, erläutert durch Träume der Metaphysik* ('Dreams of a Ghost-seer explained by Dreams of Metaphysics'), part serious, part mocking, the author confessing in his preface to 'a certain humility that he was so simple-minded as to track down the truth of some tales of the sort mentioned'.[18] The initial problem, in disucsssing the veridity of these alleged 'spiritual' experiences, was to determine what the word 'spirit' means. What is spirit in itself? And if by definition it is 'non-material' how is its presence to be detected? What is the relation between spirit and matter, soul and body? In what he calls 'a fragment of esoteric philosophy'[19] Kant deliberately entertains the idea of a spirit-world, subject to laws of its own. It would consist of all created minds, whether embodied or not, the sensitivity of animals, and indeed everything in nature to which sentience can be attributed. But the two 'worlds' of spirit and matter will have no connection with one another unless accidental or as the result of divine intervention. On this assumption contact with the spirit-world might take the form of imaginative visions such as those claimed by Swedenborg. However, Kant does not defend his assumptions very seriously, and as to when or where it might be proved he admits to total ignorance. Against it, rather, he sets 'a fragment of vulgar philosophy',[20] according to which experiences of the kind under discussion would be written off simply as hallucinations for which those subject to them ought to receive medical attention. Kant himself declines to opt definitely for either view; let his readers decide as they please. All the same, and turning away from these obscure matters, Kant raises the question whether metaphysical speculations, which of their very nature transcend the conditions of normal experience, are in any better case. The existence of spirits is a metaphysical supposition, yet visionaries like Swedenborg assert that they have had experience of them although they cannot be proved objectively true. Metaphysical speculations, on the other hand, are, or pretend to be, purely rational and so capable of demonstration. The problem of metaphysics therefore is the problem of the limitations of our knowledge, about which Kant had already learned something from Hume.[21] Cause and effect are cognizable only through sense-experience and so cannot be applied to any reality beyond sense-experience. That there is such a reality Kant does not deny;

but he most emphatically questions that it can be known with the rational certainty metaphysicians have claimed for it. Moreover, it is a mistake to argue that morality is itself dependent on truths of a metaphysical order, in particular the expectation of reward in a life hereafter. 'It would seem', says Kant, 'more fitting with human nature and the purity of morals to base our expectancy of a life to come on the sentiments of a virtuous soul than to reverse this order and base good conduct on our hope of the next world.'[22] 'Let us then', he concludes, 'leave to idle brains all pretentious doctrines which deal with objects of speculation and concern so far removed from our real world.' As he wrote to Mendelssohn (8 April 1766): 'It is neither fickleness nor frivolity but the lessons of prolonged study, which make me hold it the wisest course to strip metaphysics of its dogmatic garb, and to meet its pretended science with scepticism.'[23]

The Latin dissertation Kant wrote for his professorial inauguration in 1770, *De mundi sensibilis et intelligibilis forma et principiis*,[24] marks the transition from the 'dogmatic' stage of his philosophical development to the 'critical', on which his fame as a thinker has ever since rested. But in accepting his own acknowledgement of his debt to Hume in accomplishing this passage we should certainly not overlook what he could also well be said to owe Leibniz. Hitherto he had seen Leibniz mainly through Wolffian spectacles, but in 1765 the latter's *Nouveaux essais sur l'entendement humain* was published, the manuscript having lain unregarded for sixty years in a Hanover library. It made a deep impression on the philosophically-minded throughout Germany, and three years later all Leibniz's works became available in Louis Duten's great edition.[25] Kant studied the *Nouveaux essais* with the closest attention and with important consequences for his own ideas, not only on epistemology but on the whole problem of the relation of scientific methodology to metaphysics. The Duten edition, moreover, acquainted him with Leibniz's correspondence, dating from 1700, with the English divine Samuel Clarke, in which the German thinker contended, as against Newton as well as Clarke, that space and time are not independent realities or inherent qualities of things in themselves. They are, that is to say, *phenomenal*. As Kant himself puts it, time is *aeternitas phaenomenon*, space *omnipraesentia phaenomenon*. However, he could not endorse Leibniz's view that they represent only a confused form of thinking; for were this so, how (for example) could geometry, which pertains to space, be the exact science that it is? Leibniz was mistaken in supposing time and space to be systems of relations abstracted from particular situations and apprehended only inadequately. Instead we have to understand them as forms of our sensibility by which we can, in fact, attain to clear and certain knowledge of things.

Epistemologically Kant's position here was intermediate between that which he at first maintained and which he afterwards described as 'dogmatism', and that which he was to reach during the seventies and to identify as 'critical'. Thus he distinguishes between two orders of knowledge, the sensible and the intellectual, by which terms he does not of course mean knowledge which is clear in contrast to that which is more or less confused. On the contrary, knowledge that is sensible can be quite clear, whilst intellectual knowledge – and metaphysics offers some prize instances – may be puzzlingly confused. What he refers to is not the quality of our knowing but its *objects*, as either sensible (*sensibilia*) or intelligible (*intelligibilia*).

The knowledge we have of the *sensibilia* is arrived at from what is given in sensation, subject to the – for us – inevitable and immediate conditions of space and time. The latter Kant refers to as 'concepts', but describes as 'pure intuitions': i.e. they are not the product of reflection, and are 'pure' because known *a priori*, in advance of experience and not as a result of it. Time, Kant explains, is not a 'real' and 'objective' thing; it is not a substance or an accident or a relation, but a subjective condition necessitated by the mind's own constitution. It relates to our experience of simultaneity as well as succession and is an indispensable means whereby we coordinate *sensibilia*.[26] The same is true of space. This likewise is not objectively real; again, it is neither substance, accident nor relation; and it is subjective, of the mind itself as it performs its task of coordinating external *sense*.[27] Thus time and space together are the *a priori* forms which give order and coherence to our experience of the world about us. Were we not to see things in this way, were we to try to conceive of them as substantial to the external reality *to be known*, parts of the 'objectivity' without which there could be no knowledge, then we should find ourselves involved in inextricable confusion – faced by (to use Kant's own term) 'antinomies'. In a word, what the mind actually knows is 'appearances' (*apparentiae*). But it is obvious that our apprehension of these appearances is spontaneous and instant, and not at all a matter of subsequent thinking *about* experience; though clearly to understand that this is so does require reflection, and is attained only subsequently, as part of the work of philosophy. What Kant calls the logical use of the intellect, however, is intrinsic to the very act of knowledge. For this is how sense-experience is built up into an ordered scheme of cognition and the empirical sciences become possible.

Kant's account of sensible knowledge, at this stage of his thinking, can be followed without too much difficulty, since he is plainly set on the path which was to lead to the first of the great *Critiques*. But he is concerned also with intelligible knowledge, knowledge which has no sense-component and which is purely intellectual or rational in character. How, then, is such an intelligible world to be conceived? Kant evidently still holds the view that we do have knowledge of it, and knowledge of it as it is, *per se*.[28] Such knowledge, when ordered and elaborated, yields us the science of metaphysics, the content of which, as not being dependent on the senses, must relate to a world entirely beyond sense – to the spiritual realm, and supremely God. However this knowledge is not intuitive or positive. As Kant stresses: 'An *intuition* of intelligible objects is not given to man, but only a *symbolic* knowledge.'[29] Objects that are non-sensible, spiritual, can be cognized only under the form of concepts or universal ideas, not directly. But this would seem to leave a gap between *intelligibilia* and the intellectual shape, so to say, in which our minds represent them. Can we, then, be sure that in this realm valid knowledge, as distinct from arbitrary mental constructs, is at all possible?

Kant has an answer to this, but one which indicates fairly clearly that the doubts about metaphysics expressed in his *Dreams of a Ghostseer* have not been allayed, although he is not yet ready to abandon his view that knowledge of supersensible realities is open to us. A further question concerns the material to which, in such knowledge, the logical use of the intellect can be thought to apply in a fashion corresponding to the sense-data that constitute the 'matter' of sensible knowledge. To meet it we have to note Kant's distinction between the intellect's 'logical' use and what he thinks of as its 'real' use. For what the latter does is to generate its own 'material' in the form of concepts which are non-empirical in character, but which, at the same time, cannot be designated 'innate ideas' in the Lockean sense, since Kant is at one with

Leibniz – from whom in other respects he diverges – in rejecting this feature of Locke's doctrine. Rather are they derived from the intrinsic laws of the mind itself, and so can be rightly described as *acquired*. They comprise such notions as possibility, existence, necessity, substance and cause – in fact, those 'categories' or conditions of thought which were to occupy a central place in the 'critical' philosophy which lay ahead.[30] But in 1770 Kant had still not eliminated 'dogmatic' metaphysics altogether from his philosophical purview, inasmuch as he believed that the realities of the supersensible world are not themselves open to doubt. Nevertheless he had come to see that knowledge of *intelligibilia* cannot be of the direct or intuitive kind, but only, in his own term, 'symbolic': certainly true *in a manner of speaking*, but not an exact presentation of them *sicut sunt*, 'as they are'. Thus although it is permissible to describe God as 'first cause' the notion conveyed is not enough to tell us what God really is. In short, we are prevented by the very nature of our cognitive faculties from having a scientific knowledge of spiritual existence. Metaphysics is not excluded entirely from serious intellectual discourse, but its scope is limited, as an affair much more of method than of content, so that 'whatever is undertaken before the principles of this method have been duly worked out and firmly established, seems to be rashly conceived and fit to be regarded as a vain and ridiculous activity of the mind'.[31]

Thus in distinguishing intelligible from sensible knowledge Kant enunciates a methodological rule that principles applicable in the latter field may not be transferred to the former. Take the axiom, he says, that whatever exists does so in a given place and at a given time; it is true in regard to sensible realities, but is clearly inapplicable to spiritual, otherwise God would have to be brought down into the spatio-temporal realm of *sensibilia*. When thinking 'critically' we are able to detect the pitfalls which beset the misuse of rational concepts. In this way the world of intelligible realities is preserved from the errors of misrepresentation, testified by confusions and contradictions, to which any equation of it with that of sensible being will at once give rise. But obviously the effect of this proviso is negative rather than positive. For if God is not to be defined in spatio-temporal terms how in fact is his existence to be characterized? Any positive specification (or, in Kantian language, 'dogmatic' statement) of the mode of it is excluded. Metaphysics therefore cannot be a positive science to the extent of affording us

The Pre-Critical Period

real and substantive knowledge of God, or indeed of the human soul as a spiritual and immortal entity. For as has been observed, even to represent God as first cause, although in a sense informative, does little to lift the veil of mystery by which the true nature of the divine is concealed from us. There is no doubt, on the strength of what is said in the *De mundi sensibilis*, that Kant does believe in a supersensible, spiritual world, even though he may leave us still asking how he can be so sure, especially as all he says about dogmatic metaphysics seems to weaken the case for its credibility. In the critical philosophy Kant eventually makes his position clear enough, and metaphysical 'science' in its traditional meaning has to go. But then it is that he has to adduce rational arguments in favour of believing in supersensible realities, if not as scientifically demonstrable, at any rate as postulates of man's moral reason, apart from which his total experience as a rational being is bereft of any satisfactory explanation. It is to the theological implications of the 'critical' philosophy of Kant's later years that we must now turn.

2
The So-Called Proofs of Divine Existence

'A CRITICAL INQUIRY INTO THE FACULTY OF REASON'

The first edition of the *Critique of Pure Reason* (*Kritik der reinen Vernunft*) appeared in 1781, its publication being an event which was soon to mark its author out as the foremost philosopher of the age.[1] Not that the work was immediately acclaimed by all who were competent to judge it, and when after some six months reviews of it began to appear it was generally thought to be little more than a restatement of idealism, in essence of the subjective, Berkeleyan kind.[2] Moreover, its scholastic form, arcane terminology and prolix argumentation meant that even discerning readers found it difficult to comprehend, and Kant's purpose in writing it was not readily understood.[3] The book entitled *Prolegomena zu einer jeden künftigen Metaphysik* (*Prolegomena to any Future Metaphysics*), which came out in 1783, was planned by him as a sort of introduction to or explanation of the larger work, in view of complaints about its obscurity, but it in no way departs from the *Kritik*'s standpoint.[4] A second, revised edition of the latter was published in 1787, although how far it improves on the original remains a matter of opinion, and many students of Kant have seen no good reason for preferring it.[5]

The author's presiding aim in this taxing work was to determine the cognitive powers of the human reason and thus to ascertain, as a matter of principle, what could or could not be achieved in the orders of knowledge. Of particular concern to him was the investigation of the capacities of 'pure' reason, by which he meant reason when acting of itself and not in association with some other faculty of the mind. There were areas where reason in this sense was demonstrably capable of reaching important truths, mathematics being the signal example. But high-pitched claims were made for it in regard also to metaphysics; to the extent, that is, of asserting that by use of reason alone it is possible to attain to a knowledge of the ultimate truth about the world and to elaborate a genuine science of 'being' as it 'really' is, beyond all mere 'appearances'. Kant himself, as we have seen, at one time considered such knowledge to be a clear possibility. Gradually however doubts had arisen in his mind. These might indeed have been left unresolved but for the fact that the subject-matter of this alleged science was of the greatest intrinsic interest and significance, inasmuch as the chief problems of metaphysics were the existence of God, the freedom of the human will, and the soul's immortality. One could not think of any higher to which the human intellect could finally address itself. What troubled Kant was the question whether such knowledge was certain and reliable, or only pretended and dubious. Metaphysics, he recollected, had once been called 'the queen of the sciences', and the elevation of the matters with which she dealt would on the face of it justify a title so horrific.[6] Unfortunately this elevated subject had turned out to be the field of endless conflicts, neither yielding verifiable knowledge nor pointing to conclusions that had won anything like universal consent. Why then is it, Kant asks, that here no sure path of science has yet been found? Is it perhaps impossible to discover one?[7] But although the failure of the metaphysical enterprise had led many to become sceptical of its claims the objectives which metaphysicians have in view cannot properly be of indifference to the inquiring human spirit.[8] On the contrary, the urge to think metaphysically seems to be an impulse natural to it. Hence what is needed, if either indifferentism or dogmatic pseudo-science is to be avoided, is a 'critical inquiry into the faculty of reason with regard to all the cognitions to which it may strive to attain independently of all experience'.[9] In short, what can be known by the exercize of reason *per se*? The purpose of the work he had taken in hand was to examine this problem systematically and to propose an answer.

THE CASE AGAINST RATIONAL THEOLOGY

With the wider epistemological issues raised in the *Critique* we shall not here be concerned. What is germane to our study of Kant's theological views is the way in which he treats the question of natural theology in that part of the work which he designates

'Transcendental Dialectic'.[10] But we have to recognize as essential to his position his contention that the forms of intuition, space and time, and what he calls the pure categories of the understanding – the conditions under which *any* object has to be conceived if it is to be an object of experience in space and time – have no proper application beyond what is given in sense-experience. That is to say, for the possibility of such *a priori* synthetic principles, of which the ideas of substance and cause provide obvious instances, we have to pay the price of limiting their application to the world of what is or can be experienced, to *phenomena*. When we try to extend the application of such notions – cause and substance again providing ready examples – to things in themselves, to *noumena* (in Kant's terminology), or appear to reason 'realistically' about the cause of the phenomenal universe *as a whole*, we only entangle ourselves in conceptual muddles, 'antinomies', which it is outside the power of the human understanding to resolve.

Kant distinguishes four such antinomies, each with its thesis and antithesis. The thesis of the first is: The world has a beginning in time, and is also limited spatially. Of this the antithesis is: The world has no beginning and no limit in space. The thesis of the second is: Every compound substance in the world consists of simple parts, and nothing anywhere eixsts but the simple and what is composed of it. The antithesis is the contrary of this. The thesis of the third antinomy is: Causality according to the law of nature is not the only causality from which all phenomena can be deduced. In order to account for these other phenomena it is necessary also to admit another causality, that of freedom. The antithesis, however, is: There is no freedom, but everything in the world takes place entirely according to the laws of nature. The thesis of the fourth is: There exists an absolutely necessary Being belonging to the world, either as a part or as a cause of it. But again the antithesis denies this.[11] In each instance Kant is at the pains to show that the case for the antithesis is as arguable logically as that for its opposite. In none of these matters therefore can we be sure that the conclusion we opt for is other than illusory; which means that metaphysical propositions, at least of the traditional speculative kind, cannot be admitted to the order of objective or scientific knowledge.[12]

The problems dealt with in the latter part of the 'Transcendental Dialectic' arise from an attempt to conceive of a whole which shall

The So-Called Proofs of Existence 43

include both the known world and the mind that knows. This attempt, which Kant speaks of as the 'Ideal of pure reason', introduces the proofs, long familiar in the field of natural theology, of the existence of God as the Supreme Being in whom all possible perfections are united in a concrete individuality. Clearly, on what we have seen to be Kant's premises, no proof of divine existence is possible; the very nature of human knowledge precludes it, as Kant's fourth antinomy purports to show. But he is not content with such a blanket exclusion. He wishes, rather, to exhibit how the entire chain of reasoning which constitutes these allegedly rational demonstrations is at point after point weakened by fallacies. There are, he concedes, three types of argument possible, viz. the ontological (in the second of the two forms in which it is stated by Descartes),[13] the cosmological (which he finds in Leibniz and Wolff), and the physico-theological, as he likes to term it (set out by the deist Reimarus). In his 'Only Possible Ground for a Demonstration of God's Existence' we noted (see above, pp. 30–2) that it is the first of these alone, though in a modified form, which he admits as plausible. But now he disallows it altogether. Nevertheless he treats it with much seriousness, since it is the nerve of the whole case for a rational theology, its validity indeed being the condition, in the final resort, of the other two.

In the *Critique*, accordingly, the ontological argument is dealt with first. In the 'Only Possible Ground' Kant disclosed the fatal flaw in it to be its treatment of existence as itself a predicate or attribute, which it is not, inasmuch as existence is no part of the content of a defining idea. What the argument involves, he now points out, is that the concept of a perfect being implies of necessity the actual existence of such a being. Reasoning starts, that is, with a definition, that of *ens perfectissimum*, and just as the mathematician draws from a mathematical definition all the consequences which are entailed by it, so, by the terms of the ontological argument, the very definition of a perfect being requires the latter's existence, existence being regarded as one of the perfections without which the being thus defined could not be the sum of all perfections. Kant agrees that to assume the existence of a triangle and at the same time to deny that it has three angles is contradictory, but there is no contradiction at all, he says, in denying both the triangle and its three angles.[14] And it is exactly the same with the concept of an absolutely necessary being: if the existence of that being is denied, then the entity itself, with all its predicates, is likewise denied and no contradiction is incurred. For what does the idea of a perfect (i.e. unconditioned) being consist in? That simply of a being which cannot but exist, whose non-existence is an impossibility.[15] Yet how does one pass from the *idea* of such a being to its actuality? The concept in itself affords us no certainty that there is in this necessary being something that renders its non-existence impossible. All it states, in effect, is that if the non-existence of a being is impossible such a being is necessary. The concept itself is only a logical determination; merely to suppose something to be the case will not of itself do anything to establish its reality:

> As logic abstracts from all content, anything at all may serve as a logical predicate; nay, the subject may even be predicated of itself. But a determination is a real predicate which adds something to the conception of the subject and enlarges it. Hence it must not be assumed in the conception of the subject.[16]

The real, as Kant observes, contains no more than the possible:

> A hundred real dollars do not contain a cent more than a hundred possible dollars. The one signifies the conception, the other the object as it is set over against the conception; but if the object contained more than the conception, the conception would not express the object, and therefore would be an inadequate conception.[17]

In reply to Kant's criticism it is sometimes urged that unless what we are obliged to think ties in with the real consistent reasoning cannot be sustained; and clearly unless there is coordination and correspondence of the thoughts we think with the reality around us total scepticism becomes unavoidable. If we start with ideas which we are confident have some purchase on reality and work out their implications logically then our conclusions have a good claim to be taken as true. But this very reasonable view is a long way from proving that the concept of God as a being of determinate character whose defining attributes are not strictly to be inferred from data of experience must of itself imply his existence. Even if we prefer to speak of God simply as the infinite being, *ens realissimum*, who (or which) must be definition possess all reality, and that as such he (or it) must include existence, Kant's objection is still not met. In fact, to affirm that a being which contains all reality must be real is no more than a tautology. At any rate the conclusion thus reached, if not open to denial, is yet so empty of specific content as to be worthless for any positive theological purpose. But the concept of a deity whose attributes at all approximate to those of the God of Christian theism has such specific content that by no means can the concept itself logically require its factual counterpart. The divine as it may exist in the mind of the believer cannot offer proven assurance that this same divinity is as real as the believer himself. That this discrepancy persists is the very reason that the existence of God continues to pose a question which rational argument is unable conclusively to answer.[18]

Kant turns next to the cosmological argument, which from contingent existence infers necessary existence. 'If anything exists', it runs, 'an absolutely necessary being must also exist. Now I at least exist. Therefore there also exists an absolutely necessary being. The minor premiss contains an experience; the major premiss reasons from an experience in general to the existence of a necessary being.'[19] Kant's primary objection to this line of argument – though he discovers in it a whole nest of fallacies – can be anticipated: that it attempts to pass from an idea of causation which is applicable only within the sensible world to one of causation whereby something altogether transcending the sensible world is causally operative upon and within that same world. But this is not legitimate. The principle of causality is valid only for the conditions of sense-experience, where it plainly is meaningful; we cannot use it when we try to go beyond those conditions. Again, the argument assumes that the necessary being required to explain contingent existence is the *ens realissimum*, the Supreme Being of rational theology, i.e. God,[20] whereas the idea of a necessary being is indeterminate. For how are we to identify its (or his) attributes? The concept of the *ens realissimum* tells us nothing at all in this respect; it is an abstraction intended to serve as the ground of all phenomena indiscriminately. In any case, to maintain that the most real or perfect being exists *necessarily* is to reintroduce the fundamental mistake of the ontological argument, that there is a logical transition from concept to reality. However, it might be said, in qualification of Kant's criticism here, that if the argument simply affirms on the basis of experience the *existence* of a necessary being in order to account for that experience than the ontological proof is not invoked. But even so, the essential fault of the cosmological argument remains: namely, that its appeal to the efficacy of 'God' as the world's ultimate cause fails because we can have no knowledge either of the existence of such a being or of the way in which ultimate causality would operate even if we did. Theologically, once more, the notion lacks content.

Kant concludes that the whole idea of a supreme being is an ideal of reason, functioning, that is, as a principle for producing the greatest possible unity in phenomena. As such it is simply – if in its way importantly – a *regulative* principle or 'Idea', instructing us to view all connection in the world *as if* it proceeded from an all-sufficient necessary cause.[21] But it cannot establish the objective existence of what it quite reasonably points to.

The third of the arguments, the physico-theological, or as it is more usually named, the argument from design, stands higher in Kant's estimation as being psychologically, at least, the most impressive of them:

> It is the oldest and simplest proof of all, and never fails to commend itself to the popular mind. It imparts life to the study of nature, as it was itself suggested by that study, and receives new vigour from it.[22]

Yet under scrutiny it is found to be no more cogent than the other two, on which indeed it is dependent. But in many case Kant leaves us in no doubt, even before he comes to examine it in detail, that for him the argument cannot succeed:

> All laws [he reminds us] pertaining to the transition from effects to causes, yea, all synthetic extension of our knowledge, relate solely to possible experience, and thus to the objects of the sensible world; and it is only in regard to the latter that they have meaning.[23]

The main steps in the argument are as follows: (1) There are everywhere in the world indications of the adaptation of means to ends, evidencing an intelligible purpose. (2) This adaptation is certainly not intrinsic to the nature of things, but rather is contingent, something extraneous and accidental. Accordingly, (3) there must at least exist one cause, 'wise and sublime', of this adaptation, or possibly more than one. It is not to be identified merely with 'the blind, all-powerful productiveness of nature', but must be intelligent and free. (4) The unity which the inner harmony of the world thus exhibits is analogous to that of a skilfully constructed artifice, justifying the inference that there is one, and only one, such cause. But plausible though it is so far as it goes, to what does such argumentation lead? The most it can do, Kant thinks, is to prove an *architect* of the world, whose activity is very largely limited by the adaptability of the material in which he works. It cannot prove an omnipotent *creator* of the world, as a fully theistic doctrine would demand.[24] If we expect the argument to take us further than this we have to reinforce it with the cosmological proof, which in turn must lean on the ontological. But, as we have seen, any form of argument which thus relies, whether directly or indirectly, on an appeal to a concept alone to establish existence is fallacious.[25] Hence all attempt to prove divine existence by speculative reasoning collapses, and no transcendental theology can be based upon it.

This 'transcendental' (in Kantian parlance) or 'natural' theology is therefore ruled out, a casualty of Kant's epistemological ban on speculative metaphysics, though also by his logical critique of the particular arguments traditionally deployed in its behalf. But although Kant is emphatic that reason in its purely speculative use is incapable of proving the existence of a Supreme Being it is certainly not true that he turns his back on philosophical theology altogether.[26] Belief in God, as he stated at the close of the *Only Possible Ground*, may not be in the strict sense rationally demonstrable, but it is nonetheless of the highest importance actually to believe in God, and to show how that belief can be rationally supported is a major part of his endeavour when he comes to study the capacity of reason not only in its theoretical but in its practical aspect. For he is convinced that it can be sustained by what he describes as 'moral theology'.[27] He will demonstrate later, he says, how the laws of morality do not merely presuppose the existence of a Supreme Being but rightly postulate it – although only of course from a practical point of view – 'as these laws are themselves absolutely necessary in another relation'.[28] For it is in the realm of our moral experience that the idea of God assumes its true significance. If we cannot rank it among the certitudes of the scientific reason yet it can become the centre of a 'faith' that is not simply an emotional gesture but a matter of reasoned conviction. To gain this true perspective, however, negative criticism, a clearing away of illusory notions, is necessary. But Kant, though he sometimes was referred to as *der Allzumalmende*, the all-destroyer, was no Hume, and scepticism was not congenial to his mind. As he declared in the Preface to the second edition of the *Critique of Pure Reason*, the 'doctrine of morality' and the 'doctrine of nature' may each be true in its own sphere – something that could never have been shown had not criticism previously established our unavoidable ignorance of things-in-themselves, limiting all that we know, in the exact sense, to phenomena. 'I have, therefore, found it necessary to deny *knowledge* of God, freedom and immortality, in order to find a place for *faith (Glaube)*.'[29] Such a faith, for Kant is, notwithstanding, a rational attitude, not a mere 'hunch', nor an arbitrary 'will-to-believe' overriding non-belief. For if divine existence cannot be proved neither can it be disproved. And when this is recognized reason is free to engage in a very salutary work of constructive thought: able, that is, to correct our 'knowledge' of God – should it be possible to obtain such knowledge in some other way – to bring it into harmony both with itself and with all our other intelligible aims, purifying it from all that is inconsistent with the concept of a Supreme Being and any admixture of empirical limitations.[30] Although such a concept, Kant adds, is for purely speculative reason a sheer ideal, it still is a 'perfectly faultless' one, 'which completes and crowns the whole of human knowledge'. Not that he was unaware of the difficulties presented by the very *idea* of a supreme, transcendent, self-conscious Being. As he himself elsewhere admits, 'unconditioned necessity', as the ultimate support of all things, although to our ordinary ways of thinking an indispensable assumption, is nevertheless to the rational understanding (*Verstand*) 'the veritable Abyss', before which the inquiring mind stands aghast. For that this absolute necessity should be conceived of as a wholly self-existing Being, beyond whom nothing subsists save that which exists solely through his own will, is something that well-nigh paralyses thought.[31] Yet in spite of this seemingly destructive treatment of any attempt to secure religious belief on logical grounds Kant never resigned himself to a purely agnostic position and always preserved his own faith in the divine, attached as this was to his unshakable ethical principles.

How he proceeds to construct a 'moral theology' which will make good the deficiencies of speculative theology we must now investigate.

3
The Moral Argument

KANT'S ETHICAL TEACHING

The foundations of Kant's philosophy are to be discovered in his ethical teaching, for what as a thinker concerned him more than all else was man's sense of moral obligation and what it implies. It is to be expected, therefore, that his approach to the philosophical problem set by religious belief should be that of a moralist. In the realm of sensible knowledge we have to do with *phenomena* only – with things as they appear to us, subject to the conditions which thought itself imposes through its own forms and categories. Of *noumena*, or things-in-themselves (*Dingen-an-sich*), we can have no knowledge, given the limitations which the rational understanding places on our minds. Conceived as a kind of phantom existence behind phenomena – phantoms, however, that are never apprehensible by the reason and hence of necessity remain unknown to us – these things-in-themselves could well be said to serve no rational purpose except as the purely notional supports without which phenomena could not present themselves to us. In other words, the 'real' world is simply the world we actually know; one which, accordingly, sets no bounds to the reach of knowledge. What we call nature, or the natural order, is on this supposition void of significance if, as it were, detached from the framework of rational consciousness, which in fact is the only end-in-itself. The aim of philosophy is to arrive at that which can be seen as the ultimate or supreme end of existence – that whereby all else can be justified and the reasoning mind at last attain its full and lasting satisfaction. To this supreme end all phenomena are relative: they are significant only as referring to it. And this end can be nothing other than the rational consciousness itself, whose own end, or good, is *in itself* exclusively. This insight is the basis of Kant's ethics and parallels that by which the rational consciousness is likewise the fount of knowledge. In the latter case the source of the categories, the pure Ego, stands, so to say, outside the categories;

in the former, the source of all ends – again the pure Ego – is 'above' any of the particular ends which derive from it. In either case the subject is superior as determining and not as being itself determined. Whether as to theory or practice, to thought or action, the rational consciousness is the final explanatory principle, the one absolutely necessary point of reference. But as regards both knowing and doing this explanatory principle or necessary point of reference remains, as Kant's critics have always been prompt to observe, abstract and formal. As the pure reason, of itself, knows nothing in particular, so the moral imperative, of itself, prescribes no specific duty.

But in what sense does Kant consider the subject to be self-determining, deciding for himself, that is, what ends he should pursue? Here an all-important distinction must be drawn. Under one aspect of his being man is part of nature and thus necessarily submissive to nature's laws at every level, mechanical, chemical, biological. In this respect therefore his life is capable of explanation according to the principles of the objective sciences. This, however, is no more than an external view, even if it includes psychology. But in its 'inwardness' the rational consciousness, Kant insists, is not determined in this way. Intelligence has the capacity to understand the situation in which it finds itself, relating particular experiences to a general law, and in turn expressing rational purpose in action. It is by his rationality and volition that a man differs from an animal, even though he himself has an animal nature which he cannot change. Consequently man is free in a way that an animal certainly is not. He can envisage ends and appreciate values, recognizing above all the distinction between good and evil. This capacity is what raises him above the merely natural plane and renders him subject to law of another kind. Intelligence is not simply an instrument to enable him to satisfy his instinctual desires; indeed it will usually act as a power to check and control them. For the capabilities with which the possession of intelligence invests a man will make him responsible for the manner in which he conducts himself in life. In short, he realizes the force of the word 'ought', distinguishing between inclination and obligation. Hence it is on this side of his being that he admits the rule of law. For the moral law, unlike the laws of nature, does not compel; its sway is freely accepted because rationally approved. And in this rational approval and free accep-

The Moral Argument

tance man fulfils his proper being. He perforce lives under the conditions of the natural order, but his spiritual orientation is to the moral order, which alone is the sphere of his freedom. The concern of moral philosophy is to investigate the basic meaning of moral obligation, to perceive what exactly it signifies to say 'I ought'; or to put it rather more technically, to examine the *a priori* principles of moral action – in isolation, that is to say, from elements which are empirically derived. In this its function is the counterpart of the critical investigation of the *a priori* principles of scientific (as also ordinary) knowledge.[1]

The clearest statement of Kant's ethical theory is contained in his *Grundlegung zur Metaphysik der Sitten* (*Fundamental Principles of the Metaphysic of Morals*), first published in 1785 (2nd edition, 1786), and had he written nothing else on ethics this little work – it is quite short – would still have become a classic in the subject.[2] Penetrating as its discussion is, Kant here expresses himself with an eloquence and warmth of feeling all too rare in his other writings. His one aim, he states in the Preface, is to examine and make clear what is 'the supreme principle of morality', a study 'altogether complete in its intention and one which should be kept separate from all other moral inquiry'.[3] The ethical problem arises for man because he is only partially rational, the other side of his nature being sensual. Accordingly, many of his actions are prompted by sensual impulse alone, with his reason acting as little more than, in Hume's phrase, 'the slave of the passions'. But on the non-sensual side of his nature man can and does act rationally, and it is here that moral criteria are effective. For when a man acts morally he does so for no ulterior motive, but purely from the recognition of what is his duty; duty being defined by Kant as 'the necessity of an action done from respect for the law'.[4] The moral worth of so acting consists not in the purpose to be achieved by it but in the 'maxim' or principle which directs it. What determines morality, then, is *intention*. I may not be able to secure the ends I seek, since attainment of them is unlikely to depend on myself alone, so that it is not enough to judge of their moral worth simply by their actual outcome. But if my intention in acting is pure then the ethical value of what I endeavour to do is already established. On the other hand, if my action is prompted by considerations of personal advantage, no matter how praiseworthy my aim may be in itself, it is not moral:

The pre-eminent good [which we call moral] can consist only in the conception of the law in itself (which can be present only in a rational being) so far as this conception and not the hoped-for effect is the determining ground of the will.[5]

Further, the criterion of a moral act is that it be done according to a maxim which could be universalized: 'That is, I should never act in such a way that I could not will that my maxim should be a universal law.'[6] Kant's view is no doubt rigorously abstract, but it is determined by the clear distinction he draws between man regarded, on the one hand, as a moral agent, and, on the other, from 'the viewpoint of anthropology'. Were ethical principles merely the outcome of his empirical nature or the pressures of his environment they would have no claim to override the promptings of inclination or fear. Instead the moral command is *categorical*, without qualification. The force of the word may be judged by contrasting it with commands that are no more than hypothetical. The latter assume the desirability of certain ends or objectives and simply prescribe the necessary, or at any rate the most appropriate, means of securing them. Thus they are no more than instrumental or prudential. But the moral law is of a different kind altogether. The imperative is absolute, addressed to man purely as a rational being. This it is which makes the categorical principle of universality possible.

The categorical imperative, or the pure form of universal obligatory law, is, says Kant, 'the sole fact of pure reason'. That such a command is conceivable rests on the idea of reason, or the rational will, as self-legislative, and the law which propounds it is one that any rational being must recognize as binding. This is what Kant means by the autonomy of the will, which he sees as 'the supreme principle of morality',[7] and as opposed to all heteronomy, which would represent it as subject to laws that are not the result of its own rationally willed legislation.

Whether we care to accept Kant's account of moral obligation as it stands is not a matter which we can discuss here. It has been subjected to much criticism since his time, especially on the grounds of its abstractness and formalism.[8] For what strikes the reader of the *Grundlegung* immediately is the way in which Kant detaches moral obligation, or the sense of duty, from its emotional and social contexts – a feature of his ethical theory which has been widely held to be among its least convincing aspects. By no means, it has been urged, can the absolute End be reached simply by abstracting from particular and real ends, and if the noumenal self is to be nothing other than a notional point of unity it cannot be isolated from the rationality inherent in our concrete experience of the world about us, a criticism which was pressed and elaborated by Hegel in distinguishing Kant's *Moralität*, as he preferred to call it, from his own doctrine of *Sittlichkeit*.[9] Nevertheless, it would be a serious misunderstanding of Kant's attitude to think of it as merely formalistic and legalist. On the contrary, it was, after its somewhat dry fashion – and Kant always eschewed unction – sincerely religious. His famous words about the two objects of his veneration being 'the starry heavens above and the moral law within' are surely indicative of this.[10] Indeed, he sees the moral law as holy, and complete accord with it in living would itself be holiness – 'a perfection' (the choice of word is very significant) 'of which no rational being in the world of sense is at any time capable'.[11] There can be little doubt, one would suppose, that this religious respect for the holiness of the moral law was imbibed by Kant in the days of his pietistic youth. Further evidence of this virtually religious regard for the moral imperative is afforded by his insistence on goodness of will. 'Nothing in the world, indeed nothing even beyond the world', he declares right at the beginning of the *Grundlegung*, 'can possibly be conceived which could be called good without qualification except a good will.'[12] That there are very many other goods needs no saying, but they are capable of misuse, thus promoting evil. A good will, however, is intrinsically good, and does not merely earn the description, so to say, on the strength of good deeds. In Luther's theology, Kant would have known, faith is not simply the product of good works, but their precondition. It is not therefore fanciful to note in Kant's moral teaching something not unlike the same kind of conviction. A good will comes of a reorientation of outlook: in a word, of *conversion*. Between good and evil there can be no compromise; duty is sacred. In fact, as we shall see, in his *Religion within the Limits of Reason Alone* he even speaks, in biblical parlance, of one's becoming 'a new man' by 'a kind of rebirth, as it were a new creation'.[13] In the event, of course, there will be gradual reform, with the building up of a virtuous character. But the adoption of the law of holiness into one's maxim – to use Kantian terminology – is in principle the matter only of a moment.[14]

GOD AS A POSTULATE OF THE PRACTICAL REASON

In 1788, three years after the appearance of the *Grundlegung*, came that of the *Kritik der praktischen Vernunft* (*Critique of Practical Reason*), although the intervening period had witnessed the publication not only of the second edition of the *Kritik der reinen Vernunft* but that also of the *Metaphysische Anfangsgründe der Naturwissenschaft* ('Metaphysical First Principles of Natural Science') in 1786.[15] The *Critique of Practical Reason* was devised on a plan close to that of the earlier work, but with the purpose of extending the range of its author's philosophical inquiry to cover the whole realm of man's moral experience, to the degree at least of providing a systematic account of the *a priori* or *formal* elements in morality. More specifically, its purpose was to show the rationality of moral obligation as universal and necessary – that pure reason of itself can determine the will. For were the will not rationally determinable morality, in Kant's view, would be an illusion; conduct then would be the outcome only of instinctive volition, of impulse or desire, and thus be subject to the laws of material causality. The sense of obligation, of the force of 'I *ought*', would have no real meaning, since freedom, the power of rational choice, would be lacking. Whether Kant succeeds in demonstrating Hume's opinion that 'reason alone can never be a motive of any action of the will' to be false – or, to put it more positively, in showing exactly how reason is able to control action on the ground that 'ought' necessarily implies 'can' – is indeed a question very much open to discussion.

In the second Book of the *Critique*, headed 'Dialectic' – the first Book is devoted to 'Analytic' – Kant rounds off his ethical system with a statement of his concept of the *summum bonum, das höchste Gut*, 'the highest good', evidently feeling that his account of duty, although not in any way to be qualified, nonetheless needed to be brought into closer relation with the facts and conditions of human nature. The term *summum bonum* comprises, he points out, two quite distinct ideas. It may mean either the *supremum bonum, das oberste Gut*, 'the supreme good', or *bonum consummatum, das vollendete Gut*, 'the completed good'. The supreme good is *bonum originarium* in the sense that it is not subordinate to anything else, that it is a good in its own right. The completed good is good not only in this respect, but also as not being a part of a larger whole of the same kind. Hence it is *bonum perfectissimum*. Moral goodness, as Kant understands it, is certainly to be characterized in the first of these two senses; it is good in itself, and in no way dependent on anything other than itself. Yet it is not the entire good, which we ordinary mortals wish and seek to obtain. The complete good includes happiness (*Glückseligkeit*), not merely as a personal and probably biased desire, but as judged by unbiased reason, 'which regards the production of happiness in the world as an end in itself'.[16] Virtue without happiness would be virtue no less, nor the less admirable, whereas happiness without virtue would be an affront to our moral feeling. But if it were possible to unite virtue with happiness then a still greater good, 'the complete good', would be realized:

> Inasmuch as virtue and happiness together constitute the possession of the highest good for one person, and happiness in exact proportion to morality (as the worth of a person and his worthiness to be happy) constitutes that of a possible world, the highest good means the whole, the perfect good, wherein virtue is always the supreme good, being the condition having no condition superior to it, while happiness, though something always pleasant to him who possesses it, is not of itself absolutely good in every respect but always presupposes conduct in accordance with the moral law as its condition.[17]

The union of virtue with happiness, Kant concludes, is a demand of our moral consciousness itself, which thus is moved to postulate the existence of a power capable of bringing it about. And such a power can be identified only with God. But before proceeding to examine this argument in detail – and for Kant it replaces the supposedly rational 'proofs' as the ground of religious certitude – we must take a brief look at the role of the practical reason in Kant's philosophy more generally.

The categorical imperative is the key to his thinking when he seeks to advance beyond his 'critical' theory of the nature of human knowledge to a completed philosophical view of the world. On the principles involved in the former this enterprise would not have been possible. But the idea of the categorical imperative has implications which enable us to comprehend reality from a different angle, so to speak. These are what Kant designates as 'postulates' of the practical reason, and they are at once seen to correspond with the three Ideas which in the *Critique of Pure*

Reason form the subject-matter of metaphysical speculation, namely God, freedom and immortality. They are not, says Kant, theoretical dogmas but presuppositions which are *practically* necessary. They do not extend our speculative or theoretical knowledge, but rather give objective reality to the ideas of speculative reason in general, and so justify it in the use of conceptions which it could not otherwise venture to regard as even possible.

Taking the last of these first, we see that immortality rests upon the practically necessary condition that existence should be of sufficient duration to permit of the complete fulfilment of the moral law. The second, freedom, arises from the necessary presupposition that ultimately we are independent of the world of sense and are capable of directing our wills in conformity with the law of an intelligible universe, i.e. the law of freedom. The first, the idea of God, relates to the necessity of presupposing a supreme, self-existent good as the condition under which the highest good may be realized in an intelligible world. These topics are severally treated in the 'Dialectic' under the headings of rational psychology, cosmology and theology respectively. Their character, however, must not be misunderstood. From the standpoint of pure reason both the Idea of the self as the noumenal centre of unity of experience and the Idea of God as 'the supreme and necessary unity on which all empirical reality is founded' are no more than 'points of view' (*Gesichtspunkte*) from which reason confers systematic unity upon its experience. As such they are, as we have already noted, 'regulative principles' or 'formal rules' – in modern parlance, a heuristic device – for the organization of experience. They cannot be scientifically established as constitutive.[18] Instead, we have to see reality *as if* it accorded with them: *as if* the successive states of consciousness were unified in a single subject-substance; *as if* all phenomena were in fact a totality made up of an indefinitely extended causal series; *as if* the world – as we have to think of this totality – were the work, finally, of an intelligent creator. Given this limitation of them we have to recognize that these 'transcendental Ideas' are 'as natural to the reason as are the categories of the understanding'.[19]

The practical reason, then, affords us clear indication as rational beings of what the moral imperative involves if we are fully to comprehend it. Through it we arrive at a 'moral belief' or 'moral certainty' as to the coherence and unity of our experience in this world, not only as knowing subjects but as moral agents. For we

The Moral Argument

learn to see the postulates as the conditions which, in the light of reason, must be held to obtain if the moral law is to be obeyed. In this sense, although not theoretical certainties – for this they cannot be: we cannot know, for example, that there is a God – they nevertheless are matters of rational belief, of a rational faith (*Vernunftsglaube*). This qualification of their status as rational truths is, on the other hand, no mere *pis aller*, for where there is complete rational certainty no room is left for the disinterested moral will, the exercise of which is an essential function of our humanity.

Let us take the postulate of free will first, although the word 'postulate' may not seem a very appropriate term to apply to Kant's view of freedom, inasmuch as he sees it, rather, as a fact, as something we need not doubt to be among the things we know (*scibilia*). At any rate it follows directly from the primary datum of the moral law, even if in itself it cannot be proved. A more accurate account of it would be that it is the condition of the possibility, the *ratio essendi*, of the categorical imperative. For the idea of obligation under the moral law itself implies the freedom to obey it. 'As practical reason or as the will of a rational being the will must regard itself as free. That is to say, the will of a rational being can be a will of its own only under the idea of freedom, and therefore in a practical point of view such a will must be ascribed to all rational beings.'[20] In plain language, if I *ought* to do a thing then in principle I *can* do it, otherwise the command would be meaningless. Thus morality and freedom are mutually conditioning, the moral law being the *ratio cognoscendi* of freedom. But freedom implies that in the noumenal sphere the will is not subject to the sequence of causality as it is in the phenomenal. This involves the notion of a man's conduct being explicable from two quite different angles, the 'intelligible' and the 'sensible'. The fact that I am subject to determining antecedents in the life I live in and through the senses does not excuse disobedience to moral commands which remain perfectly valid for me as a rational being. Indeed, even if my past life has been one of repeated acts of moral disobedience yet, according to Kant, every time I exercise my will in choosing I am in a position to make an entirely fresh start, for I am still free to obey. Empirically, that is, I will have developed a settled character that sufficiently explains my actual conduct. Nevertheless as a rational being it cannot be said that my freedom to will the good and obey the law's command has been abolished.

That this dualistic view of human character and freedom is one that most people are likely to regard as plausible cannot well be claimed. For the kind of division which Kant envisages between the rational and the empirical, the noumenal and the phenomenal, is surely not to be sustained, since if a man is not free under his phenomenal aspect – if his behaviour is wholly or largely explicable in terms of his physical constitution or psychological disposition or personal environment – then it cannot be said that he is free. By sticking to his rigorously abstract method of analysis, by appearing to contend that freedom consists in there being no predetermination of motives, Kant offers a concept of freewill which is wholly suppositious. But the point of Kant's argument is, we may agree, acceptable if he be taken to mean that man as man is aware of a moral ideal to which his action should always be referred and which he can acknowledge as his 'true self' and the real ground of responsible conduct on his part, despite even his strongest inclination to disregard it. However, we must leave further discussion of Kant's position and move on to a consideration of his second postulate, that of the soul's immortality.

The moral law requires of us complete conformity with its demands in both mind and heart in order to promote the *summum bonum*. Were it possible to meet this requirement fully we should have achieved holiness, which Kant also describes as 'a perfection of which no rational being of the sensible world is capable at any moment of its existence'. Unless therefore the final goal of the moral imperative is to remain for ever unattained by a rational being – whose vocation nonetheless is to achieve such holiness – then its demands must be held to be eventually attainable by an unending progress or approximation towards the ideal. 'But', Kant maintains, 'this infinite progress is possible only under the presupposition of an infinitely enduring existence and personality of the same rational being; this is called the immortality of the soul.'[21] Thus again the categorical imperative obliges us to accept a belief, not itself rationally demonstrable although also not logically impossible, as a postulate of the pure practical reason. Without it the moral law would be seen to impose an absolute requirement which the conditions of our mortal existence show to be an impossibility. Not surprisingly, from this argument, like its predecessor, many readers of Kant have demurred. It embodies, they might object, assumptions about the nature of the moral law that are unwarrantable, and that the law is not the 'absolute' which

Kant so intransigently insists that it is. Or does he not, on his own showing, they will ask, contradict himself by suggesting that its fulfilment is never more than an *objective*, whether in this life or another – something like the fabled shores of Ausonia which ever recede as the traveller approaches them? For in that case immortal life, were we even able to conceive it as having conditions which continue to present a moral challenge, would yet offer no certainty that holiness is finally attainable. In a word, moral perfection, as Kant would have us see it, is impossible. But does this not of itself reveal the essentially 'religious', rather than the strictly 'rational', nature of the moral law? In orthodox theology redeemed man is called to a 'divine' sanctification which never, here or hereafter, in the end confers divinity upon him.

But we now must go back to the postulate of God's existence, which Kant also maintains to be implied by the categorical imperative. The highest good, he says, is attained only when virtue and happiness are combined; not that virtue should be pursued for the sake of happiness, for that would deprive morality of its properly disinterested character by introducing an ulterior motive, as still less that happiness should be sought in disregard of virtue, which would be offensive to our moral sense. But if the pursuit of virtue renders a man worthy of happiness – and happiness is something we all by our very nature desire – then it is from every point of view fitting that the two should be united. We must therefore postulate the existence of a Cause of nature as a whole – our own as sensible beings and that of the external world wherein we live – which yet is distinct from nature, and which is able to connect happiness and obedience to the moral law in complete harmony with one another. The only power adequate to accomplish this is divine:

> As a consequence, [Kant continues] the postulate of the possibility of a highest derived good (the best world) is at the same time the postulate of the reality of a highest original good, namely, the existence of God. Now it was our duty to promote the highest good; and it is not merely our privilege but a necessity connected with duty as a requisite to presuppose the possibility of this highest good. This presupposition is made only under the condition of the existence of God, and this condition inseparably connects this supposition with duty. Therefore, it is morally necessary to assume the existence of God.[22]

The reader's immediate response to this argument is not likely, it has to be admitted, to be very favourable. He will see it as factitious and unconvincing, unimpressive and unappealing both to the doubter and the believer. Against the charge, however, that Kant is not being consistent with his own principle of duty purely for duty's sake and that morality has to be disinterested,[23] we have in all fairness to note that Kant takes care to press the point that the existence of God is not the condition of morality *per se*, but only of morality as an indispensable factor in achieving the highest good. All the same, any close consideration of this moral argument will soon reveal the difficulties it presents.

A METAPHYSIC OF FAITH

But first we have to raise a query of a more general sort. We cannot, says Kant, arrive at any knowledge of God by way of the speculative reason; but this is not to say that for him the very idea of God is without meaning, for were this so any discussion of it in terms of its truth-value would be idle. When he states that it cannot be either affirmed as true or denied as false on the ground of *speculative* reason he intends to imply, as the subsequent *Critique* makes a great effort to show, that God can yet be known by the *practical* reason. The question that obtrudes itself here, though, is how one can be rationally justified in asserting as much: how it is that speculative or theoretic reason can possibly *know* that there is an order of reality and truth of which, by its own methods, it can have no knowledge. And it is very doubtful whether Kant ever lets us have a satisfactory answer. One can only observe that the philosopher, while unable to provide a strictly logical account of belief in God, inasmuch as the principles of his critical doctrine precluded it, yet found that belief to be so deep-rooted in his own mind and heart that he was obliged to look for some alternative explanation, not in the 'scientific' reason but in the 'moral'. This recourse, however, introduces the whole problem of whether the idea that there are two altogether distinct levels of truth-affirming reason is really feasible, or to suppose that what cannot be cognized at one level is nevertheless accessible at the other. It is a problem that touches the quick of Kant's philosophy.

But according to that philosophy there is 'an absolutely necessary practical use of reason', namely the *moral* in which it inevitably goes beyond the bounds of sensibility:

> From the critical point of view the doctrine of morality and the doctrine of nature may each be true in its own sphere; which could never have been shown had not criticism previously established our unavoidable ignorance of things-in-themselves and limited all that we can know to mere phenomena.[24]

This would seem to indicate that we not only have some kind of cognitive apprehension of things which, owing to the constitution of our minds, we are unable to cognize in any fully intellectual or theoretical manner, but that the limits of speculative reason are such that practical reason has scope enough to operate in its own sphere unimpeded by limitation from the former. *Speculative* reason, that is, does not deny the existence of God or write it off as impossible, but it is only through the medium of the *practical* reason – by reflection on the full implications of the absolute moral imperative – that we can move to the position of cognizing divine existence as an objective truth. In short, whilst pure reason does not tell us that the concept of God is an impossibility, it is practical reason alone – the moral consciousness – which can make the concept real to us. Rational faith may give entry to a realm of knowledge which for theoretic cognition must remain closed.

This certainly would be a conclusion of the highest importance for the claims of theistic belief if the reasoning which leads to it could be shown to be sound, as Kant himself was evidently convinced it is. But what precisely does it mean to argue, as Kant does, that it is 'morally necessary' to assume the existence of God? Is he saying that in order to account for the ultimate end of morality – i.e. a state of things in which virtue and happiness are wedded – the existence of God *must* be posited? If so, then it would appear that God is being adduced as a causal explanation – indeed the only such explanation – of how this comes to pass. For the alternative, as Kant himself states, would be to regard the moral laws as no more than empty figments of the brain', and morality therefore as lacking any finally rational basis.[25] But if the argument is, as it unquestionably looks to some critics to be, an appeal to a transcendent cause in explanation of man's experience as a moral being, then how can it be described as other than *speculative* in intention and purpose? In that case it would simply be furnishing a variant of the metaphysical type of argument as propounded by Descartes, say, or Wolff; and in fact the moral argument for theism has frequently been used by religious thinkers since Kant's time quite expressly as a legitimate inference from data of experience.[26] But if looked on in this way Kant's 'postulate' becomes vulnerable to the very criticisms which he himself has made of similar forms of speculative 'proof'.

But there is an alternative interpretation which would eliminate any transcendent reference in the use of the word 'God', although whether it is one which Kant himself would have endorsed, even though at times his own language seems to point to it, is a debatable matter. According to this view the statement 'God exists' would not involve the positing of a supersensible being having the attributes with which divinity is traditionally associated in theistic religion, but would instead indicate a disposition of the will, a moral attitude or intention. It could be put somewhat as follows: Morality is such that it places us under obligation to promote the *summum bonum*, in the confident assurance, moreover, that that realization of the *summum bonum* is an attainable end and that happiness, in the measure that the highest good is realized, will accompany it. Thus when I speak of God I do so not as implying an ontological reality but as expressing a moral determination; that is, I express my intention to seek the highest good and my conviction both that this can be achieved and that in striving for it I shall also deserve happiness. In brief, I shall be acting, or resolving to act, in a way that marks alike my obedience to the moral law and, therewith, my hope and expectation that my natural inclination to self-fulfilment will be met. In using the term I am articulating or declaring the basic orientation of my life as a rational being, disclosing my fundamental moral attitude or stance.[27]

Kant believes that herein lies the essence of Christianity as distinct from the ethical doctrines of either the Epicureanism or Stoicism of antiquity; for while the former based morality on happiness without regard to obligation, the latter dwelt only on obligation without regard to happiness. In both cases the true character of morality was misconceived, either as something much less than worthy of rational man or else as imposing an excessive demand upon his actual nature.[28] An ethics, however, in the context of which it is appropriate to speak of God is furnished, Kant maintains, by Christianity. To quote his own words:

The moral law does not of itself promise happiness, for the latter is not, according to concepts of any order of nature, necessarily connected with obedience to the law. Christian ethics supplies this defect . . . by presenting a world wherein reasonable beings single-mindedly devote themselves to the moral law; this is the Kingdom of God, in which nature and morality come into a harmony, which is foreign to each as such, through a holy Author of the world, who makes possible the derived highest good.[29]

Kant then points out that the Christian principle of morality is not itself theological, for were the moral law simply delivered to us by God it would in principle be alien, heteronomous, whereas, he says, it is 'the autonomy of the practical reason' in that it does not make the knowledge of God and the divine will the foundation of moral law. Nevertheless he does contend that the moral imperative, along with the conception of the *summum bonum* as the final end and object of the practical reason, leads on to religion, which for him connotes 'the recognition of all duties as divine commands', although primarily they are 'the essential laws of any free will in itself'. There is, then, Kant concludes, a knowledge of God indeed, but only for practical purposes; theoretical knowledge is impossible. So belief in God is simply a practical commitment. A righteous man may say: 'I will that there be a God, that my existence in this world be also an existence in a pure world of the understanding outside the system of natural connections, and finally that my duration be endless. I stand by this and will not give up this belief, for this is the only case where my interest inevitably determines my judgment because I will not yield anything of this interest'.[30]

Any practical resolve to pursue the highest moral good is therefore the only intelligible way of affirming divine existence, theoretical reason or 'intuition' being excluded. Apart from this practical attitude, this direction and purpose of the will issuing in moral action, I can know nothing of God and am unable to speak of him after any fashion that would imply an affirmation of the understanding, however general. My 'faith' implies no logical judgment, no assessment of probabilities, but only an assurance that in discharging my duty purely for duty's sake – that is, with such complete moral integrity as may be possible for me – I shall not fail to attain happiness, not only as a rational but also as a sensible being. Thus metaphysical theology is for the author of the *Critiques* altogether void of content. This at least is what one side of his teaching would seem very plainly to assert, and if it stood alone Kant must surely be taken to have rejected theism outright. At any rate to the ordinary believer his use of the word 'God' would be entirely arbitrary and misleading. But to be fair to the philosopher himself, he evidently had no wish to go that far; for when he denies that one can *know* God it is only when this knowledge is claimed on a metaphysical basis. He does not maintain that *all* knowledge of God is impossible; on the contrary, it is available to us through the 'practical reason'; by this medium we can affirm that God exists and accept that religion has an intelligible content. The question is whether Kant's position here is self-consistent, for whilst with one part of his mind he arrives at a conclusion which refuses us such knowledge, with another he will permit it. But can the assertion that we do have knowledge of God, albeit 'practically' grounded, be intelligibly advanced without implying at least some residual truth-judgment such as can be made only at the 'speculative' or 'theoretical' (or, we may add, 'common-sense') level? For if the transcendent world lies wholly beyond the reach of cognition it is difficult to see how 'willing' (as likewise 'feeling') can repair the deficiency.

The conclusion the reader is very likely to draw from the pages of the 'Dialectic' is that Kant is really trying to have it both ways. He rules out the metaphysical approach because incompatible with the principles of his critical philosophy, but at the same time he is not content with an ethic which makes no reference to belief in God. Thus he introduces the concept of 'practical reason' in order to preserve the theistic dimension in terms of a 'moral faith' (*moralischer Glaube*), meaning thereby an assurance that in the end virtue and happiness are coincident. But practical reason of itself can give us no knowledge of what is or is not the case in the order of external reality; its sole function is to designate a subjective moral attitude, a volitional disposition. Its 'mood' is the imperative, not the indicative, its concern that of doing, not that of reflecting. But obviously action presupposes at least some measure of reflection, and morality presupposes something about the nature of reality the truth of which can be assessed only by rational inquiry. It is along these latter lines, in fact, that the argument from morality on behalf of theistic belief has usually proceeded. In that form, however, it is an argument which has to rely on the 'theoretical reason' and so becomes exposed once again to the sort of criticisms which in any serious discussion of the claims of natural theology will be brought against it. Kant's attempt to sustain the argument 'practically' and without resort to metaphysical considerations must, then, be deemed to be unsuccessful – if, that is, we interpret him as simply endeavouring to use another type of 'proof' to do what the metaphysical arguments failed to do.

IMMORTALITY

But before leaving the *Critique of Practical Reason* we should take note of Kant's argument for immortality, since it too forms part of his 'moral theology'. Speculative reason can of course no more prove the truth of this doctrine than it can prove divine existence, although the first *Critique* did not preclude the possibility that it could be true. The problem raised by the concept of the *summum bonum*, however, is capable of solution only on the assumption that immortality, like the existence of God, is true, so that it too is a postulate of the practical reason. The moral law, that is, obliges us to achieve the highest good possible in this life; yet if complete submission of the will to the moral law is the attainment of holiness it obviously is a state of being not realizable under the conditions of sense, which provide continual inducement to disregard the moral imperative. When, therefore, we understand both that holiness is demanded by the moral law and that it is impossible of achievement in this world, we have to recognize that its possibility depends upon conditions of a wholly different kind, such as would obtain only in a non-physical world and allow the will, by an infinite progress, to reach perfection:

> This infinite progress is possible . . . only under the presupposition of an infinitely enduring existence and personality of the same rational being; this is called the immortality of the soul, and the latter, as inseparably bound to the moral law, is a postulate of pure practical reason.[31]

For an ordinary mortal 'cannot hope here or at any foreseeable point of his future existence to be fully adequate to God's will, without indulgence or remission which would not harmonise with justice. This he can do only in the infinity of his duration which God alone can survey'.[32]

Here again the reader is likely to find himself puzzled by Kant's reasoning. The argument, he sees, involves two principles: the first is that 'ought' implies 'can'; for what I am under obligation to do I must be able to do; the second, that I am likewise under obligation to attain holiness, complete moral perfection, which, on the other hand – as Kant admits – I cannot do. Yet taken together they are incompatible, whilst to abandon either the one or the other would be to destroy the argument altogether.[33] Further, if the soul has unending 'time' in which to strive for the ideal of holiness it is difficult to understand how it also can continue to be in need of happiness, with the consequent peril to an essential element in the case for believing in God, as Kant presents it. Thirdly, and perhaps most obviously, how can a moral struggle be carried on when the conditions no longer obtain which originally gave rise to it? Moral effort, which implies the eventual overcoming of all sensual desire or personal disinclination in order to fulfil one's duty, surely pertains only to the world of sense. It would seem, then, that Kant's defence of immortality is no more solid than his argument for a divine being. But if his logic at this point is indeed so faulty a vital component of his system – for he himself views it as such – would have to be dropped, so that the entire concept of a knowledge obtained through practical reason becomes only very dubiously valid.

Bearing in mind the force of Kant's criticism of speculative metaphysics one wonders how it is that he could seemingly have been unaware of objections like these. For it might look very much as though Schopenhauer's quip, that Kant only smuggled in by the back door what he had thrown out at the front, has its truth.[34] But in regard to the postulates of both immortality and God it is important to realize just what Kant is trying to do. It is not – let us be clear – that he rejects the whole notion of metaphysical *truth*. What he bars is the old style of metaphysical *argument*, deployed in the confidence that this truth can be established in much the same way as truth in the physical order, so that we can have an 'objective' knowledge of it independent of the conditions of subjective consciousness itself. For the moral consciousness is to him a factor that cannot be left out of account if man's knowledge *in its entire range* is to be explained. God and immortality, that is to say, are not simply objects of the rational understanding, access to which is afforded by the logic of ordinary reasoning unaffected by moral considerations. On the contrary, except on the basis of the moral consciousness we know nothing of them. We come to believe in them only by reflection on morality and what it implies.

To be a little more explicit. In the case of belief in immortality, what Kant is saying is that we have an obligation to pursue the life of virtue in obedience to the moral law, but being the finite and sense-bound creatures that we are, the attainment of virtue involves great moral effort, a continuing moral struggle. With complete moral victory, however, all striving would cease and a state of holiness be achieved, so that to reach such a state must also be seen as obligatory. Yet it is one which, under the conditions of finitude, is actually unattainable. Hence it follows from what the moral law itself demands that an unending life – a life hereafter, that is – is something which must be believed in – even though the belief may not in fact be present to the mind – if our recognition of the categorical imperative is to satisfy our rational nature. In the case of belief in God, a state of things in which happiness would be proportioned to virtue is not within mortal man's capacity, however sustained his effort may be. But without conjunction of happiness and virtue the *summum bonum* as the aggregate of all moral ends, would not have been attained. Nevertheless, his persistence in the way of virtue denotes confidence that the highest good will be realized and hence belief that a Power or Being exists who uniquely is able, as the omnipotent and wise creator of all things, to bring this conjunction about. Belief in God therefore cannot be separated from belief in the possibility of the *summum bonum*. What, in essence, Kant is telling his reader is this: Examine your moral consciousness – an integral part of your rational nature – and you will discover that belief in God, as likewise in the soul's immortality, is a necessary consequence of the obligation it lays upon you. You will accept it, that is, as a matter of rational *faith*.

4
Teleology

'THE CRITIQUE OF JUDGMENT'

The third of Kant's *Critiques*, *Die Kritik der Urteilskraft* (*The Critique of Judgment*, or more accurately, *The Critique of the Faculty of Judgment*), appeared ten years after the first, in 1790.[1] However, despite the fact that its author tried to impose on it the same structure as we find in the earlier works – although it has to be said that the second, *The Critique of Practical Reason*, is itself only artificially and to its detriment made to fit the pattern of the first – it really consists of a series of appendices, each more or less self-complete, to what has gone before, the only connecting motif between the several sections being the idea of *purpose*. *The Critique of Pure Reason* had dealt with the problem of our knowledge of the causally determined world of nature, its successor with the world of freedom and moral action; the instrument of the one was theoretical or speculative reason, that of the other, practical – the moral consciousness and its implications. But the two worlds were apparently sundered; theoretical reason was inapplicable to the second, practical reason to the first. Yet the world of freedom could not be thought of as wholly separate from that of causal necessity unless altogether incapable of influencing nature, in which case the principles of practical reason could not be translated into effective action. Kant was well aware of this dichotomy and evidently felt that he could not leave the resultant dualism unresolved and the two differing orders or modes of man's rational apprehension unreconciled. Nature accordingly needed to be looked at afresh to discover whether it might reveal some aspect of its being that could be seen as a link between them by admitting the possibility of freedom and purpose. It belongs to the very idea of freedom, Kant states, to actualize in the world of sense the end proposed by its laws, so that nature, in compliance with the law of its form, must at least be capable of harmonizing with that end. Hence 'there must be a ground of unity of the supersensible that lies at the basis of nature, with that which the concept of freedom practically contains'.[2] Such a principle, while not yielding a knowledge of the sensible world, and thus having no realm of its own, would nonetheless enable the mind 'to make the transition from the theoretical to the practical standpoint'. Or putting it in terms of philosophical understanding, what is required is a bridge to join theoretical philosophy with moral, so rendering possible a rational linkage between knowledge of the natural order and that of the moral. Kant locates this connection in the faculty of judgment, described by him as 'the faculty of thinking the particular as contained under the universal'.[3]

The *Critique of Judgment* is of great interest as to its subject-matter, but it is not without its difficulties. Kant himself considered it to be 'the crowning phase of the critical philosophy', and the vindication of his entire system. But the form of the book, with its subdivisions suggested, as in the first *Critique*, by formal logic and seeming often to have little enough connection with the topics discussed under them, presents a somewhat curious alignment of formal system and discursive content, and for many commentators since Kant's time it only provides further evidence of inconsistencies in his thought which they had detected all along. But from Kant's own standpoint the argument of this concluding treatise was vital to his scheme as a whole, and he had no doubt that its component parts do possess a significant unity. We can take account of it here only so far as the concept of teleology, which he discusses in the latter part of the book, relates to his idea of the divine; but it is necessary to have some grasp of his thesis if we are to follow his reasoning on this particular theme.

Kant distinguishes judgment (*Urteilskraft*) from understanding (*Verstand*), the principles of which are of course specifically, and much more fully, the subject of the first *Critique*. The understanding, as he sees it, is the faculty of rules, whereas judgment is disclosed in the application of such rules to individual instances. We may regard it as the element of individuality and spontaneity in all thinking, something for which no rules can be discovered. Judgment, in fact, cannot be taught; it is a purely personal faculty which rational beings possess in varying degree, and has the character of insight; in a way it is akin to genius. What Kant's inquiry amounts to, then, is this: Can the mind (*das Gemüt*), in its intercourse with individual persons in all their variety and difference, be guided by any general rules or principles or criteria? The point of the question can be made clearer if we relate it, as Kant himself does, to the subject of causation. This, according to him, is an *a priori* principle of the understanding, and thus is an essential constituent of all experience; but it tells us nothing about particular causes. These have to be investigated empirically, and the personal knowledge, skill and judgment of the investigator make up a highly relevant factor. Indeed this is what Kant means by the *faculty* of judgment, and its province, in the present instance of causation, includes an indefinite number of causal laws or principles. But this multiformity can be reduced by scientists to some kind of unity by assuming continuity in nature; they thus discern in their collective knowledge something very much more coherent than a mere aggregate of separate rules or principles. These assumptions, Kant points out, differ from the principles or rules of the understanding, in that whereas the latter provide the indispensable conditions of all experience, the former have no such necessity, and in fact the unity posited or assumed has never actually been attained – a failure that in no way invalidates the experience on which the drive to unity is based. It is this directing, guiding idea which, as we already have noted, Kant describes as 'regulative'; its use is heuristic, helping to advance knowledge. Unlike the categories of the understanding regulative ideas are not constitutive of phenomena. They lead us towards the view that nature is, as Kant has it, *purposive to the understanding;* they suggest an order in nature which systematic investigation endeavours to trace there. This assumption, although not strictly demonstrable, may be made, however, with increasing assurance and profit.

'PURPOSE' IN NATURE

According to Kant, then, the faculty of judgment assumes as a regulative principle the teleological aspect of the natural order – that nature would not, in truth, be intelligible without our reading into it the idea of intent. But in the first part of the *Critique* he devotes a good deal of space to the consideration of art, because in our judgment of beauty too, he thinks, we are interested in it from a sense of general purposiveness. Indeed for him aesthetic judgment is the supreme act of the faculty of judgment. It looks on a particular object as giving aesthetic pleasure for its own sake, as an intrinsic source of satisfaction, without attempting to relate it to any particular desire or to bring it under some general rule or concept: it is simply disinterested. But although aesthetic judgment might appear on the face of it to be only a matter of individual feeling we do believe it to be no mere reflection of the observer's idiosyncrasy but to have universal validity:

> Since the delight is not based on any inclination by the subject (or any other deliberate interest), but the subject feels himself completely *free* in respect to the liberty which he accords to the object, he can find reasons for his delight in no personal conditions to which his own subjective self might alone be a party. Hence he must regard it as resting on what he may also presuppose in every other person; and therefore he must believe that he has reason for demanding a similar delight from every one.[4]

This universality, however, is not objective but subjective. Aesthetic judgment is not determined by any rule or concept and in this respect is quite different from morality. A simple way of putting it would be to say that whilst a thing of beauty is significant, it has no *specific* significance. Its meaning cannot be framed in a scientific statement nor abstracted from its form; nonetheless we regard it as possessing *meaning*. That we think of an aesthetic judgment as free while at the same time claiming for it universal validity may be explained, says Kant, by the notion that a beautiful object is such that its contemplation kindles and enhances the two faculties of the intelligence, the imagination and the understanding, in their proper proportion and harmony. It is for this reason that art also can be described as 'purposive to the understanding'.

The sense of beauty thus seems to induce in us a more concrete view of the world, in which any sharp distinction between what is and what ought to be begins to lessen, and the antithesis between determinism and freedom to be overcome. Although art is neither science nor ethics, it yet is an intensely real part of our rational experience. It seems to have a purpose, but not one that can be particularized (*Zweckmässigkeit ohne Zweck*). In this sense aesthetic judgment can be regarded also as teleological, at any rate subjectively speaking, and from it Kant makes a natural transition to the question of teleology in nature. But when we recall his interest in the argument from design – albeit that he allows it no probative force – it should come as no surprise to the reader of the *Critique of Judgment* that its author's lengthy reflections on teleology are made to bear directly on his philosophical or 'moral' theology.

Kant's main criticism of the design argument in its usual form was that it could at most do no more than establish the existence of an intelligent architect or artificer – or even possibly a plurality of them – working upon independent pre-existent material, and not an omnipotent and omniscient Creator in the full theistic meaning. In the *Critique of Judgment*, however, with its more searching discussion of the argument, he entertains the idea of design in nature in a less external manner:

> We do not [he observes] say half enough of Nature and her capacity in organized products when we speak of this capacity as being the *analogue of art* (*Analogon der Kunst*). For what is here present to our minds is an artist – a rational being – working from without. But Nature, on the contrary, organizes itself, and does so in each species of its original products – following a single pattern, certainly, as to general features, but nevertheless admitting deviations calculated to secure self-preservation under particular circumstances. We might perhaps come nearer to the description of this impenetrable property if we were to call it an *analogue of life* (*Analogon des Lebens*).[5]

The difficulty with this approach, as Kant immediately points out, is that we still are left with a problem on our hands; for if we conceive purposive causality as actually operating within matter we are evidently assigning to matter itself a property (hylozoism) which contradicts its essential nature, a course which would mean 'the death of all science'. On the other hand, if we associate it with a soul connected with the body concerned we resign ourselves to a supernaturalism no less fatal to scientific inquiry. Strictly speaking, therefore, the organization of nature is not analogous to any causality known to us. Thus the 'analogue of life' idea is really of little help, and we are driven to conclude that the concept of a thing as in itself a material purpose is not to be thought of as a constitutive concept of the understanding or of reason; but it may rightly serve as a regulative principle for the reflective judgment, to guide our investigation of objects of this kind by at any rate a distant analogy with our own purposive causality generally, and as a basis for reflection upon their ultimate ground. In this respect the teleological concept has to be seen as an appropraite *maxim* for controlling our study of organisms. But the question of the actual character of nature's seeming purposiveness must remain open, for we cannot in fact decide whether within nature itself the mechanical and the purposive may not somehow be combined in a single principle.[6]

In all this Kant treads very cautiously, being careful to avoid coming down on the side either of sheer mechanism or of an inherent purposiveness. Rather does he present the issue as an antinomy, the thesis of which states that all production (*Erzeugung*) in the natural order has to be judged possible according to purely mechanical laws, and the antithesis, that some products (*Produkte*) of physical nature cannot be so judged. Actual contradiction, however, does not arise so long as these two propositions are not converted into 'constitutive principles of the possibility of objects'. For reason is unable to prove the truth of either, because although teleology cannot be demonstrated there is 'no determining principle of the possibility of things according to mere empirical laws of nature'. What the antithesis says is that there may be bodies the mechanical origin of which is unknown to us, but even if we cannot state positively that a given organism is explicable in terms of the mechanism of nature we are able to affirm – as indeed we must do – that human reason is not in a position to pronounce organisms to be inexplicable by mechanical laws alone, with the consequence that we have to look at them in the light of the principle of final causes. Thus Kant seeks to preserve the universality of mechanical causation as essential to discursive understanding, while at the same time maintaining that for an intuitive understanding mechanism and teleology may be conjoined. In a somewhat earlier work, *Über den Gebrauch teleologischer Principien in der Philosophie* ('The Use of Teleological Principles in Philosophy') (1788), we even find him asserting quite plainly that because in an organism each part is both means and end in respect of all the rest, explanation solely according to physico-chemical laws is insufficient and the idea of teleology is indispensable. 'To abandon teleological grounds of explanation in order to make room for physical grounds in the case of organized beings regarding the preservation of their species is wholly unthinkable.'[7]

Kant's solution to the problem is, therefore, that both mechanism and teleology have to be seen as regulative principles only, in that if the two together result in an antinomy neither of them can be taken as constitutive of reality. Mechanism assumes that reality is a complex of recurring or interchangeable parts whose changes are necessitated, whereas teleology regards the world as inexplicable unless purpose is introduced as an operative agency in change. From the strictly scientific angle purposive agency in nature is inadmissible, but from that of freedom, as required by morality and religion, mechanism cannot offer the final answer. Thus although neither mechanism nor purposiveness provides the sole key to the ultimate nature of reality, together they tell us that much can be accounted for by looking on it as a machine, and much also by seeing in it a field of purpose. A broad enough view of nature will allow that our understanding of it is consistent with either principle, each being used as far as it will appear to take us.

Teleology cannot, then, be established on a theoretic or scientific basis, although it influences science by interpreting nature as though it constituted an organism using mechanical causality in order to realize its own forms and ends. But if philosophy may accept that mechanism and teleology are not incompatible, it has a wider interest in the latter to the extent that it conceives nature as a single vast system of which man is the supreme end. Without man, Kant declares, the whole creation would be a mere desert, in vain and without final purpose; although he hastens to add that it is only as moral beings that we recognize in man the purpose of creation.[8] Philosophy is impelled to ask why nature exists, and can supply no answer to its question without prescribing some kind of destiny for it, or without imagining a being who, in creating nature, assigned to it an ultimate end; in which case nature has a relative existence only, since it exists for something other than itself. Apart from nature there is but one being who acts with a view to ends, and that is man as a rational and moral entity, free and autonomous. We may not ask what purpose man himself serves, because he is his own proper end. We do, however, become possessed of the idea that nature exists simply in order that rational and moral man may exist and fulfil himself. Teleology, no doubt, has again and again been used as a springboard for 'physico-theology', as Kant dubs it, although of course unavailingly, since the design argument is quite ineffective to prove divine existence. Indeed:

> It proves no more than this, that by the constitution of our cognitive faculties, and, therefore, in bringing experience into

touch with the highest principles of reason, we are absolutely incapable of forming any conception of the possibility of such a world [as ours] unless we imagine a highest cause *operating designedly*.[9]

Objectively, we are unable to state that there is 'an intelligent original Being'. At least, if we venture the assertion it is only because we rest it on a purely regulative principle of subjective *interpretation*. In other words, the supreme Being, or God, can never be more than an affirmation of the practical reason, of moral faith. It does not prove to the sceptic that there is a God, but simply that, if he wishes to think in a way consonant with morality, he must admit the *assumption* of the proposition under the maxims of the practical reason. Thus the existence neither of God nor his attributes is demonstrable, and theology cannot be 'scientific'; it is solely a matter of practical belief, such belief being definable as 'the moral attitude of reason in its assurance of the truth of what is beyond the reach of theoretical knowledge'.[10] So the *Critique of Judgment* ends with a theological discussion, similar to that in which the two former *Critiques* had culminated. Surely, even without the treatise to come on *Religion within the Limits of Reason Alone*, we here have evidence enough of Kant's deep-seated preoccupation with the problem which religion raises for reason, and proof enough that for him neither the one nor the other could ever be discounted.

5
Rational Theology Reviewed, and the Question of Theodicy

KANT'S LECTURES ON PHILOSOPHICAL THEOLOGY

As professor of philosophy at Königsberg it was part of Kant's academic routine to lecture each winter semester on the *Metaphysica* of Christian Wolff's pupil, Alexander Gottlieb Baumgarten, a standard text-book of Wolffian rationalism which comprised also a treatise on natural theology. Occasionally, however, he would deliver a series of lectures expressly on philosophical theology in the sense then current, and the course on this subject which he gave during the winter of 1783–84 seems to have been especially popular.[1] These lectures never saw print in Kant's lifetime, but what is now presumed to have been their text was published by K. H. L. Pölitz in 1817 as *Immanuel Kants Vorlesungen über die Religionslehre* from a manuscript in the possession of Kant's friend Rink, a second edition appearing in 1830. Pölitz claimed that his text was a 'careful transcript of Kant's own words', and it is this which was re-published by the Berlin Academy of Sciences in *Kants Gesammelte Schriften* in 1972,[2] together with three other, though shorter and fragmentary, manuscript versions of Kant's lectures. But the editor of this modern edition, Gerhard Lehmann, is somewhat dubious of the full authenticity of the Pölitz text as it stands, suggesting that it is really a synthesis of the other three. Yet there is little reason to suppose that the manuscript which Pölitz acquired from Rink was not in all essentials at least Kant's original discourses. Certainly its contents do not deviate from the teachings set out in the works Kant himself published, even if, for example, the treatment of 'physicotheology' here is less negative than is the case with them.[3]

Kant's style as a lecturer, to judge from contemporary accounts, was a good deal less forbidding than as a writer for publication. One of his biographers, Jachmann, describes it as 'always clear and attractive'.[4] His exposition was methodical, erudite and often witty, although sometimes digressive. But he evidently sought no mere rhetorical effect, and some students found his manner dry. He disliked too much verbatim note-taking on the part of his pupils, preferring that they gave his arguments as he unfolded them their closest attention. His aim was, in fact, not so much to *teach* philosophy, as though it were a fixed body of ideas, as to 'do' it, encouraging his pupils to think it out for themselves.

The interest of these lectures – assuming their substantial authenticity – is in Kant's quite impartial, some might even say, sympathetic, presentation of the concept of God formulated in rational theology of the Leibniz–Wolff type. Certainly he was well acquainted with the rationalist tradition in this regard, and he fully appreciated the view that theism as an 'ideal of reason' involves a series of coherent ideas which, if not open to theoretical proof (or disproof), are at least not subject to inner contradiction; although no doubt on examination most of the knowledge thus claimed in the name of reason turns out to be of a purely negative kind, a recognition that the diverse qualities of things finite and sensible – things, that is, as known to us – cannot correctly be ascribed to an *ens realissimum*, a being conceived as embracing all reality.[5] Kant is convinced that it is altogether natural for reason to attempt to formulate a conception of the divine, since rational curiosity itself impels us to do so. What he cannot concur with is the notion of the traditional metaphysics that theology can be transformed from an inevitable object of speculative inquiry into a theoretical science offering genuine knowledge of divine being. However, rational assurance of God's existence, even though 'objectively insufficient', can nonetheless be 'subjectively sufficient', so that what is objectively insufficient may yet be taken as true. For when we say that something transcendental is the case what we mean is that we affirm its reality although supported neither by empirical nor by *a priori* intuition, whereas of course objectively sufficient grounds permit of a determinate judgment of things intuitively.

The lectures set out Kant's views on much of the content of the traditional metaphysical theology; namely, the nature and attributes of God, his relation to the world, the divine causality, creation and providence. He also reconsiders at some length the speculative proofs of divine existence under the headings 'onto-theology', 'cosmo-theology' and 'physico-theology' respectively, although he again finds then wanting in cogency. 'All this speculation', he says, 'depends, in substance, on the transcendental concept'.

> But if we posit that it is not correct, would we then have to give up the knowledge of God?. Not at all. For then we would only lack the scientific knowledge that God exists. But a great field would still remain to us, and this would be the belief or faith (*Glaube*) that God exists. This faith will derive *a priori* from *moral principles*. Hence if ... we raise doubts about these speculative proofs and take issue with the supposed demonstration of God's existence, we will not thereby undermine faith in God.[6]

For the aridities of deism, with its idea of a God entirely transcending all experience, Kant had little time. 'The deist's conception is wholly idle and useless and makes no impression on me if I assume it alone.'[7] At the same time anthropomorphism has to be avoided, and an unthinking way of speaking of God which would appear to represent him as an object directly accessible to our mode of cognition is not only wrong theoretically but is liable, Kant thinks, to have a corrupting effect on our moral character, although, following Baumgarten, he further distinguishes between 'vulgar anthropomorphism' where God is thought of in human shape, and the 'subtle' kind, where human perfections are assigned to God but without discounting their limitations.[8] 'It is better not to be able to represent something at all than only to be able to think of it confused with errors', and he concedes the usefulness of analogy (*per viam analogiam*).[9] But this does not prevent him from suggesting the corrective value of scepticism if it compels us to recognize the importance of faith. 'If our faith', he exclaims, 'is not scientific knowledge, thank heaven it is not!' For God's wisdom is apparent in the very fact that we are unable to *know* that he exists, but rather should be required to *believe* that he does so. 'For suppose we could attain to scientific knowledge of God's existence ... then, in this case, all our morality would break down. In his every action, man would represent God to himself as a rewarder or avenger.' Such an image would force itself involuntarily upon the soul, and one's hopes for reward and fear of punishment would take the place of moral motives. 'Man would be virtuous out of sensuous impulses.'[10] Kant's statement anticipates, so English readers may recall, a dictum of S. T. Coleridge's that the existence of God 'could not be intellectually more evident without becoming morally less effective'.[11] In fact Kant's position reflects a recurrent tendency in German Lutheranism to throw knowledge and faith into antithesis. It surely is clear therefore that whatever degree of intellectual favour theological rationalism may have found in Kant's sight, as in its way a consistent attempt to show the rational strength of the idea of an *ens realissimum*, it would be a mistake to approximate his own considered thinking to it.[12]

WHERE REASON FALTERS

In 1791 Kant published an essay bearing the title *Über das Misslingen aller philosophischen Versuche in der Theodicee* ('On the Miscarriage of all Philosophical Attempts at Theodicy').[13] In it he was concerned to point out some of the difficulties inevitably to be encountered whenever believers seek reasoned justification of the ways of God to men. For the apologist will obviously have to provide an adeqaate explanation of the existence, in a world created by a supreme Being who is no less benevolent than omnipotent, of pain and undeserved suffering as well as of moral evil. This has long been a problem the solution of which has never perhaps succeeded in yielding an answer that is at once logically coherent and morally satisfying. Leibniz had discussed it at considerable length in his famous *Theodicy* (1710), in which he had sought to parry the accusation that God himself was the author of sin and indeed of evil in general. In doing so he had drawn upon a tradition of teaching that derived ultimately from the Stoics but was taken up by St Augustine and again used by Descartes in the fourth of his *Meditations métaphysiques*. To follow it he had to distinguish between metaphysical evil, or imperfection, physical evil, or suffering, and culpable evil, or sin. Imperfection can be attributed to the limitations to which all creatures are subject, although if one bears in mind that God created beings with due regard to the place of each within the entire scheme of things and takes account not of any single part merely but the universe as a whole one will come to understand that the world we know is really the best possible, in which every creature at every moment has the special perfection appropriate to it. It is only because we perceive things in isolation and abstraction that they appear less perfect than they are. Physical evil or suffering, on the other hand, is explicable either as itself a consequence of imperfection, or else of sin, through fulfilment of divine justice. In the case of culpable evil Leibniz held that the fault of Adam was not simply an imperfection but a positive force, the result of Adam's own deliberate choice. As such it had changed man's entire destiny, having introduced into the course of things the element of discontinuity which Leibniz himself wished to eliminate from his view of the universe.

This optimism, however, which Voltaire had satirized in *Candide* in the person of his Dr Pangloss, Kant was unable to share, since reason could offer no tidy way out of the moral difficulty which sin and evil are bound to pose for the believer in both God's goodness and power. In the end the attitude of Job in the Old Testament was, he thought, the only acceptable one. The facts of life as we know them to be cannot be denied without offence to moral sensibility: the plea, *sunt superis sua jura*, 'the gods have their own code', is not to be allowed; nor is that of redress hereafter any more satisfactory. But a man may preserve, as did Job, a practical faith in the divine justice, not because we think we can arrive at a fully rational understanding of how this always operates but because we are convinced that it is our duty to live in accordance with conscience, whatever the situation in which we find ourselves. But Kant well appreciated the fact that the disposition of the Old Testament hero did not win the approval of the orthodox of his day as represented by his 'comforters', and did not refrain from expressing his doubt that had Job been summoned before some modern ecclesiastical court or 'high consistory' he would have met with an unpleasant fate.[14]

This last observation was no mere generality; it had a particular point. On the death of Frederick the Great, Voltaire's friend and patron, in 1786, a new monarch, Frederick William II, acceded to the Prussian throne who soon showed himself zealous for Protestant orthodoxy. Two years later the liberal minded von Zedlitz, minister of public worship and education and an admirer of Kant's to whom the latter had dedicated the *Critique of Pure Reason*, was replaced by a certain Johann Wöllner, a former pastor and a man totally opposed to the attitudes and ideas of the *Aufklärung*. On 9

July 1788 the new minister published an edict under royal authority threatening dismissal from office, accompanied with civil penalties, of all teachers, clerical or lay, of subjects having a bearing on religion who might be found to deviate from sound biblical doctrine. Three years later a commission of three members was established with extensive powers of censorship over all books whatsoever dealing with religious matters, no publication being allowed which had not received the necessary *imprimatur*. Kant himself had always entertained a deep respect for authority and was therefore not personally inclined to treat it with contumely on this occasion, or – let it be said – to present himself as a candidate for martyrdom. But a 'Concluding Remark' in his essay nevertheless made clear allusion to Wöllner's edict and the certification of orthodoxy which it required, and spoke of a *tortura spiritualis* applied in respect of ideas and beliefs which of their very nature were not amenable to precise dogmatic formulation. Any affirmation of 'faith' made under duress or without due thought for what was involved was declared to be a lie – an 'outright falsehood', and 'impious' as undermining 'the foundation of every virtuous intention: sincerity'. 'How quickly', Kant added, 'such blind and superficial *creeds* (which readily become contemptible with an equally untrue inward creed), when they provide the means of livelihood, can by degrees bring the commonwealth to a certain falsity in thinking, is easily to be seen.'[15] No reference was made to Wöllner by name, but the author's mind was unequivocally plain. At any rate his words did not escape notice in Berlin, as he was shortly to discover when he submitted to the censor Hillmer the second of the four parts which compose his *Religion within the Limits of Reason Alone*, although the first part had been formally approved and published in the April 1792 issue of the *Berliner Monatsschrift*, Hillmer's comment then being that it might be printed, 'since only profound scholars read Kant'.

But in spite of his advancing age and physical frailty Kant was not the man merely to accept an official rebuff of this kind. His whole concern had been guided by his sense of the rights of reason and the demands of personal moral integrity. The inquiry upon which he had embarked was one that could not be inhibited by a brusque gesture on the part of the civil authority, for all the respect in which he held it, as also his full recognition that a minister of religion in dealing with his congregation, especially its younger members, was bound (as Kant puts it) 'to conform his discourse to the symbols of the church he serves'. The position of a scholar, however, was different; not only had the latter the freedom, he also had the obligation, to communicate to the educated public his own considered and critical views on the church's doctrines. It was his privilege and his duty so to do. Thus minded, Kant referred the three unpublished parts of his new work to the philosophical faculty of Jena, which was among a number of German universities possessing the right to authorize publication of books treating of religious subjects, seeking its approbation. The hoped-for *imprimatur* was forthcoming and *Religion within the Limits of Reason Alone* was published at Königsberg in 1793. But in this he incurred the government's displeasure, bluntly expressed in a missive from the king himself which chided him for his 'misuse' of his philosophy 'to undermine and debase' some of the fundamental teachings of Christianity, and calling on him to proffer a 'conscientious answer' immediately, with the further demand, 'for the avoidance of our highest disfavour', that no such offence was repeated in the future, and even threatening 'unpleasant consequences' should resistance on Kant's part be continued.[16]

Kant did indeed reply, and in terms for which he has since been criticized. The first section was by way of an apology for his published work: he wrote on religious matters simply in his character as a scholar addressing his fellow-scholars, and in a manner which the government would surely desire to encourage. His purpose was constructive: to indicate how best, in his opinion, religion could be presented to the people. But the work itself was not intended for a popular readership. In any case, if his standpoint did appear critical, it was only so of the currently favoured 'natural' religion of reason, which he himself considered to be inadequate in its theoretical aspect, and notably in its failure to deal at all seriously with the problem of evil. His own regard for Christianity was of the highest and he felt no doubt what the Bible offers for instructing the public conscience in a truly moral spirituality. In view of his years, he then went on to say, and the near approach of that time when he could expect to be called to account for his life before the Supreme Judge, he could not dissimulate. And he ended by giving the king his solemn declaration henceforth to refrain entirely from all public statements on religion whether natural or revealed, either in his lectures or in his writings. The promise, in which some have detected a rather craven submission, was kept until 1797, when the king died, Kant's view being that acquiescence in the royal will was personal to Frederick William himself and not binding after that monarch's demise. All the same, Kant did not withhold a slightly enlarged second edition of his book from public circulation in 1794.[17] The state minister Wöllner's dismissal in 1797 resulted in the cancellation of the 1788 edicts.

Part Two
Interpreting Christianity

6
The Radical Evil in Human Nature

'RELIGION WITHIN THE LIMITS OF REASON ALONE'

Towards the end of the *Critique of Pure Reason*, in the section entitled the 'Canon of Pure Reason', Kant poses the three fundamental questions which in his view philosophy should attempt to answer. They are: (1) What can I know? (2) What ought I to do? and (3) What may I hope for?[1] In a letter to Carl Friedrich Stäudlin of Göttingen, dated 4 May 1793 – on the morrow, that is, of the publication of *Die Religion innerhalb der Grenzen der blossen Vernunft* – he repeats these same questions and states that with this last book of his he had sought to complete the philosophical scheme which had begun with the first of the *Critiques*. In the new work, he writes, 'a scrupulous conscience and a genuine respect for the Christian religion' had combined with a free determination to conceal nothing and to affirm openly how he believed it possible to unite religion with 'the most pure practical reason'.[2] The letter also clearly indicates that Kant regarded the content of *Religion within the Limits of Reason Alone* as an integral part of his systematic philosophical enterprise and not simply as an addition external to it. But if he himself saw it thus his statement is nonetheless misleading should it be taken to mean that three *Critiques*, followed now by a substantial book on religion, were the outcome of a preconceived plan. For the fact is that the scheme of thought evolved in these works found expression only rather tentatively and with the modifications Kant judged to be necessary when he came actually to write them. At the outset he conceived no clear distinction between the practical reason and the theoretical, but only between a practical and a theoretical *use* of the pure reason, the field of activity of which would constitute the subject-matter of a critical investigation to be completed within the covers of a single volume. Hence the *Critique of Pure Reason* would then have sufficed to provide answers to all three questions. In the event, however, this simple design did not prove feasible. A second *Critique* had to be produced, and then a third, even though this last, as we have remarked, is really little else than an extended appendix to its two predecessors and is only so called because of its author's love of system and symmetry. The result was that when he had finished the latter Kant had in effect carried out his plan, but it had needed three volumes for its accomplishment. What these works had achieved was, in fine, the 'critical philosophy'; and indeed Kant himself had said as much in the Preface to the *Critique of Judgment*:[3]

> With this, then, I bring my entire critical undertaking to a close. I shall hasten to the doctrinal part, in order, as far as possible, to snatch from my advancing years what time may yet be favourable to the task. It is obvious that no separate division of Doctrine is reserved for the faculty of judgment, seeing that with judgment Critique takes the place of Theory; but, following the division of philosophy into theoretical and practical, and of pure philosophy in the same way, the whole Ground will be covered by the Metaphysic of Nature and Morals.

What *Religion* offers, along with other writings of Kant's such as *Die Metaphysik der Sitten* (*The Metaphysic of Morals*) (1797) and *Die metaphysische Anfangsgründe der Naturwissenschaft* ('The Metaphysical First Principles of Science') (1786), is the application of the critical principles to a particular sphere of thought. In the order of logic Kant should have produced the *Metaphysic of Morals* first, following it up with a discussion of religion. This however he did not do, and one may very reasonably suppose that the ageing author felt that it was time he set about tackling the religious problem as something which had never been far from his mind throughout life. Certainly it is not an area one would have regarded as immediately adjacent to those covered by the *Critiques*, although all three of them confront the question of rational theology. But religion, in the form in which he himself knew it, evidently raised for him a difficulty which he did not see his way to solving merely by the straight application of his philosophical principles. This difficulty was the presence in human life of what he designates as 'radical evil', *das radicale Böse*.

But how was that – an indubitable fact of the human situation –

The Radical Evil in Human Nature

to be fitted into a tightly rational philosophical scheme? To do so it was necessary, Kant saw, to take account of the answer supplied by divine revelation. The issue, seemingly lying outside the grasp of theoretical reason, was urgent. On the one hand, religion was a realm of human experience from which it was possible to gain a profound knowledge of man and his spiritual needs. But, on the other, was it not also impossible to accept it on the supernaturalist credentials and in the forms presented by the churches? A middle way had to be found; for the title Kant gave to his book was not meant to signify such an *a priori* view of religion as would render it deducible from purely rational principles, a procedure which would have set it altogether beyond what men normally understand by it. Rationalism of this kind was not what he contemplated. As he states in the Preface to the second edition:

> Regarding the title of this work (for doubts have been expressed about the intention concealed thereunder) I note: that since, after all, *revelation* can certainly embrace the pure religion of reason, while conversely, the second cannot include what is historical in the first, I shall be able [experimentally] to regard the first as the *wider* sphere of faith, which includes within itself the second, as a *narrower* one (not like two circles external to each other, but like concentric circles). The philosopher, as a teacher of pure reason (from unassisted principles *a priori*), must confine himself within the narrower circle, and, in so doing, must waive consideration of all experience. From this standpoint I can also make a second experiment, namely to start from some alleged revelation or other and, leaving out of consideration the pure religion of reason (so far as it constitutes a self-sufficient system), to examine in a fragmentary manner this revelation, as an *historical* system, in the light of moral concepts; and then to see whether it does not lead back to the very same pure *rational system* of religion.[4]

Quite evidently, this standpoint does not preclude religion, as a matter of faith, from being itself, in a broad sense, rational. That is to say, that while not everything which traditionally is part of the received belief is to be regarded as rational, it does imply that in its essence faith also pertains to the reason. Kant's purpose therefore is not in any way to revive the claims of dogmatic metaphysics – for these the critical philosophy has demonstrated to be invalid –

but to show that the Christian religion, in its historic lineaments, is conformable with what he calls 'moral theology', resting on a new metaphysics of the practical reason. What *Religion within the Limits of Reason Alone* offers us is, accordingly, a reinterpretation of Christianity solely in terms of moral values. 'Revealed' religion may thus be seen to embody truths which dogmatic metaphysics is unable to convey on its own account. For if the kind of metaphysical basis for religion which 'natural theology' purported to lay down is no longer available another is provided by the critical philosophy itself. Furthermore, it presents criteria by which the traditional content of Christianity is itself to be judged.[5] For what is contrary to reason is to be rejected, the morally acceptable sifted out from the superstitious dross; although it should also be recognized that reason may yet sanction certain beliefs which it cannot expressly justify.

Kant's method, then, is to apply reason to an object historically given and hence incapable of precise definition, not to determine that object on preconceived rational principles. In this sense Kant's 'religion within the limits of reason alone' is not to be construed as a 'religion of reason'. What he has in view is Christianity as he knew it himself, the religion in which he was nurtured as a child and which throughout his life he had seen practised around him. But this means that his approach to Christianity is not primarily theological; his interest is, rather, in the church as an institution and in the religious beliefs commonly held and taught. Indeed Kant makes little or no attempt to adopt the standpoint of the academic theologian. He illustrates his argument from a variety of sources, assembled in the course of his reading, but his references to theological writers are notable for their absence. It is difficult to believe that this omission resulted purely from ignorance; but evidence is lacking that he had read much contemporary theology. What is more surprising is that authors like Leibniz, Locke, Shaftesbury, Hume and Rousseau, who had very much to say that bore on religion and in whose works Kant was of course well versed, citing them frequently in his other writings, do not figure at all in these pages. Lutheran though he was by upbringing, and living in an environment steeped in the Protestant tradition, he never alludes to the Reformation or the Reformers, of whom his knowledge may not, in fact, have been more than sketchy. The mediaeval Catholic thinkers or the early Christian Fathers he never mentions. Yet he is by no means without a penetrative insight into and understanding of some of the main

Christian doctrines such as revelation, providence, the Trinity and the Church visible and invisible, as to which he has, for the most part, far more spiritual perception than the deists. The most plausible explanation of this silence is that it was deliberate, that he wished to limit his discussion in accordance with his particular objective – to get to what he thought of as the heart of the religious attitude. And this, for his purposes, had its fully adequate expression in the Bible: his knowledge of and reverence for the scriptures, especially the New Testament, is evident throughout. For the Bible he sees as the one authority for Christian belief and the foundation of the Christian church. But it is to the text itself that he has recourse. To the work of the biblical commentators he is indifferent, just as he is to the complicated theological structures which the letter at least of scripture had all too often been made to support. His concern is with the core of the faith, as distinct from anything that is merely adventitious, irrelevant or corrupt. But his treatment of such a doctrine as the Trinity would nevertheless have been better informed had he studied it in one or another of its classic expositions. For the truth is that in dealing with the belief and practice of historic Christianity he can never divest himself wholly of the simplistic rationalism and lack of historical sense so far characteristic of his age.

In approaching this work the reader should therefore be advised that Kant is deliberately taking up a position of independence: he intends to look at religion – which for him is the Christian religion in its Protestant form; he considers no other – simply in the light of his own philosophy and without submitting his inquiry to guidance from elsewhere.[6] As we have seen, he was but one of many who also, over the preceding century, had tried to comprehend religion 'within the limits of reason alone'; but he never refers to their undertakings. For ought that he tells us he might have been embarking on an enterprise entirely novel.

The contents of *Religion within the Limits of Reason Alone* are set out according to what appears to be a rigorously consistent scheme, but the exposition of it in detail is not always so clear and well-arranged; sometimes the procedure is confusing, while certain important topics that one would have expected to form an essential part of the text itself are simply relegated to lengthy notes. The four main sections are headed respectively:

'Concerning the indwelling of the Evil Principle with the Good, or, On the Radical Evil in Human Nature';

'Concerning the Conflict of the Good with the Evil Principle for Sovereignty over Man';

'The Victory of the Good over the Evil Principle, and the Founding of the Kingdom of God on Earth'; and

'Concerning Service and Pseudo-Service under the Sovereignty of the Good Principle, or, Concerning Religion and Clericalism.'

The theme of the work will thus be seen to be that of the struggle between good and evil in human nature. The examination to which Christian belief and institutions are subjected is based entirely upon this and upon the conditions attending it.

In his Preface Kant indicates his general view of the relationship between religion and morality along lines already familiar from his earlier works. He begins by repeating his affirmation of man's moral autonomy: because as a rational being man binds himself to unconditional laws he has in principle no need of some Being superior to himself to instruct him in his duty, nor, in the discharge of that duty, any other incentive than the moral law itself. Thus, for its own sake, morality can dispense with religion; the pure practical reason renders it self-sufficient. However, morality of necessity leads to religion, in that the question inevitably arises as to the *result* of virtuous conduct. The end must not indeed determine the will, yet apart from the idea of some desirable consequence of virtuous action such action is stultified. It cannot, says Kant, be a matter of unconcern to morality whether or not it forms for itself the concept of a final End of all things (*Endzweck aller Dinge*); harmony with which, while in no way increasing the number of our duties, nevertheless provides them with a special focus for the unification of all ends. To complete man's rational understanding of his life as a moral being he needs the idea of a *summum bonum* – 'the idea of a highest good in the world for whose possibility we must postulate a higher, moral, most holy, and omnipotent Being which alone can unite the two elements of this highest good'.[7] There is, then, and can be, no difference of substance between philosophical theology and ethics. But what the latter addresses itself to is the moral consciousness as such, founded as it is on the moral imperative; whereas religion, in its intellectual formulation as philosophical theology, while assuming this moral consciousness, is concerned to elicit the metaphysical implications of morality as the practical reason gives shape to them in its postulates. All the same, the content of religion is not intellectual perception but practice, the fulfilment of one's moral vocation. If we claim to know anything of the divine it can only be those attributes of God's nature which have their reflection in our own moral conduct. Religion, accordingly, is equivalent to morality, but as seen not so much from the standpoint of the individual moral conscience – which is what ethics, in Kant's view, presents – as, so to speak, 'objectively', as part of that divine moral order in which the individual has his essential role. Morality becomes religious, that is, when its duties are interpreted as voicing the will of God.

Finally, Kant has a care to distinguish between 'biblical theology' and 'philosophical', an observation occasioned, as we remarked earlier, by his brush with the Prussian state censorship. Biblical theology pertains to the church's public preaching and is rightly subject to ecclesiastical control; philosophical theology, on the other hand, is a territory open to full rational inspection. But although distinguishable the two ought not to be separated, since biblical theology 'will itself not deny that it contains a great deal in common with the teachings of unassisted reason':

> Were biblical theology to determine, wherever possible, to have nothing to do with reason in things religious, we can easily foresee on which side would be the loss; for a religion which rashly declares war on reason will not be able to hold out in the long run against it.[8]

Indeed between the biblical and the philosophical theological co-operation is in the highest degree desirable. That is why Kant feels justified not only as a philosopher in embarking on the investigation that he plans; he will be endeavouring to perform a task of essential value to religion itself. Only if the biblical theologian heeds what the philosopher has to say will he be forearmed against the kind of difficulties which the latter might make for him; difficulties, Kant could have added, which the rationalist and secularizing tendencies of the age had increasingly accumulated.

THE EVIL IN MAN IS WILLED

Kant begins the first Book of his treatise, which has been fairly described as 'the profoundest and most original portion of the whole',[9] by quoting the words of a New Testament writer that 'the world lieth in evil'.[10] He says that it is 'a plaint as old as history', and one certainly which he himself feels bound to endorse. Thus he at once sounds a note that by no means harmonizes with the prevailing optimism of the Age of Reason, whose characteristic spokesmen were virtually at one in affirming their belief in man's basic goodness and ultimate perfectibility. They were eager enough to recall the errors and miseries of the past, but they had every confidence that this unhappy condition would in time become only a memory. So in the words of the English scientist and Unitarian Joseph Priestly: 'Whatever was the beginning of this world, the end will be glorious and paradisaical, beyond what our imaginations can conceive'; adding, 'Men will make their situation in this world abundantly more easy and comfortable; they will probably prolong their existence in it, and will grow daily more happy'.[11] And statements like these could be multiplied from many sources.

Little wonder is it that the Christian doctrine of original sin was usually dismissed by the men of the Enlightenment as a noxious superstition and a device of priestcraft. For Kant, therefore, to open his case for rational religion by presenting a theory of the evil *inherent* in human nature was challenging to the verge of paradox.[12] Moreover it seemed to indicate a sudden change in his own point of view as consistently developed in his preceding works, for even his *Lectures on Philosophical Theology* of ten years previously do not discuss it. Yet here a doctrine of the radical evil in humanity is brought forward as the very foundation-stone of what purports to be a rigorously moralistic interpretation of religion. As Karl Barth has put it: 'One certainly does not expect, having a knowledge of Kant's ethics from his earlier writings, and looking at the rest of the contents of his teaching on religion after this beginning, to be met here immediately on the doorstep with a detailed doctrine of the problem of evil, and above all with that kind of doctrine. It is in fact the last thing one would expect.'[13] But is it really such an alien intrusion?

There was undoubtedly a streak of moral pessimism in Kant's personal disposition. Mankind, he could assure himself, was moving towards a brighter future; so much indeed, as a thinker of his time, he was almost bound to hold.[14] But he states his belief with caution; he does not commit himself to any theory of inevitable progress, as still less does he attempt to formulate a law by which it would come about. For history only too often shows up men's folly and their childish vanity and perverseness and love of destruction.[15] In any case – and here again he differs from the more usual outlook of his day – the true goal for humanity to aim at is not perfect happiness but perfect obedience to the moral law. And to achieve the good in its ideal realization – something finally impossible in this life – calls for perpetual effort and a degree of resolution not easily sustained. It is an austere view, and one which evoked the comment of the poet Schiller that Kant seemed to be saying that 'one can now at last be sure of doing one's duty when one does it with aversion'.[16] Be that as it may, Kant believed that moral purity amounts to holiness, that state of the soul to which rational man must ever aspire. But to this man's bent to falsehood, to the lie, is an ever-recurring obstacle. Indeed for Kant the lie epitomized moral evil. 'A lie', he declares, 'always harms another' – he is discussing *A Supposed Right to Lie From Altruistic Motives* – 'if not some other particular man, still it harms mankind generally, for it vitiates the source of law itself'.[17] Temperamentally Kant was not at all morose or misanthropic, but he had no illusions about the difficulty of striving after the moral ideal in the unremitting demands of duty.

It is not, then, really surprising that Kant's treatment of the religious question should have as its pivot the inescapable fact of moral evil in human life. His philosophy of religion, as set out in this book, could be said to be entirely structured upon the problem thus posed for the moral reason and upon its resolution. More, the sense of its importance and urgency imparts to his thinking on the whole subject a distinctive warmth and vigour.

Kant starts by contrasting two views of human nature and history. According to the one the world began in a state of goodness, since looked back to as a Golden Age, a life in Eden, from which, in the course of the ages, it has embarked on a long decline, a 'Fall' (*Verfall*) into evil – moral evil, that is, although physical evil is its close accompaniment – which has hurried mankind on from bad to worse in ever-swifter descent. On this view the present age represents the nadir of degeneracy and its future destruction cannot but be imminent. The other view, although much less prevalent, in that it is chiefly entertained by philosophers and educationists, is the optimistic belief that the world is steadily improving, that, from a former condition admittedly bad, things are on their way to the better. In some respects the truth of this would have approved itself to Kant: civilization had obviously made progress; but if what is meant is advance in moral goodness then he does not see it as founded on experience, and the evidence of history is formidably against it. He suggests that the whole notion of progress in this respect is really no more than a well-intentioned assumption of moralists, from Seneca to Rousseau, intended to encourage the cultivation of that seed of goodness which may be held to lie within us alongside the evil. What Kant himself proposes, therefore, is a *tertium quid*, a mediating doctrine avoiding either of the two extreme positions by arguing that man is by nature *part* good *part* bad – as much, perhaps, the one as the other. But in saying this he is not simply falling back on a bland truism, that the same men sometimes act well if also sometimes badly, and that they ought not in fairness to be judged too severely. For the demand of the moral law is not one that can be met by halves. One has to go behind the actions to the state of mind which prompts them. 'We call a man evil, not because he performs actions that are evil, but because these actions are of such a nature that we may infer them from the presence in him of evil maxims'[18] – maxims being the Kantian term for the principles which actually guide his conduct. If a man's maxims are good he will be good; if they are bad, so will he be. In falling short of the moral law, as experience everywhere indicates to be the case, men can properly be described as bad by *nature*; as having, that is, an underlying common ground constituted by morally evil maxims.

This is not to say that Kant is seeking to revive the theological doctrine, so greatly stressed by Calvinism, of man's total depravity; if there were not some good in human nature obedience to the moral law would be impossible; whereas it is obvious that men do accomplish much that is morally right.[19] In contending that man is bad by nature one is simply saying that his disposition is to adopt evil maxims; responsibility and blame remain therefore his and are not removed because of some unavoidable bias within him. Without freedom there could be no blame, since responsibility would be precluded. Thus for the 'cause' of moral evil we must look to a principle or principles voluntarily adopted. This further implies that the ultimate subjective ground of our adopting these, as essentially a matter of free choice, cannot itself be a fact disclosed in experience; one is unable, so to speak, to go behind a free act in order to explain it; which is why one cannot rightly talk of it as *caused*. What, on Kant's argument, has to be explained is the coexistence of a subjective disposition (*Gesinnung*) towards evil maxims and their actual adoption by a free act of the will. Plainly Kant is reluctant to admit that there is anything 'morally intermediate' either in actions (*adiaphora*, actions resulting simply from natural conditions) or in human characters; for where such ambiguity exists all maxims, he thinks, are in danger of losing their 'precision and stability'. In this respect he unhesitatingly aligns himself with the 'rigorists' against the 'latitudinarians', with those who take the strict course that he who adopts the moral law in its absoluteness as his maxim is morally good, and against those who prefer the 'indifferentist' or 'gradualist' view that would permit a man to be accounted morally good in some ways and morally evil in others. You cannot, that is, fulfil the moral law by adopting both good maxims and bad simultaneously. However, if the disposition of humanity in general reveals a 'propensity to evil' (*Hang zum Bösen*) then this can fairly be called natural in the sense just noted, namely, that it is the subjective ground of the possibility of deviation from the principles of the moral law. 'The will's capacity or incapacity', Kant observes, 'arising from this natural propensity to adopt or not to adopt the moral law into its maxim, may be called a good or an evil heart.'[20]

To drive this point home Kant states explicitly that evil does not lie either in man's animal nature as a living being, nor yet in his humanity as a rational being; even his personal capabilities as a responsible individual are not, in this respect, to be blamed. Nevertheless the propensity to evil is beyond all question latent and can show itself whether as 'frailty' or weakness – and Kant aptly quotes St Paul's lament in the Epistle to the Romans (7:18): 'What I would, that I do not'; or as 'impurity' of motive – a good overall intention, but intermingled with incentives other than that of duty; or as sheer 'wickedness' – corruption, perversion, depravity, a motivation altogether incompatible with that of a pure obedience to the moral imperative. Unhappily this last condition, brought about by inordinate self-love, is to be found even in the best of men. For it is not enough that a man's actual conduct conforms to the moral law, that he is *bene moratus* as recognizably a man of good morals. He should also be *moraliter bonus*, a morally good man who 'obeys the law according to the spirit'. Kant here cites St Paul again, that 'Whatever is not of faith is sin' (Romans 14:23), meaning thereby that what determines the goodness of an act is the state of mind or heart whence it springs. Hence, if the principles which determine a man's deeds are contrary to the moral law, then despite the admitted fact that his deeds are commendable he himself is not virtuous.

However, unless the propensity to evil within us can be seen as our own act it cannot be morally judged. Therefore our 'evil heart' must be of our own choosing, induced by our own will. In other words, we are ourselves responsible for being evil 'by nature'. But by what act is our individual choice of evil to be identified? Not, clearly, any particular act on a specifiable occasion. For if such act is to be judged morally it must, as Kant repeatedly states, be free, and thus not to be assigned to some cause of which it is merely the natural effect:

> It is a contradiction to seek the temporal origin of man's moral character (*Beschaffenheit*), so far as it is considered contingent, since this character signifies the ground of the *exercize* of freedom; this ground (like the ground of the free will generally) must be sought purely in rational representations.[21]

When we speak of 'acts', that is, the word can be used in two different senses: either as an act performed in time, in the course of an individual's life – one that is empirical or phenomenal – or as an 'intelligible' act cognizable only through reason without the conditions of time. This latter connotation may be likened to the 'original sin' (*peccatum originarium*) of the theologians, as the ground or precondition from which the adoption of principles contrary to the moral law inevitably proceeds. It is not something acquired in experience, a habit or disposition built up over the years; nor can it, in the nature of the case, be assigned to a 'cause'. Its origin must be rational (*Vernunftsursprung*) if it is to qualify as ethical; but if it is inexplicable in terms of empirical conditions it must be taken simply as a fact of rational human existence. 'The rational origin of this perversion of our will whereby it makes lower incentives supreme among its maxims, that is, the propensity to evil, remains insensible to us.'[22] In fine, it is in our nature to choose the evil, yet the choice is also itself rational and responsible. Although man's faculties or capacities are in themselves good, he yet deliberately wills what is bad.

Such is the problem by which Kant as a philosopher sees himself confronted; and it has to be confessed that his idea of a rationally willed act 'outside' time is not at all an easy one to grasp. Nor is the transition from an original or 'normal' condition of innocence to one of sin readily explicable; especially as on Kant's argument it has to be immediate: one passes from innocence to sin *directly*. In the Bible this is represented in narrative form by the story of Adam's fall, and Kant's discussion of the subject in the light of Genesis – although he disavows any intention of offering scriptural exegesis – is of much interest. Adam, he observes, adopted into his maxim of conduct the ascendency of the sensuous impulse over the incentive which springs from the law – and thus occurred sin'; and he adds: '*Mutato nomine de te fabula narratur*'[23] – 'Change but the name, and of you the tale is told'.[24] We act daily after the same fashion, and continue to do so. This may be taken to mean that the moral law views every act as an *original* use of our freedom, and can accept no excuse for the misuse of that freedom in the cumulative consequences of past misdoing, even though such consequences are so real as to have become a 'second nature to us'. What Kant wishes us to understand, then, is that the choice of our evil maxim – 'sin', in religious language – is essentially an ethical fact independent of time and circumstance and intrinsic to every evil action. And this, as a universal characteristic of humanity, may be represented under the biblical symbolism as having occurred once and for all in the first man's primal fault. 'In Adam all have sinned.'[25] Indeed, according to Kant, the Genesis story exactly parallels his ethical analysis. Even the figure of the tempter-spirit in the guise of a serpent indicates that the ultimate origin of the evil impulse is inconceivable by us. For whence came the spirit's own evil? In the last resort we are left only with an enigma.

Kant, then, gives an account of the origin of evil, but not an explanation of it, much as, in his *Fundamental Principles of the Metaphysic of Morals*, he admits the impossibility of any subjective explanation of the freedom of the will, telling us that 'every being which cannot act otherwise than under the idea of freedom is thereby really free in a practical respect'.[26] Similarly, if sin is imputed to man it must in reason proceed from his free decision. But why this decision is made Kant is unable to say. We have only to admit the fact of it, along with such illumination of the mystery as is afforded by the biblical myth of the fall, recourse to which he deems to be necessary.

Some among his contemporaries were frankly scandalized at

this sudden appearance within his philosophical system of the assertion that man, whose natural goodness the age of Enlightenment had been extolling for near a century past, was in truth flawed by a radical disposition to evil, as still further that Kant should have taken this belief in the presence of an essentially non-rational factor in human life as the starting-point for a philosophy of religion ostensibly determined by rational considerations alone. It could even be seen as a betrayal of intellectual trust. Thus Goethe wrote complainingly to Herder (7 June 1793) that Kant, having spent a long life shaking out of his philosopher's cloak all kinds of prejudices which were dirtying it, had 'slobbered on it with the blot of radical evil so that even Christians would be enticed to kiss its hem';[27] while Herder himself was later sarcastically to observe that this new philosophy of religion actually went beyond scripture in proclaiming man's sinful nature.[28] Were this radical evil really to exist, he objected, the moral imperative itself would amount to no more than a formality, with no effective force. Schiller likewise confessed himself puzzled and disappointed by Kant's strange conviction on this matter. Was he not backing away from 'reason' and towards the realm of 'revelation'? Christian believers no doubt would thank him for his support, but they would nonetheless continue to disregard the philosophical foundations on which his thought properly rested.[29]

How then are we to account for Kant's belief that the evil in human life is a power not to be explained away? Clearly he felt himself unable to share the optimistic view that elements in human nature which might seem to belong only to its lower or more primitive levels time would surely remove. Nor evidently did he think that the more ameliorating influences of education would result in the automatic improvement of the individual as person and citizen. Either view was unsatisfactory; the latter as having little basis in experience: men do not so easily repent of their sins; the former as suggesting that any badness in human nature can be attributed to factors for which mankind has no real responsibility: that sin is no more than a state of pristine undevelopment still lingering on but eventually to be sloughed off. Instead he sees sin or evil as a fact to challenge the moral consciousness profoundly, at all stages of life; and one therefore of the origin of which we cannot give any ready account. Neither responsibility before conscience nor the evidences of experience, that is, are to be denied.

CONVERSION

However, although Kant maintains that evil is embedded in human nature – not simply as a condition of man's finitude, nor yet as an inherent defect of either his sensible or his rational constitution as such, but through his adoption of a maxim or principle of conduct which is contrary to the moral law – he nevertheless believes it possible for man to gain the mastery over it because of the essential freedom of his will; inasmuch, that is, as he is at liberty to choose a right maxim. It may well be asked, of course, how a corrupt tree can bring forth good fruit. But Kant's point is that in the human situation the tree, although corrupt, is not wholly so. For were man totally evil the moral imperative would have no meaning for him, whereas he in fact does recognize the command of duty even in his corrupted state. The moral law still faces him, and he understands, at least basically, what its demands are. This implies that his original disposition for good is ineradicable, and on the strength of it he has it in him to change his evil condition to one of good. 'For despite the fall, the injunction that we *ought* to become better men resounds unabatedly in our souls; hence it must lie within our power. . . . It must indeed be presupposed throughout that a seed of goodness still remains in its entire purity, incapable of being extirpated or corrupted.'[30]

But this does not mean that the change is brought about only gradually, by a slow and difficult transmutation of our nature into something better. Empirically no doubt the latter is likely to be the case; a man does not become visibly good in the twinkling on an eye; for even were it possible for him to do so there could be no certainty that improved conduct denoted a real change of heart. As Kant sees it – and he quotes St John's gospel, chapter 3, verse 5 – there has to be a re-birth, a new creature. On this he is very explicit: If a man is to become not merely *legally* but *morally* good (pleasing to God), that is, one endowed with virtue in its intelligible character (*virtus noumenon*), and who, knowing something to be his duty, requires no incentive other than the representation of duty itself, this cannot be brought about through gradual *reformation* so long as the basis of the maxims remains impure, but must be effected through a *revolution* in man's disposition.[31] What has to be altered is the supreme subjective ground of all our maxims, so that we are truly renewed in 'the spirit of our minds'. The change, as Kant avers, must be revolutionary; as radical, that is to say, as was the original act of sin. And, we are bound to think, as inexplicable; but when it is accomplished – although we fail to grasp rationally *how* it is achieved – then moral progress, aided by moral education, is possible. What matters is that there should be a fundamental reorientation of the individual's life. For without it moral effort would be unavailing, a mere ploughing of the sands. But when an altogether new maxim begins to show itself in growing virtue our moral self-betterment is still no reason for self-congratulation, for what we have succeeded in doing is no more, if no less, than our duty. Rather, 'the one thing in our soul which we cannot cease from regarding with the highest wonder, when we view it properly, and for which admiration is not only legitimate but even exalting, is the original moral predisposition itself in us'.[32] Kant even goes so far as to declare that it is the very incomprehensibility of this predisposition, which as he claims announces a divine origin, that must necessarily raise the spirit to the point of exaltation and strengthen it for whatever sacrifices man's respect for his duty may require of him.

It is certainly appropriate to speak of this renewal of mind and heart as a *conversion*, but we must note that the change is a purely moral one, depending entirely, it would seem, on the individual's own resolution and firmness of will. Kant uses biblical language to describe it, but his choice of text is such as to omit any allusion whatever to the means whereby, in the belief of the New Testament writers, the 'new birth' is effected.[33] Religious conviction, that is, is not invoked by him. Protestant doctrine laid the heaviest stress on faith, or rather grace working through faith, as the only ground of good works; without it – and it is described as salvific – moral exertion alone will not create the 'new man'. In this all-important respect Kant's teaching stands in clear opposition to orthodox Christianity. Yet strangely enough, it is always the pattern of Christian doctrine that Kant has in mind when expounding his 'rational' religion. This means that the conceptual framework remains religious even if the content is purely ethical.

Thus in a way that recalls the Reformers' stress on a supernatural righteousness, Kant repeatedly refers to the *purity* of the moral law as the supreme ground of our maxims, in reverting to which we must adopt it whole, 'in its entire purity', if it is to be an adequate incentive to the determination of the will. 'Original goodness', he, 'is the holiness of maxims in doing one's duty, merely for duty's sake.'³⁴ And he expressly contrasts the Christian moral standard with that of the ancients:³⁵ the Christian ideal is the ideal of holiness, of moral purity of heart; theirs was simply virtue, moral strength.³⁶ Conversion is essentially the restoration of moral purity and the moral life an ever-continuing progress towards holiness. Hence the necessity of its being radical, if advance is to be sustained. Purity is not a matter of degree, for not to be pure is to be impure. Again Kant's insistence on a complete change of heart is an echo, after its fashion, of Luther's insistence on justification as full, not merely partial. For both the philosopher and the religious teacher effective progress in moral living must depend on a fundamental spiritual renewal.

Conversion, then, as Kant would have us understand it, is not an empirical act or event but an 'intelligible' decision of the rationally directed will such as goes to the root of all other decisions. Christian teaching is right therefore in seeing it as the difference between salvation and perdition, between heaven and hell. But as in Christian teaching the 'moment' of justification has to be followed by a continuous process of sanctification, so for Kant the 'non-temporal' adoption of an altogether new maxim has to be succeeded by a course of conduct, indefinitely prolonged, that will result in an actual state of moral goodness. As Kant is careful to point out:

> If a man reverses by a single, unchangeable decision, that highest good of his maxims whereby he was an evil man (and thus puts on a new man), he is, so far as his principle and cast of mind are concerned, a subject susceptible of goodness, but only in continuous labour and growth is he a good man.³⁷

In the sight of God, who 'penetrates the intelligible ground of the heart' and who comprehends the unending process of ethical amelioration as a unity, it is equivalent to being actually good, or as a theologian would put it, to being *accounted* righteous before God. But in the eyes of men, who have to measure the strength of their principles and their advance in moral goodness according to their success in overcoming their sensuous nature, the course of their lives must appear as 'an ever luring struggle towards the better', and hence as only a gradual reformation.

So, to fall back on the language of theology, Kant's morally 'converted' man is *simul justus et peccator*, at once righteous and a sinner. Judged from without, his actions may still be far from wholly righteous, but inwardly he has taken the decisive step, having changed his basic maxim from bad to good, from self-love to commitment to duty for its own sake. But the question can still be asked: Is he now a truly *righteous* man or not? Or at any rate, is his decision not again reversible? He may be making every effort to conform his conduct to the recognized standards of morality, but can he be sure that a real change of heart has been wrought in him? It is pretty certain that Kant, with his well-known dislike of religious emotionalism, of *Schwärmerei*, would not have been satisfied with any mere assertion of or appeal to feeling; nor would he have recognized the testimony of some alleged inner illumination. His own attitude would have more readily found utterance in St Paul's words (Philippians 2:12): 'Work out your own salvation *with fear and trembling*', even though he realized the dangers of such an injunction when carried to extremes.[38] At the same time he is aware that complete uncertainty about the actual direction of one's moral volition would provide no proper climate for effective moral action. Moreover, one can try to take stock, as it were, of one's ethical progress from time to time, and if such progress seems really to have been achieved he may fairly believe himself genuinely 'to have turned over a new leaf' and that further moral advance may be hoped for.

But is it not at least possible that he may fall away from his resolution for good and revert to an evil state of mind and will? Kant does not expressly consider this possibility, and indeed it is difficult to imagine his regarding it very seriously. For would such an oscillation back and forth, from good to bad and from bad to good, be compatible with the behaviour of a rational and responsible person? Plainly his view is that if moral conversion has been well-considered and sincerely intended then it will not be reversed. Similarly one could ask whether an earnest religious conversion, brought about by what the believer holds to be divine grace, is not open to a contrary experience. However, Kant recognizes that such a relapse into evil could be:

> true of him who, despite good resolutions often repeated, finds that he has never stood his ground, who is ever falling back into evil, or who is constrained to acknowledge that as his life has advanced he has slipped, as though he were on a declivity,

evermore from bad to worse. Such an individual can entertain no reasonable hope that he would conduct himself better were he to go on living here on earth.[39]

As Kant sees it a such man's 'conversion would have been no conversion at all, but only a self-deception'.

Nevertheless we still have not entirely disposed of the problem as to the possibility for one who on Kant's view is morally changed or 'converted' actually to do wrong, since unachieved perfection in moral conduct must, one supposes, inevitably mean the occasional performance of acts that are contrary to the law of duty. Yet how, if the individual's choice of new and good maxims is sincere, can he really – if infrequently – defy the moral law? Kant certainly would not have argued that conversion results in immediate virtue, in clearly recognizable 'newness of life'; he is only too well aware that the reform process is gradual; and he also concedes that a man can never be wholly sure of the genuineness or the durability of his change of heart. Thus there is bound to be moral failure, despite the recovered will to good. All the same, do not bad actions, on Kant's reckoning, proceed from the *radical* evil in human nature, so that the heart is not after all regenerate? It would seem that it is only on the theological principle of 'righteous but still a sinner', that the wrongdoer is, *coram Deo*, righteous through the *imputed* righteousness of Christ, that the gap between intention and achievement can be bridged. As Luther, in his *Commentary on the Epistle to the Romans*, says of the condition of justified sinners: 'In reality they are sinners, but in the eyes of the merciful God they are righteous, because God judges them to be such according to his mercy; in their standing they are righteous, but they know themselves not to be so; they are sinners in fact but righteous in hope.'[40] However, this essentially theological doctrine is a good way off from the positions Kant so inflexibly maintains in his moral philosophy. Hence his attempt to account for the moral shortcomings of one who has in principle redirected his entire moral orientation towards the good appears insecure. The theological doctrine is not inconsistent with attributing conversion to the grace of God, and sin to the corrupted will of man. But Kant's effort to attribute both the good and the evil to one and the same human volition, which yet must adopt the maxim *either* of duty *or* of self-love, surely indicates a discrepancy in Kant's reasoning that does not admit of easy resolution.

But does he intend us to understand that the success of moral conversion depends entirely on our own strength of will, or does he in any way envisage supernatural co-operation? The latter he certainly does not rule out. Some supernatural aid, he grants, may be necessary for a man's becoming good, or at least better, but whether this co-operation consists merely in the abatement of hindrances or affords positive assistance, Kant by no means qualifies the principle that 'a man must first make himself worthy to receive it, and must lay hold of this aid (which is no small matter) – that is, he must adopt this positive increase of power into his maxim, for only thus can good be imputed to him and he be known as a good man'.[41] Christianity, Kant claims, more than any other religion recognizes the responsibility which rests on each and every individual to do whatever he can to raise himself morally – and he cites Luke 19:12–16 in this connection – urging that it is on this condition alone that a man can hope that what is not within his power to achieve will be supplied through co-operation from above. But he adds that it is not absolutely necessary that we should know exactly what such co-operation involves, since if we did we might well form different conceptions of it, albeit in all sincerity. Hence although such knowledge is not essential to us, it is quite essential, Kant holds, 'to know what man himself must do in order to become worthy of this assistance'.[42]

These observations are bound, from a theological point of view, to introduce the conception of divine grace; and Kant does not omit to give it serious consideration. At the end of this whole first section he mentions it as a *parergon* of his main concern to view religion 'within the limits of reason alone', by which he means that matters dealt with under this classification do not properly belong to his subject but 'border upon it'. They include works of grace, miracles, mysteries, and means of grace, and are discussed by him in sequence during the course of his book. These topics, he explains, reason does not dispute as being possible or even real, but 'she cannot adopt them into her maxims of thought and action'. He regards them as 'morally-transcendent' ideas and has to point out the damage which is likely to result from them when they are brought into religion and made part of its substance.

In a still later work, *Der Streit der Fäcultaten* ('The Controversy between the Faculties'), published in 1798, Kant addressed himself specifically to the question of the philosophical interpretation of religious doctrines in an attempt to determine the proper spheres of intellectual discipline represented by the academic faculties of theology and philosophy respectively.[43] He perceived no real difficulty in settling the matter. The biblical theologian, he argued, derives his teachings not from reason but from the Bible, in order to maintain sound church doctrine; beyond scripture he has no need or title to venture. But in so far as the philosopher also is a theologian his province has to be that of reason alone, and he supports religious belief solely to the extent that it can be shown to rest on principles of reason common to all men.[44] Within this perspective the territories of the biblical and the rational theologian do not overlap. Nevertheless the matter is not really so simple, for the Bible, while admittedly the unique authority for the biblical theologian, is not composed exclusively of narratives and 'statutory' or positive doctrines, and in that respect at all events his concern too must submit to reason, since clearly any 'revealed' truth presenting itself in human shape ought to be interpreted in a manner worthy of its putative author, God. Thus reason can fairly be said to be 'the supreme exegete of scripture'.[45] On the other side of the picture the rational theologian is not to be thought of as constructing a religion purely from abstract principles; he has, rather, to take religion as he finds it, examining its 'revealed' doctrines in a rational light and seeking to discriminate between such as are acceptable and those that are not. Now as Kant views it, it is in this area that the inquirer encounters the *parerga* of reason: they themselves are not part of rational theology, but they certainly lie at its confines, and the rational theologian should take them into account:

> Reason [Kant states], conscious of her inability to satisfy her moral need, extends herself to high-flown (*überschwenglich*) ideas capable of supplying this lack, without, however, appropriating those ideas as an extension of her domain.[46]

In other words, ideas of this order are not necessarily contradictory of reason and may well have a certain practical interest. Reason's attitude could be described, Kant suggests, as a *reflective faith*, distinguishing itself from a *dogmatic* one purporting to be a form of knowledge in a way that reason can only regard as dishonest and presumptuous. What is called for, then, is a *parergon*, or 'by-work', of a kind to remove difficulties that may obstruct the path of moral practice. These difficulties, arising from an exaggeration of the supernatural dimension of the ideas in question, are to be classified as follows: (1) imagined inward experiences ('works of grace') leading to *fanaticism*; (2) alleged external experiences ('miracles') leading to *superstition*; (3) supposed enlightenment as to the supernatural 'mysteries') suggesting *illuminism*, 'the illusion of the adepts'; and (4) hazardous attempts to manipulate the supernatural ('means of grace') resulting in *thaumaturgy*.

In this opening section of his treatise Kant restricts his attention to the first of these *parerga* – works of grace (*Gnadenwirkungen*). Taken in its usual theological meaning of a supernatural power operating on a man's will, grace is a concept that cannot itself be brought within the limits of reason. In the realm of the supernatural 'all reason ceases', inasmuch as it is impossible to frame a *theoretical* definition of works of grace sufficient to show that they are not natural effects, for the concept of cause and effect, as Kant has already been at such pains to demonstrate, cannot be extended beyond matters of sense-experience. Nor is it possible even to accord the idea a *practical* application, since such a use of it would presuppose a positive effort for good *on our part*; whereas merely to wait upon the operation of grace implies exactly the opposite, because then the accomplishment of good would be not our own act but that of another. In any case it is contradictory to think that one can achieve anything by doing nothing. Therefore, although we are not in a position to deny that works of grace do occur, they must remain incomprehensible to us, and so can have no place in a religion circumscribed by reason.

Kant's own view is that if supernatural aid is a possibility, in spite of the fact that we neither can have sensible awareness of its operation nor believe in it on the evidence of personal feelings, then we should endeavour to make ourselves worthy of it by moral exertion, in treading the difficult upward path of holiness. The orthodox Protestant doctrine, that 'grace is all' and that moral obedience in itself is no ground of justification, is one therefore that Kant was bound to reject as dangerous to the supremacy of the moral law. Yet considering his own profound sense of original sin, the mystery of which he did not minimize, and his stress on conversion as distinct from observable improvement in moral conduct, one has to conclude that Kant could not take a purely rationalizing view of moral obligation. He even can find a place for the doctrine of the forgiveness of sins, in that conversion, the adoption of a new life-maxim, may be held to be in God's sight that finally achieved 'holiness' which the actual conditions of life in this world render impossible. His own 'rational' notion of grace, although the word itself is of course absent from his philosophical vocabulary, is fairly well indicated in a passage in the *Streit der Facultäten*, in which he tells us that if one understands by *nature* the drive in man to promote his happiness, but by *grace* the principle, deep-rooted in him, of obedience to duty, of purely disinterested morality, then clearly not only do nature and grace differ but they often are in conflict. If however one understands by nature, in the practical sense, the power (*Vermögen*) of realizing certain general ends through one's own resources, then grace is nothing other than human nature as controlled by inward reverence for the moral law, by the sheer force of the sense of duty.[47] How it is we have this inner recognition of moral obligation we are unable ultimately to explain, but because we are ignorant of its cause we think of such a disposition to good as produced in us by the divine as a work of grace, since its spring is not simply within ourselves. Thus Kant would seem really to bring grace and nature together as one, so envisaging a condition of things in which rational beings single-mindedly devote themselves to fulfilling the moral law. For 'this', he declares, 'is the Kingdom of God, in which nature and morality come into a harmony that is foreign to each as such, through a holy Author of the world, who makes possible the derived highest good'.[48]

7
Good and Evil in Conflict

THE OPPOSING PRINCIPLES

The second Book of *Religion within the Limits of Reason Alone*, 'Concerning the Conflict of the Good with the Evil Principle for the Sovereignty over Man', deals, as its title indicates, with the struggle between the original good in man, as testified by his recognition of the moral law, and the deep-seated propensity for evil in him which formed the subject matter of the first Book. The very name by which, since the days of the Stoics, the activity of this original good has been designated, namely *virtue* (*areté*, *virtus*, *Tugend*) – a word signifying courage and valour – implies the presence of an enemy to be overcome. It is a word Kant likes, despite its frequent misuse and the derision it sometimes evokes; it conjures up resolution and energy in contrast with the 'lazy and pusillanimous' spirit that mistrusts itself and hangs back, looking for help from outside. Yet the Stoics' emphasis on moral effort was to some extent countered by their mistake in seeing as the enemy merely the undisciplined inclinations of our animal nature, of which of course we are all aware; whereas the real foe to be met is one who screens himself 'behind the reason itself' and thus is all the more insidious. The Stoics set wisdom against folly simply, instead of against the wickedness lurking in the human heart itself and undermining human nature with 'soul-destroying principles'. For the natural inclinations are not in themselves evil; on the contrary, they are good, not being opposed to the moral law. What is opposed to the moral law is a perverted *will*. That the curbing of our natural appetites faces difficulties is not in doubt, but the will is not directly antagonistic to them; it needs only to discipline them because of their unruliness. The Stoic perspective therefore was not wrong, but it was inadequate, as not getting to the spring of the problem. At this point Kant aptly cites Ephesians 6.12: 'For we wrestle not against flesh and blood' – i.e. the natural inclinations – 'but against principalities and powers' – i.e. against evil spirits. Christian insight is here profounder than the Stoic ethic, since the evil spirits of which the Bible speaks are to be taken as figuring an evil *principle* which the will itself has adopted and which *per se* has nothing to do with the promptings of animal instinct. As Kant observes, Christianity represents moral goodness in its difference from evil not in the disparity between heaven and earth (nature), but in the antagonism of heaven and *hell*, where the difference is as that between light and darkness. Between heaven and hell there is no middle course, no gradation; rather are these realms separated from one another by an immeasurable gulf. Nor does the Devil – if we so wish to unite and personify the powers of evil – constrain us to do what is against our will. 'It is all one', says Kant, 'whether we place the seducer merely within ourselves or without, for guilt touches us not a whit less in the latter case than in the former, inasmuch as we are not led astray by him at all were we not already in secret league with him.'[1] If the Devil is our ally it is only because we choose to have him so.

THE GOOD PRINCIPLE PERSONIFIED

If God's creation is looked at from the moral point of view then its only possible end, Kant states, can be *Mankind in its complete moral perfection*. But this end, this ideal, is something that has to be thought of as eternally existent in the divine mind, as proceeding from God's very being. Hence man in his moral perfection, in his ideality, is no created thing but, in biblical language, 'his only-begotten Son', the Word through which all things were made and without which nothing exists which was made.[2] To this absolute ideal, or moral archetype and pattern, it is man's universal duty to raise himself, in and by the power supplied by the ideal itself. Also, because we are not ourselves the creators of the ideal and because it established itself in the human rational consciousness without our comprehending how human nature could ever have been rendered capable of receiving it, it is quite appropriate to say that it has come down to us *from heaven*. Indeed, recognizing the evil in our own nature, who possibly could claim that the ideal is actually, or ever could have been, our own creation? More feasible is it to speak of it as having descended to man and assumed humanity – which in itself, let it again be said, is not evil. Thus

Kant turns to the doctrine of the incarnation as alone expressing the humanly realized moral ideal in all its perfectness.

> Such union with us may therefore be regarded as a state of *humiliation* of the Son of God [the allusion is to Philippians 2.6ff.] if we represent to ourselves this godly-minded person, regarded as our archetype, as assuming sorrows in fullest measure in order to further the world's good, though he himself is holy and therefore bound to endure no sufferings whatsoever.[3]

The historical example thus set before us, as of one who goes about disseminating good by both word and deed, is completed by the afflictions, even to the extreme of an ignominious death, which he endured wholly undeservedly for the sake of the world and even of his enemies. It is characteristic of Kant, the reader will feel, that he should so emphasize the worth of a moral disposition by drawing attention to the obstacles it is bound to encounter and the effort required to surmount them, victory in the end being won in the face of the direst onslaughts. However, he insists that the only way for man to please God and gain salvation is through a practical faith in the incarnate Son of God; a faith, that is, whereby he makes his own the disposition of which the incarnate is the ideal examplar.[4]

That this moral ideal is also objectively real is certified by our morally legislative reason. because we recognize that we *ought* to conform to it it follows that we must be able to do so. We do not, then, actually need a specific historical instance of its fulfilment in order to convince ourselves of its possibility, any more than we need the attestation of miracles to substantiate its authority. Such reliance on external testimony would only be a sign of moral unbelief, of our lack of faith in the moral ideal itself, and actions arising from it would not be morally valuable. In any case no actual embodiment of the ideal could ever be proved as such, since what really is in a person's heart as distinct from what appears in his actions – an inward holiness of disposition, that is – can never be known with strict certainty. It is also in line with such thinking for Kant to suggest that the idea of a 'truly godly-minded' man who is our perfect moral pattern need not be supposed to be other than naturally begotten or to be elevated above the frailties of human nature; rather would it make the adoption of his personal example all the more difficult. In fact, were he to be regarded as superhuman, to the degree that his absolute purity of will was simply innate and not achieved by effort, he could no longer be a credible example. The truth is, Kant thinks, that speculations about the nature of the Son of God have no relevance to our obligation to fulfil the moral ideal which he is taken to represent. For the moral ideal we see in him was likewise that present to his own mind, as the gospel record shows, except that the failings we are only too conscious of in ourselves are not evident in him, as that same record depicts him. Thus he is rightly portrayed as asking, 'Which of you convinceth me of sin?'[5] To that extent he remains a valid pattern for all men to try to adopt as their own, although we have to grasp the magnitude of the difficulties which stand in the way of making its adoption possible.

The first of these difficulties is that of our being able to realize in act the moral perfection which the law demands, as stated in the gospel saying: 'Be ye perfect' – i.e. in the conduct of your lives – 'as your Father in heaven is perfect', and which is set before us as a model is the moral ideal of the Son of God on earth. For the distance between the evil condition from which we perforce have to start and the consummate good to which, as rational beings, we are obliged to aspire, is so vast that its achievement in time is impossible. We may earnestly strive for the ideal, but how can a good intention, even when translated into action, count for that maximum of attainment which, great as it might be, always falls short of its end? The solution of the difficulty turns on the fact that it envisages man only in his phenomenal aspect, whereas the truth is that a good disposition is good *in itself*, regardless of time, and so is judged by God, 'who knows the heart', as a completed whole. It is this disposition itself which is pleasing to God, however inadequate a man's achievement may have been at the moment when his existence was terminated. The second difficulty, to which, like the first, allusion has already been made earlier in our discussion, is how one can be certain that this new disposition to good will be sustained. It could no doubt be said that the resolution always to act rightly must be such as to preclude any further inclination to evil. Nevertheless reliance on a mere feeling of revulsion towards evil is spiritually hazardous: 'Man is never more easily deceived than in what promotes his good opinion of himself';[6] although Kant admits that if we lacked all confidence in our moral determination it is unlikely that we should be able to persevere with it. But we would be justified in hoping to continue our moral progress, since if the underlying principle of our actions is indeed good each advance will give us strength for the future, enabling us to press on with ever-mounting courage. Moreover, 'the good and pure disposition of which we are conscious . . . creates in us, though only indirectly, a confidence in its own permanence and stability, and is our Comforter (Paraclete)' – an echo of the teaching of St John's gospel – 'when our lapses make us apprehensive of our constancy'.[7] And if after this life another awaits us we may well expect to continue in the course on which we have embarked here, just as one who, by contrast, repeatedly fails can only come to see in his failures the corruption rooted in his disposition.

At this juncture Kant adverts, in a lengthy footnote, to the question – which however he stigmatizes as 'childish', because if an answer were forthcoming the questioner would still be none the wiser – whether the punishments of hell will be terminable or everlasting. Such speculations he considers likely to have an undesirable moral effect, for should the first of the alternatives be believed it might encourage the idea that by determination one could 'stick it out'; if the second is accepted then complete immunity from punishment could be secured in spite of 'a most abandoned life' by a death-bed repentance that may well not be sincere, even though the whole purport of the doctrine is to teach the contrary. Dogmatic statements on the subject are therefore to be avoided as pertaining to matters of which in the nature of things we can have no knowledge. We have simply to look at it from a practical point of view, content to infer from the way in which we have conducted our lives on earth whether or not we shall at the last be pleasing to God. On this topic as on many others we should confine our judgment to *regulative* principles, which can properly be applied to the moral life.

The third difficulty which Kant detects, and the one which he also deems to be the most serious, takes us on to newer ground. It is the possible objection that whatever a man may have done in the way of acquiring a good disposition, and however steadfastly he may have persevered in conduct conforming with it, he still cannot expunge the guilt (*Schuld*) of his former life, which remains as a debt (*Verschuldung*) that he is unable to pay off. Also he cannot regard the fact that he has, since his conversion, incurred no new debts, as having itself discharged the old ones. The resolution of this difficulty, as Kant would see it, is that, in view of the morally converted man's change of heart resulting in a new disposition pleasing to God, the penalty which formerly might have been appropriate is no longer so, because he now is morally a new person; yet – and here Kant harks back to the classical Anselmic theory of the atonement[8] – satisfaction must be rendered to 'Supreme Justice', in whose sight no one who is blameworthy can ever be guiltless. But on account of his 'newness of life' the debt of the old, corrupt life may be thought of as discharged in the eyes of God. The change, however, from a corrupt to a good disposition – 'the death of the old man', 'the crucifying of the flesh' – is itself a sacrifice and 'an entrance upon a long train of life's ills' which the changed man freely accepts – in that he now makes the moral idealism of the Son of God his own – as his due punishment, although incurred by the 'old man' that he once was. What the latter, that is, would have felt as an evil, the former acknowledges as a good. Physically of course it is the same man who suffers for his guilt, and rightly so, but because of his new disposition he is in the sight of his judge another and a different person. As Kant expresses it, this new moral disposition, which in its purity – like indeed to the purity of the Son of God – the converted man has personally assumed, bears, as *vicarious substitute* – again like the Son of God, it may be said – the guilt of sin for him. 'As saviour' – i.e. the 'Son of Man' ideal within him – he thus 'renders satisfaction to supreme justice by his sufferings and death; and *as advocate* he makes it possible for men to hope to appear before their judge as justified'. The difference between this interpretation and that of orthodox theology is, Kant argues, that the suffering which in the one case will last throughout life is pictured in the other as a death endured once for all by the representative of mankind.[9]

This surplus which, over and above the profit coming from good works, is thus imputed to the 'new man' can be reckoned an act of *grace*, albeit fully in accord with eternal justice. Although it may not appear, Kant suggests, that this view of justification has any *positive* use, religiously or morally, since the good disposition has in fact already been acquired and the knowledge that this is so will itself always be of comfort to the individual concerned, it yet has a decided *negative* benefit in that 'only the supposition of a complete change of heart allows us to think of the absolution, at the bar of heavenly justice, of the man burdened with guilt' – something for which no external religious act, whether of prayer or praise, can ever be a substitute.[10]

That this account of salvation as a process taking place wholly within the individual consciousness, expressing and resulting from one's personal moral self-reorientation, contrasts with the objectivity of the divine act as presented by orthodox Christianity, is scarcely open to question. On Kant's view the vicarious sufferings of Christ are no more than a symbol for the remorse and misery of the repentant sinner consequent upon his former misdeeds, and one moreover that is essentially different in its nature from what it is intended to signify. In the Christian theology of the atonement Christ's sufferings were borne voluntarily, 'for us men and for our salvation', by one who himself was without sin; whereas in our case the sufferings endured are not without justification, and when accepted by us as due punishment serve as a spiritual discipline proper to that moral effort needed for advance along the new road of life that we have chosen. Such suffering may indeed be thought of by the penitent sinner as 'like' Christ's, but it can never, for the believer, be identified with his. For all its elevated ingenuity Kant's argument is unable to conceal the vital difference between an abstract moral ideal and its living embodiment in the reality of an historical personage. An internalized 'Son of God' may succeed in avoiding the obvious difficulties inherent in affirming a divine incarnation under specific historical conditions, but only by equating salvation with a course of moral regeneration the sole ground of which is the individual's own decision and tenacity of will. Kant's 'moral theology', that is, cannot admit the idea of redemption (*Erlösung*) in the sense which, basically, it has always carried in Christian belief. It is noteworthy that the word itself occurs but once in his book, and then only in a context which depreciates its meaning.

THE DEVIL'S CLAIM TO LORDSHIP OVER MAN

The second division of Book Two is concerned with the legal claim of the evil principle to sovereignty over man, and resistance to it by the good. Kant opens his discussion by recalling how holy scripture, 'in its Christian portion', presents this moral relationship in narrative form by depicting the two conflicting principles – 'opposed to one another as are heaven and hell' – in personal guise. For not only do they pit their strengths against one another, they also endeavour to establish their respective claims legally to man's domination, as though before a supreme judge, the one in the shape of his accuser, the other in that of his advocate.

Good and Evil in Conflict

In the beginning (Genesis 1.28) man was given proprietary right over all earthly goods (*dominium utile*), if on condition of his holding it only as tenant of, or trustee for, his Creator and Lord (*dominus directus*). But immediately an evil being made his appearance – although whence came his evil character is unknown – who through his fall – for originally he was good – had forfeited all the property he might have enjoyed in heaven and now wished to gain another on earth. However, inasmuch as he belongs by nature to a higher order of existence, that of spirit, he derived no satisfaction from earthly and material goods, seeking instead to acquire dominion over spiritual beings, human souls, by causing man's first parents to be disloyal to their sovereign lord and to become dependent on himself. In this way he achieved paramountcy here as 'prince of this world'. Why God did not at once exert his power to overthrow the usurping traitor and destroy his realm at its first inception may well of course be asked.[11] The explanation, Kant thinks, is to be found in the fact that Supreme Wisdom, in its control and government of rational beings, treats them in accordance with the principle of their freedom, so that whatever befalls them, be it good or evil, is really imputable to them. And because the options are thus open a 'kingdom of evil' was set up in defiance of the good principle, an authority to which all men, who are naturally descended from Adam, have become subject by their own consent, simply because they could not resist the allurement of this world's goods. Yet despite the ubiquitous power of evil the good principle, through its claim to sovereignty over man, exercised some authority by means of a form of government – namely, the ancient Jewish theocracy – established solely for the public and exclusive honouring of his name, although the subjects of this authority in fact remained in thrall to no other incentives than worldy goods, and thus could be ruled only by a system of rewards and punishments in the present life. For this reason no other laws befitted them than such as were partly prescriptive, laying upon them burdensome ceremonies and observances, and partly ethical, although the latter were themselves purely civil, resting on external compulsion without the inner moral disposition being in the least considered. This scheme of things, however, did nothing to reduce the kingdom of darkness, but served merely to sustain remembrance of the inalienable rights of the original proprietor. All the same, it was among these people, at a time when they had become all too conscious of the evils of the sort of hierarchical constitution under which they lived – having also learned from the Greek philosophers, Kant suggests, whose ethical doctrines of freedom had gained some influence over them, thus making them in a sense already ripe for revolution – that there suddenly appeared a prophet whose wisdom was purer than any of his predecessors' – indeed 'as pure as though it had descended from heaven'[12] – and who by both his teachings and personal example showed himself to be truly human, but who also, on account of his original innocence, was not implicated in Adam's guilt, so that 'the prince of this world had no part in him'.[13]

At this point Kant finds it appropriate to allude to the doctrine of the virgin birth as purporting to secure such a person from man's innate propensity to sin. The impulse behind the belief he can to some extent appreciate: shame, for example, at the sensual pleasure inseparable from natural generation, or even from the fact that sexual union would seem to relate us to the common animal species 'far too closely for the dignity of humanity'. It is notions like these, with their confusion, as Kant sees it, of the sensual and the intellectual, that have led to the idea of a human birth independent of sexual intercourse and therefore not soiled by moral blemish. But the whole subject, when one ponders its implications, amounts in Kant's opinion to no more than idle speculation, since the doctrine has no practical bearing except as a symbol of humanity raising itself above the temptation to evils that would hinder its victorious resistance.

But whatever the explanation of the sinlessness of this man so 'well-pleasing to God', the prince of evil felt his own power to be threatened by him, especially if others were to follow his example. Therefore he first tested his integrity by offering to make him 'deputy-governor' of his entire kingdom were he pay homage to him as its rightful owner. But because this ruse failed he subjected him to persecution and finally to a most ignominious death. Nevertheless he achieved nothing, being unable to subdue a perfectly good man to his will. He no doubt gained a *physical* victory, and to that extent the good principle was worsted, but he could not secure a moral one. Thus was the principle itself defeated. 'This death ... was therefore a manifestation of the good principle, that is, of humanity in its moral perfection, and an example to everyone to follow.'[14] In reality of course it was only a signal instance in time of what has been a continuous process – the resistance of evil by good – since the beginnings of the human race. However, as an example to others this pattern-life was never more aptly described than in the words of the gospel: 'He came unto his own, and his own received him not; but as many as received him, to them gave he power to be called the sons of God, even to them that believe on his name.'[15] Kant takes this to mean an example by virtue of which the gates of freedom are opened to all who, like him, are willing to die to everything that binds them to life on earth, to the great detriment of their moral state. So, then, the supreme exemplar of the good principle gathers together 'a people for his possession, zealous of good works',[16] while abandoning to their fate those who prefer moral slavery to freedom. The result of this long struggle with evil was not, in truth, the *conquest* of the principle, because its kingdom still endures, but the breaking of its power and the setting up of another realm, a new moral order, whither those who have fled the kingdom of the prince of this world may seek refuge. But in this world those who adhere to the good principle must always be prepared to endure physical suffering and other tribulations as persecutions by the evil principle.

Thus does Kant view the history of salvation as delineated in Christian doctrine, transposing it from the mystical to the moral plane; a transposition which for practical purposes shows its spirit and rational meaning to be valid and binding for all men in all ages. 'There exists absolutely no salvation for mankind apart from the sincerest adoption of genuinely moral principles into his disposition.'[17] Opposed to it are not so much man's natural inclinations, although these are often blamed as the enemies of the good, as a 'certain self-incurred perversity', in which the entire human race shares and which can be conquered only by embracing the principle of moral goodness in its full purity, at the same time understanding that this principle was part of our original nature and that man has always to strive to preserve it from impure elements and allow it to permeate his whole disposition. Only so can the evil principle be successfully resisted. On the other hand it is in vain if, from want of this assurance, we fall back either upon superstition (*Aberglaube*), which involves no essential change of heart, or upon fanaticism (*Schwärmerei*), which likes to invoke supposed inner illuminations. 'We should acknowledge as a mark of the presence of goodness in us naught but a well-ordered conduct of life.'[18] It is a duty to read scripture itself only in a way that harmonizes with 'the most holy teachings of reason'.

MIRACLES

Thus Kant ends his second Book, but he appends to it a 'General Observation' in which he discusses the second of his four *parerga* of rational religion, namely *miracles*, a subject for long prominent in the Enlightenment religious debate. He admits that when one religion is being superseded by another, as was the case with Judaism, 'a religion of mere rites and observances', on the rise of Christianity, based as this was on 'the spirit and the truth', that the latter, in order to gain the necessary authority in the sight of ordinary men, should have claimed the sanction of miraculous occurrences. However, to be able to win over the adherents of the older religion to the new, the coming order had itself to be interpreted as the authentic fulfilment of its predecessor and therefore as having all along been providentially designed. Hence the adventitious appeal to the evidence of miracles can now be dropped, the new faith being able to maintain itself on rational grounds. That in the birth of a new religion there is an element of mystery, even of what some may consider the miraculous, need not be questioned; certainly the person of the teacher of 'the one and only religion valid for all worlds' – his appearance on earth, his life and sufferings and his eventual leaving of it – may well be thought of as one continuous miracle; as too, in a manner of speaking, may be the historical record which purports to authenticate all these occurrences. But Kant is emphatic that in using such historical accounts there should be no insistence on their providing of themselves the means whereby a man will make himself pleasing to God. That can be achieved only by the performance of one's duty.

Of miracles in general Kant remarks that while reasonable people are not disposed categorically to deny that they have ever occurred, they do not allow this reservation any effect in practice. In theory there might be such things as miracles, but they are not to be taken into account in the affairs of life (*Geschäfte*). A reflection of this attitude is the widely entertained belief that although miracles may have happened of old the incidence of new ones is not seriously to be considered; the former could indeed be admitted without fear of untoward consequences, but there would be no telling what results any 'new workers of miracles might have upon the public peace and established order'.[19]

Kant's definition of miracle is that it is an event the operative law of whose causes are and cannot but remain absolutely unknown to us.[20] For the origin of miracles may be diversely judged: they could be ascribed to demonic powers as well as to divine, or to angels as well as to God – though Kant slyly adds that 'good angels (I know not why) give us little or nothing to say about them'. Even in the case of *theistic* miracles not much can be positively understood regarding them. If God controls the natural order no less than the moral then we can be said to have knowledge of the laws by which he operates; but should he occasionally deviate from these laws we can have no conception of that according to which he brings the miraculous event to pass. 'Here reason is as it were crippled, for it is impeded in its dealings with respect to known laws, it is not instructed in anything new, and it can never in the world hope to be thus instructed.'[21] In the case of miracles attributed to diabolic agency reason is still more obviously flouted. The upshot is that in the actual conduct of life the miraculous must always remain supernumerary. It attests nothing, but rather must itself be subjected to rational and moral criteria.

On reading the few paragraphs that Kant here devotes to the question one may feel that his treatment of miracle is somewhat desultory and even evasive, as though, with the Prussian censorship in mind, discretion for him had proved the better part of critical valour. The truth however would seem to be that Kant's own thought on the matter had varied. Thus in two of his *Reflexionen*, dating from 1760–63,[22] he considers the natural order of things to be defective enough to justify at least the possibility of divine intervention as a needed corrective; and any such special action affecting the order of nature would have to be described as miraculous and expressive of God's perfect will. It does not signify in principle that we are unable to identify any specific act of this sort. The 'critical' standpoint adopted later was clearly bound to modify this position, and Kant's subsequent views are concisely stated in a short piece on miracle (*Über Wunder*) dating from the period 1788–90, although not published until after its author's death.[23] By this time he had come to the conclusion that miracle is theoretically impossible: miraculous occurrences would have to take place in space and time; all spatial modifications involve movement, and movement produced by a miracle would necessarily require an extra-phenomenal cause. Yet the law of action and reaction implies that both effect and cause relate only to the sensible world, and miraculous movement would not be covered by this law. Thus its cause would have to lie outside the world in pure space; but the idea of movement in pure or 'absolute' space (i.e. a total void) is self-contradictory. The same holds of a miraculous event in time; its cause would have to be extra-temporal, in 'absolute' time (i.e. immeasurable time) – again a contradiction. Metaphysically, that is, the divinely established order of being can admit of no exception to its regulative principles, while epistemologically science can likewise admit of no exception to the laws by which it comprehends nature. It is this latter consideration particularly which it is Kant's interest to stress.

When therefore in *Religion* Kant returns to the problem of miracle his concern is not with the theoretical issue of its possibility but with belief in its occurrence. The reason for this change of perspective, quite apart from the risk of censorship, may well have been his desire, in a book dealing expressly with the meaning of Christianity as he understood it, not to alienate the sympathies of friends of his such as Stäudlin and Matern Reuss.[24] Miracle was still a theologically sensitive matter; that it may have a place in faith Kant does not dispute, but the effectiveness of this belief he sees as only very limited, and he quotes John 4.48, 'Unless you see signs and wonders you will not believe', to support his opinion that appeal to miraculous testimony is really indicative of moral timidity. Thus he obliquely criticizes the current orthodoxy with its heavy reliance on 'evidences': faith, he thinks, should not arise from intellectual constraint. But he refrains from embarking on any penetrating discussion of the signification of the gospel miracles from a moral aspect. For this, it may be suspected, would have led him on to the theme of supernatural grace, on which his comments are ever studiously veiled.

8
The Victory of Good Over Evil

THE ETHICAL 'STATE OF NATURE'

The subject of the third Book of *Religion within the Limits of Reason Alone* is, as Kant phrases it, 'The Victory of the Good over the Evil Principle, and the Founding of the Kingdom of God on Earth.' The Book consists of two main sections, the first of which he describes as a 'philosophical account' of how this comes about. In the opening sub-section he registers his belief that moral man can resist evil successfully, otherwise his struggle would be pointless, but that he does so, as he soon learns, only to deliver himself from the *sovereignty* of evil. That is to say, he will always be at risk from its actual *power*, and if he is to assert his freedom against perpetual attack he must 'ever remain armed for the fray'. But this continuing state of peril is really his own fault, and the question is how he is to extricate himself from it. The moral danger to which he is constantly exposed is to be located, however, not in his own 'gross nature' as an individual but in human society itself. Simply as an individual his needs are comparatively few and he has no great difficulty, so Kant believes, in satisfying them: it is not his being poor that a man minds so much as in fearing to be despised by others for his poverty. In other words, his passions are aroused as soon as he finds himself among his fellow-men. And this is not because they are necessarily very wicked. 'It suffices', says Kant in a tone of characteristic pessimism where society is concerned, 'that they are at hand, that they surround him, and that they are men, for them mutually to corrupt each other's dispositions and make one another evil.'[1] Hence a condition of things that must be seen as being socially caused can be overcome only by social means: a society will have to be created the express purpose of which would be the upholding of ethical ideals and of countering evil with united forces. Moreover, such a society, committed to maintaining the laws of virtue, would eventually have to extend the scope of its influence to cover the entire human race. Reason itself demands no less. A union of mankind so orientated may be called an 'ethical society', and in so far as its laws are publicly recognized an 'ethico-civil society' (*ethischbürgerliche Gesellschaft*) or an *ethical commonwealth*.[2] This may well exist within the political commonwealth and even in respect of its membership be identified with it; in any case it must have the latter as its basis – a clear echo here of the Lutheran tradition of the relationship of church and state. Its essential principle differs, nevertheless, in being that solely of promoting virtue *without* the sanctions of the law. For in the discharge of this task coercion will have no place. 'Woe', Kant exclaims, 'to the legislator who wishes to establish through force a polity directed to ethical ends'. For in so doing he not only would achieve the very reverse of an ethical polity but also undermine the political order itself and render it insecure.[3] Good behaviour can to some extent be enforced by law, as Kant no doubt would have admitted; but his concern is with moral actions, which in order to be moral must be free.

This ethical state, or 'kingdom of virtue' (*Reich der Tugend*), as Kant also terms it, has objective reality in that it is men's duty to establish it. Yet the actual isolation and cross-purposes of individuals in what he calls the 'ethical state of nature' (*ethische Naturzustand*) inevitably militates against cohesive action to secure the good, so that willy-nilly society's own members act, in effect, as 'instruments of evil'.[4] This condition is obviously undesirable, so that it is every individual's duty to endeavour to become a member of an ethical community. The ethical state of nature, it should be noted, can and does easily exist within the political commonwealth itself, where, although a juridical order has been established, with each citizen subject to the public laws, the public authority, as we have just remarked, cannot itself bring about 'a kingdom of virtue'. Only to the extent that an ethical commonwealth must rest on public laws and possess a constitution based on these laws are they who freely pledge themselves to enter into this ethical state 'bound . . . to agree to its limitations, namely to the condition that this constitution shall contain nothing which contradicts the duty of its members as citizens of the state'.[5] In practice, as Kant observes, this limitation, given genuineness of ethical commitment, is of little account. Furthermore, because virtue is an ideal presented to the entire human race the idea of an ethical commonwealth must finally be extensive with mankind itself, and therefore immeasurably wider in scope than the political commonwealth. Thus what is envisaged is an ethical totality of which any particular society is no more than a special form of representation. Indeed a number of such societies coexisting with no positive relationship to each other would itself be an example of that same ethical state of nature which the realization of a realm of virtue aims to supersede.

THE ETHICAL COMMONWEALTH AS A CHURCH

In the following sub-section, headed 'The Concept of an Ethical Commonwealth is the Concept of a People of God under Ethical Laws', Kant enlarges on this theme of man's obligation to leave the ethical state of nature for membership of an ethical commonwealth. Men have never failed to recognize, he reminds us, that a 'brutish' condition of mere lawlessness is one only of injustice and strife, and thus have come to establish political order. Similarly the ethical state of nature is itself one of open conflict between principles of virtue and a condition of inner viciousness which the natural man strives to abandon as soon as possible. Hobbes's account in *Leviathan* of the state of nature as *bellum omnium contra omnes* – 'a war of all against each' – Kant regards as correct enough if for the word *bellum* we substitute *status*; it is sufficient that everyone has to be armed against everyone else.[6] The duty to quit this wretched state of things he considers to be *sui generis* – not an obligation simply of individuals towards one another but of the human race towards itself, the species of rational creatures being 'objectively, in the idea of reason, destined for a social goal', i.e. the promotion of the highest social good.[7] However, an ethical commonwealth as 'a universal republic based on the laws of virtue' is an end that cannot be achieved by individual effort alone; its attainment must be a *common* objective, to be reached by the united endeavours of men of good will. As an 'idea of reason' it thus implies, Kant maintains, another – that of a higher moral Being through whose providential working it becomes possible for individuals to realize their common end.

Kant goes on to argue that if an ethical commonwealth is eventually to be established the individuals who constitute its membership must be subject to laws capable of being looked on as commands of a common lawgiver. In the case of a juridical commonwealth this common law-giver would of course be the will of the people themselves, expressed in legislation limiting the freedom of each to those conditions which would render it consistent with that of the rest. But in an ethical commonwealth this cannot be so, inasmuch as there the laws would be specifically designed to promote the *morality* of actions – an inward quality not subject to external control – and not merely the *legality* of actions as matters of common observation. Hence the law-giver of an ethical commonwealth must be conceived of as a Being in regard to whom the laws of morality – the laws, that is, of the autonomous will, binding on the conscience in their own right – can at the same time be accepted as divine commandments. Such a Being must be one 'who knows the heart', penetrating the depths of all men's minds and able to bring it about that each receives the due reward of his actions. 'But this', says Kant, 'is the concept of God as moral ruler of the world'. Thus an ethical commonwealth is to be thought of only as 'a people under divine commands', indeed 'a People of God' whose laws are the laws of virtue.[8] In contrast with this would be the idea of 'a rabble of the evil principle', actively propagating evil in conscious opposition to a people of God 'zealous of good works'.[9]

Incidentally, Kant points out that the notion of *statutory* divine commands, distinct from the laws of the state, are not on his principles possible. For a juridical commonwealth of this kind would be a theocracy the government of which had become the responsibility of a priestly hierarchy. But such a constitution, resting as it would do only on a historical basis, could not account for the morally legislative reason that every rational being recognizes in his own conscience. Of this, however, Kant will have much more to say later, as we shall see. Nevertheless he does affirm, in accordance with the perennial tradition of Christian moral teaching, that any duty, when seen as a duty, even though it be imposed by the arbitrary will of a human law-giver, should be respected as of divine commandment. The saying, 'We ought to obey God rather than men',[10] simply means that if authority commands anything that is directly opposed to the law of morality it ought not to be obeyed. What the saying does not signify is that ecclesiastical ordinances have priority over the laws of the state.

In the next sub-section Kant propounds the view that the idea of a 'People of God' can be realized in institutional terms only in the form of a *Church*. But he ruefully admits at the outset that the 'sublime' concept of an ethical commonwealth, once it has received historical embodiment, will markedly deteriorate. It becomes an organization and therefore subject to the defects to which all organizations are prone, human nature being what it is. But though the ultimate achievement of a 'moral people of God' is something God himself alone can effect, men are not on this account to remain idle, pursuing their own concerns and leaving the work to Providence. Rather must they proceed as though everything depends on them. What, then, is to be done?

Although an ethical commonwealth 'under direct divine moral governance' is, says Kant, a Church, in so far as it is not an object of possible experience but simply a conception of the totality of all righteous persons in a morally governed universe, it is *invisible*.[11] A visible church, on the other hand, is more than an ideal archetype, in being an actual union of men forming a body consonant with that ideal. Explicitly, it is a congregation under *authorities* – pastors, teachers, the clergy – whose responsibility it is to administer the affairs of its invisible supreme Head. As such they are aptly described as servants of the church. The true church is that which manifests the ethical kingdom of God on earth as fully as human conditions allow. But as the traditional Catholic ecclesiology recognizes the true church by its 'notes' (*notae*),[12] so too does Kant by adducing certain marks or tokens corresponding to the four classes of the categories as formulated in the *Critique of Pure Reason*. These are:

1. Universality (*Allgemeinheit*), i.e. quantitatively or numerically considered. If it is universal the church has to be one. It is founded upon such basic principles that in spite of variations in inessentials it must constitute a single body, without division into sects.
2. Nature (*Beschaffenheit*) i.e. as qualitatively considered. Inasmuch as a church's unity is not dependent on other than moral forces it is pure, being without either superstition or fanaticism.
3. Relationship (*Verhältniss*), i.e. it is to be seen as free, in respect both of the internal relations of its members and of its external relations to the state. This freedom is not to be impaired either by a hierarchy or by the false democracy of illuminism, under which the whim of each and every man becomes for him authoritative.
4. Modality (*Modalität*), i.e. the unchangeableness of the church's

fundamental constitution, even though in the lesser matter of administration it may well change according to time and circumstance. The principles on which it is established are determined by its end, or the idea of its purpose. But Kant points out that a church as 'a mere representative of the city of God' has nothing about it that really resembles a political constitution: its own polity, that is, is neither monarchical (as having a pope), nor aristocratic (as subject to bishops), nor democratic (as in the case of sectarian *illuminati*). It is best likened to the family of an invisible Father, whose 'only Son', knowing his Father's will and yet standing in a relation of kinship with the rest of the family, imparts this knowledge to them more clearly. The latter, honouring the Father in him, 'enter with one another into a voluntary, universal, and enduring union of hearts'.[13]

REVELATION, CHURCH DOCTRINE AND SCRIPTURE

Kant now turns to consider the fact that each particular church is always based on faith in an historical revelation – ecclesiastical faith (*Kirchenglaube*), as we may call it – the soundest credentials of which are to be found in sacred scripture. A truly universal church, he states, must rest on a pure religious faith (*ein reiner Religionsglaube*); one, that is, which is grounded in reason alone and so capable of being accepted and shared by all men, as distinct from an 'historical' faith supported only by certain alleged happenings. For the latter can extend its influence no farther than information regarding such occurrences is able to reach, an area which in the nature of things must ever be more or less restricted. Yet because of what Kant judges to be a 'peculiar weakness' of human nature purely rational faith never suffices of itself for the establishment of an institutional church. Regrettably, ordinary men are not disposed to believe that perseverence in a morally good life is all that God requires of them in order to become citizens of his kingdom. Instead they understand their obligation to him to demand some special divine service that depends for its acceptability in his sight not on its intrinsic moral worth but on the condition that it is specifically offered to him. They think of God, that is, as a human potentate wanting to be honoured visibly by his subjects and glorified by their declarations of submissiveness. 'We treat duty, so far as it also is a divine command, as the prosecution of a transaction with God, not with man.'[14] Thus it is that the concept of religion as essentially *divine worship* arises.

The question, then, is one of knowing how God is truly to be served. For the divine will may be thought of as imposing laws that are either merely *statutory* (*statuarische*), or on the other hand purely *moral*. The latter can be known to any man simply through the reason that is in him; indeed the very concept itself of deity derives solely from consciousness of the moral imperative and reflection upon its implications. However the former – statutory divine laws – cannot be known from reason alone but only through revelation (*Offenbarung*), which, whether it be delivered publicly or to an individual privately, would have to be an historical and not a purely rational faith if its means of propagation were to be either oral tradition or the written word. Even so the obligatory nature of these injunctions could draw its force only from the moral law 'through which the will of God is primordially engraved on our hearts'.[15] Hence the only possible answer to the question of true divine service is that it is to do God's universal moral will. Statutory commands, of necessity, are only contingent and on that score incapable of universal application. It is not they who cry 'Lord, Lord' merely, but 'they who do the will of God' who are pleasing to him.[16]

Although this is undoubtedly so, a moral commonwealth or 'divine state' on earth would still require organization, a public covenant, thus becoming a recognizable church. Accordingly the further question arises of how God is to be honoured under these special conditions, since it appears that what is demanded by them is something over and above the fulfilment of moral duty as such. This cannot be met, it seems, out of purely rational considerations but only by statutory regulations based on an historical revelation. But if any such form is inevitably contingent likely to be manifold in its particulars, it could not be seen as obligatory unless from divine statutory provision. Even then the task of determining its form or forms in detail rests with us, and our efforts in this respect may not at first be very successful. Nevertheless we should not cease to strive for their betterment, learning to avoid previous mistakes. Certainly we have no reason, says Kant, 'straightway to take the laws constituting the basis and form of any church as divine statutory laws; rather is it presumptuous to declare them to be such in order to save ourselves the trouble of still further improving the church's form, and it is a usurpation of higher authority to seek, under pretence of a divine commission, to lay a yoke upon the multitude by means of ecclesiastical dogmas'.[17] At the same time a church system may rightly be judged to have been divinely ordered if it is entirely in harmony with moral religion, and especially if it appeared so suddenly that no sufficient intellectual preparation for it had taken place in the public mind.

Kant has already remarked on the evident human inclination to prefer a religion of prescribed ritual observances, a *cultus*, as something pleasing to God in and of itself; and examples can be cited, he believes, of the way this is manifested: ecclesiastical faith is seen to precede a purely moral one; temples, as buildings consecrated to public divine worship, came before churches, which properly are meeting-places for moral instruction and exhortation; priests, as ordained stewards of formal religious rites, similarly came before ministers (*Geistlicher*, or teachers of religion). Priests indeed still command greater veneration among the populace, and Kant notes that this fact would itself indicate that a sound religious faith, propagated in the same form everywhere, is more adequately preserved by *scripture*, which having fixity is relatively more stable, than by *tradition*, which is subject to variation and change. 'A holy book arouses the greatest respect even among those (indeed, most of all among those) who do not read it, or at least those who can form no coherent religious concept therefrom.'[18]

Kant ends this sub-section with a few observations on what belief in a divine revelation involves. First, he distinguishes between true religion, which is unique, and *faiths* of various kinds. But differing faiths, and hence churches, can preserve true religion within them. Common usage however equates religion with ecclesiastical creeds and confessions, no doubt because the latter are much in evidence, whereas the former, which concerns men's moral disposition, is hidden. This error is very difficult to eradicate, not least when we speak of 'religious strife', when what we really mean is 'wrangles over ecclesiastical faith'. Furthermore, an ecclesiastical body's claim to be the one universal church denotes in practice that a man who declines to belong to it is condemned as an unbeliever, and even he who only partially dissents is denounced as heterodox, and should he continue to assert his membership of that church, although at one with it on certain matters of faith, he is dubbed a heretic, and being held to be 'more culpable than a foreign foe' is excommunicated. 'Right' ecclesiastical faith, on the other hand, is called orthodoxy, although admittedly it may be either despotic or liberal. But narrowness and exclusiveness of outlook are confined neither to Catholics nor to Protestants, but are readily to be discovered among both.[19]

For Kant, then, the visible church is the manifestation, or *schema*, of the kingdom of God on earth, its doctrines and institutions providing the media for the transmission of a pure religious faith. But how precisely does he understand the relationship between the visible reality and the invisible? He affirms clearly enough that the visible church, with its dogmas, laws, discipline and ministry, is as necessary to the realization of the ethical commonwealth as is the state organization to society in general. Thus it is not, as some of the church's more hostile eighteenth-century critics accused it of being, merely a means whereby a power-hungry priesthood had exploited the ignorant masses for its own advantage. On the contrary, the visible body is only a further instance of a concrete reality giving appropriate expression to an intelligible idea; man is a rational being, but also sensible and finite, and his life is constituted of both elements. Yet it is no less clear that Kant is reluctant to go all the way towards accepting the church simply in its actuality as an historical phenomenon. He finds it to be necessary at a certain level, so to say, but not intrinsically so, in the way that the state is intrinsically necessary to the social order. Hence it is essentially a 'free' institution, which the individual is at liberty to join or not, as he deems fit. And as is well known, Kant himself stood aloof from the church of his day and declined to assist at its worship even in the round of his official duties. At the same time he did not consider that the form taken by religion, as contrasted with its moral substance, is a matter of indifference. Rather is the form itself also of importance, in that ecclesiastical doctrines and institutions are always to be judged by the standards of purely moral faith and thus are ever open to improvement. But he did not believe that such improvement was likely to be automatic or continuous, and the history of religion shows that there have been times of regress as well as progress. Not that he offers any detailed critique of the course of church history, since his knowledge of it seems to have been little more than sketchy, and in any case his feeling for history and the historic past was itself markedly limited. He was a man altogether of his own century, the rationalist assumptions of which appeared to him to furnish the proper criteria for determining what a true religious faith should be and for assessing church doctrine in their light. It was therefore quite logical for him, in the ensuing section of this third Book of *Religion within the Limits of Reason Alone*, to proceed to discuss how 'ecclesiastical faith has pure religious faith as its highest interpreter'.

Kant takes it as incontrovertible that no church can sustain the claim to universality on the basis only of a *revealed* faith; the historical circumstances and conditions in which it arises and to which it is subject render this impossible. Yet it is equally obvious that men are not content with the abstract and look around for concrete evidence of what is presented to them as a truth of reason. Accordingly if an empirically-grounded faith, depending on contingencies, is to serve as the vehicle of moral faith it will have to be explained in a manner to align it with the universal principles of rational religion. Unless any particular feature of historical religion can be shown to have inherent moral value it cannot be held to carry the authority of a divine ordinance. Sometimes a moral interpretation will look forced, and may well be so; but it will be preferable to the literal interpretation where this is morally valueless or even noxious. Such a procedure, Kant observes, is nothing really new. The sacred writings of pagan antiquity were often construed so as to bring out their moral content at the expense of the literal sense. Thus the Greek philosophers were able to excuse the crudest polytheism as symbolically representative of the attributes of a single divine Being, and it has long been customary for Christians to interpret the imprecatory psalms of the Old Testament in such a way as not to justify vengefulness. In other words, scripture, so far from being the source of moral principles, must be read in accordance with them. Later Judaism, the Moslems and the Hindus in interpreting the Vedas have all judged it necessary to do much the same thing, because it has always been felt that, as against the literal meaning of a text, the basic insights of moral religion are integral to human reason itself. No dishonesty is incurred by this, even though the later interpretation may not reflect the intentions of the original authors. It is sufficient that their words may be so understood. In any case the purpose of studying sacred writings is to make men better. 'The historical element, which contributes nothing to this end, is something which is in itself quite indifferent, and we can do with it what we like.'[20] Historical facts simply as such can have no moral significance. Furthermore, even if a particular writing is believed to be a divine revelation the test of its genuineness in this respect can only be human improvement, which is the goal of all religion. The spirit of God, which guides us into all truth, not only instructs us but imbues us inwardly with the basic principles of conduct. If the scriptures are to be rightly studied the incentive for doing so must be the search for the spirit within them.

But the fruitful study of scripture calls too for scholarship. If men demand a divine revelation they presumably also need historical certification of its authenticity. Obviously complete certainty on this head cannot in the nature of things be attained – men are unable to ascend to heaven to find out – but it is possible, from evidence other than that of the actual content of the revelation, to investigate the manner in which the faith was first introduced. Historical scholarship is necessary therefore to sustain the authority of a church founded upon holy scripture, even though it affords no more than an assurance that nothing relating to the origin of such scripture renders its acceptance as divine revelation impossible. Scholarship is likewise requisite for scriptural exegesis, since how is the multitude of the unlearned, who read it only in translation, to be at all sure of its meaning? The exegete thus must be familiar not only with the original languages but with the historical circumstances in which the text was produced. That is why the pursuit of the methods of historical scholarship, and the publishing of the results ensuing from it, should not, Kant urges – and he wrote from personal experience, as we have seen – be hindered by government censorship. For when such censorship is exercised it amounts to laymen compelling the clergy, the accredited teachers of religion, to conform to their own views. The state's duty is to ensure that there is no lack of competent scholars in this field, having standing and authority in the church, to whose consciences the state entrusts this responsibility. It has no right of itself to intervene in matters where informed opinion differs.

What Kant will not allow is that the interpretation of scripture should be determined by some kind of inner illumination or feeling. No doubt the man who uses scripture as a practical guide to conduct will come to satisfy himself that it is indeed 'of God';[21] but moral experience is not the same thing as emotion; nor is feeling itself any evidence of direct divine influence. In fact the appeal to feeling, something that is personal to each individual, all too easily degenerates into fanaticism.

Thus Kant concludes that there is no norm of ecclesiastical faith apart from scripture, and no true exposition of it other than what is provided by reason and scholarship. And even of these the first alone is really valid, the second being no more than doctrinal, aimed at establishing church teaching in any given historical situation as a definite and lasting system; in which case, Kant presciently observes, belief itself could finally come to mean nothing better than trust in biblical scholars and scholarship. This may not say much for human nature, but the reasonable safeguard against it is that the scholars' researches should ever be open to public discussion and they themselves preserve a due intellectual humility.

WHAT THE COMING OF THE KINGDOM OF GOD MEANS

The seventh and final section of this first part of Book Three sets out what in Kant's view the coming of the kingdom signifies. He sums it up in the phrase 'the gradual transition of ecclesiastical faith to the exclusive sovereignty of pure religious faith'.[22] This happens when an historical or ecclesiastical faith realizes that its purpose is simply to prove itself the vehicle, so to speak, of moral religion and that this purpose is attained only as it approaches the ideal of pure religious faith. The process, however, does not occur without doctrinal conflict, so that an historical church actually in such a state of transition can be designated only as the church *militant*, even if the prospect before it be that finally of becoming the church *triumphant*. The faith of an individual with the moral capacity for eternal happiness can similarly be termed a saving faith, by contrast with one which is expressed only in a religion of divine worship (*gottesdienstlichen Religion*) and which Kant describes pejoratively as a drudging or mercenary faith (*fides mercenaria, servilia*). The one is free and moral, the other servile, induced only by hope or fear.

Saving faith, Kant himself holds, comprises two aspects, the one relating to what a man is unable of himself to accomplish – making good, as in the eyes of a divine judge, his own wrongdoing in the past; the other, to what he himself can and ought to do – performing his moral duty. The first involves belief in the ecclesiastical doctrine of the atonement or reconciliation with God through the work of another; the second, recognition of how we can become acceptable to God solely through the pursuit of a good life. These two aspects are moreover inseparable, although we perceive this only in assuming that one is the source of the other: we suppose, that is to say, either that faith in the atonement and forgiveness of sin itself results in a moral life, or else genuine determination on our part to live such a life will create in us a belief in our absolution or acquittal. Thus we are faced by an antinomy, for both are apparently true yet also contradictory. How are we to resolve it?

As regards the first position it is obvious that were it simply a question of professed belief any man would adopt it. But is it in the least likely that a reasonable person will in all seriousness imagine that he need only accept formally the atonement doctrine as true to secure the complete erasure of his guilt and the ability thereafter to pursue a virtuous life? Such a notion would be feasible only if he thought of his belief as 'instilled in him by heaven' and hence as something the attainment of which demands no further effort. If not, then he would have to view the gift of faith as wholly conditional upon his first doing all he can to better himself morally. But in that case the purely ethical concept clearly is to be preferred to one which exists only in church doctrine.

Yet if men are indeed corrupt by nature, as Kant consistently maintains they are, how can anyone believe in his ability, simply by trying hard, to make himself acceptable to God, when he is well aware that he is still held in the grip of the evil principle and sees no means of his own of releasing himself from it? If he really can do nothing to save himself, and at the same time finds it impossible to believe in an atonement wrought on his behalf by another, what hope has he left? Thus it would seem that faith must after all precede good works, as orthodox Protestantism affirms. The difficulty might not be insuperable if we could fully understand the grounds of our human freedom, but unfortunately we do not. Practically, however, we can ask ourselves whether we are to begin with faith in what God has done for us, or with what we ourselves should do to render us worthy of divine help. In Kant's opinion there can be no doubt which of these two is the right course.

The first of them, that requiring faith in a vicarious atonement, turns on a theoretical idea, whereas the second is straightforwardly practical and moral. On the one view acceptance of ecclesiastical doctrine is held to be a duty, while the active pursuit of goodness by the aid of a higher power presents itself as a matter of grace; but on the other the order is reversed: atonement 'from on high' (*höhere*) is to be seen as an act of grace, while to lead a good life is an unconditional duty. The former is often criticized, not without justice, as superstitious as well as hypocritical, in knowing how to combine an unworthy mode of life with the profession of religion; the latter as rationalist or unbelieving, uniting virtuous living with indifference or open antagonism to revealed truth. The knot of the problem, however, need not be cut. Kant thinks it possible to unravel it.

This can be done if, instead of demanding a prior empirical belief in an actual historical appearance of the God–Man (Christ), and the specific act of atonement rendered by him, is substituted faith in a moral archetype or pattern of humanity that *in itself* is well-pleasing to God. The ideal, that is, is more important and more effective than any alleged signal instance of its fulfilment ever could be, in that the principle of a good life is open to all men to embrace, regardless of time or circumstance. By following the moral ideal as such it may be, and indeed theoretically should be, possible to realize it in an individual instance; but by starting from the individual instance it would not be possible, so Kant argues, to deduce therefrom the maxims of a good life:

> In the appearance of the God–Man on earth, it is not that in him which strikes the senses and can be known through experience, but rather the archetype, lying in our reason, that we attribute to him (since, so far as his example can be known, he is found to conform thereto), which is really the object of saving faith, and such faith does not differ from the principle of a course of life well-pleasing to God.[23]

And as regards the atonement, where according to theological dogma a single historical individual, 'of whom reason tells us nothing', by his personal holiness and merit rendered satisfaction alike for himself, in discharging his duty, and for others, in respect of their sins, a purely moral view confines itself to the injunction to strive for a holiness which is inherently acceptable to God, in the confidence that the divine love towards man will finally make good whatever falls short of the latter's moral perfection. These two disparate positions are to be found, Kant claims, in all forms of religion, in that all teach both a doctrine of expiation and an insistence on moral rectitude, though also at times in conflict with each other, priests complaining about the neglect of public worship and moralists about the decline of virtue.

Thus at last will the empirical and adventitious come to be discarded, the rational and the necessary assuming its place with the emergence of a true religious faith. The leading-strings of ecclesiastical tradition, with its many regulations and observances – serviceable though these may have been in their time – will be seen to be dispensable, or, unless dispensed with, a fetter. What Kant deems to be the 'humiliating distinction' between clergy and laity will similarly disappear, equality arising from true freedom; though also without anarchy, since the law which the believer will now recognize as binding on him is nothing other than 'the will of a World-Ruler revealed to him through reason'.[24] This consummation is not, we are told, to be expected from an external revolution the accompaniments of which are invariably undesirable, but from a process of gradual development. Kant's conclusion is therefore that 'we have good reason to say that "the kingdom of God is come unto us"',[25] once the principle of the gradual transition of ecclesiastical faith to the universal religion of reason, and so to a divine ethical state on earth, has become general and has also gained somewhere a public foothold, even though the actual establishment of this state is still infinitely removed from us'.[26]

HISTORICAL RELIGION

The second division of Book Three is devoted to what Kant presumes to offer as an 'historical account of the gradual establishment of the Good Principle on earth'. Unfortunately it reveals what to the modern reader is perhaps the least satisfactory aspect of its author's thinking, its all but total lack of historical perspective and hence of historical understanding. He starts off by telling us that, strictly speaking, there can be no universal history of religion, in that true religion, i.e. 'pure moral faith', cannot be institutionalized and must always remain a matter solely of individual perception. It is only of institutional religion, 'ecclesiastical faith', of which an historical account may be given, and this is broadly to be characterized as 'nothing but' a narrative of the persisting conflict between a religion of outward ordinances of one kind or another and genuine moral faith. Indeed a mere description of the multiform beliefs of diverse peoples, whose religions – so Kant supposes – have no connection with one another, would be pointless because of the absence of the underlying unity necessary for historical comprehension. Historical faith acquires significance only when inquiry is confined to that portion of humanity which has already recognized the problem raised by the difference between 'the faiths of reason and of history' and the need for solving it. In Kant's opinion this must limit our interest to Christianity alone; Judaism has to be excluded as having no essential relationship – i.e. no real unity of ideas – with the religion which, historically, grew out of it.

Kant's presentation of the Jewish faith, it has to be said, is a purely external one and discloses no sympathetic perception whatever. He sees it as no more than a collection of merely statutory laws supplying the basis of a political organization; such moral dimension as it has was added later and constitutes no integral part of the Jewish religion. He even goes so far as to declare Judaism to be no real religion at all, but simply a 'union of a number of people who, since they belonged to a particular stock, formed themselves into a commonwealth under purely political laws and not into a church'.[27] That this political state assumed the form of a theocracy is of no consequence. Although the name of God is invoked the deity of the Old Testament is nothing other than 'an earthly regent, making absolutely no claims upon, and no appeal to, conscience'. In merely imposing commands from the observance of which no moral betterment can be expected he is quite evidently not the moral Being who ultimately must be the object of any religious faith worth the name. Judaism is also to be dismissed as having no belief in a future life, for Kant flatly denies that any religion is conceivable which does not teach it. To the deep moral and religious sensitivity of the Jews, as their scriptures display it, Kant seems to have been impervious.

By so denigrating the religion of the Jewish people Kant is able to sever Christianity from its historic spiritual root. As 'scripture' the Old Testament falls out of the picture, the Bible being virtually equated with the New Testament. The new religion, no longer tied to the old statutes, or indeed to any statutes at all, was such therefore as to become a faith valid for the whole human race and not for a single people alone. Even though to some extent prepared

The Victory of Good Over Evil

for by Judaism – so much Kant does concede, because in later times something of the wisdom of the Greeks had percolated into it, enlightening it with at least the conception of virtue – it arose suddenly. 'The Teacher of the Gospel' – Kant seems studiously to avoid speaking of 'Jesus' or 'Christ' – announced himself to be an envoy from heaven:

> As one worthy of such a mission, he declared that servile belief . . . is essentially vain and that moral faith, which alone renders man holy . . . and which proves its genuineness by a good course of life, is the only saving faith.[28]

His life and his death, the latter 'unmerited yet meritorious', provided an example consonant with the archetype of a humanity pleasing to God. Thereafter he is represented as returning to heaven. But although the teaching of Christianity's founder was in itself sufficient for a 'moral self-improving faith' and accordingly had no need of miraculous attestation, claims were soon made on behalf of that founder's own status and personality, so giving rise to an historical faith of a kind needing verification by miracles. This in turn called for an 'inspired' book to document them, with a suitably 'learned public' for its readers. After this manner did Christianity become the ecclesiastical religion we are familiar with, although much of its early history is obscure and we still remain largely ignorant of the moral effect of its teachings upon its first adherents. However, since the time when Christianity took its place in the forefront of western civilization it has, Kant opines, 'served in no way to recommend it on the score of the benificent effect which can justly be expected of a moral religion'.[29] Hence for Christian history itself he has precious little to say of good. What we have to deal with is for the most part a record of 'mystical fanaticism', a noxious glorification of socially useless celibacy, superstitious miracle-mongering, a power-seeking hierarchy, a presumptuous orthodoxy battening on false interpretations of scripture, a Christendom rent by unending disputes on matters of creed, the Eastern part of it subjected to a meddlesome state, with the Western no less in thrall, at the price of civil and cultural confusion, by a self-styled 'viceroy of God' – all this and much more, 'when surveyed in a single glance, like a painting, might well justify the exclamation: *tantum religio potuit suadere malorum*'.[30]

Kant's own age alone offers hope of a brighter future. It is an enlightened age in which the seed of the true religious faith is being sown, albeit only by a few. But if its growth is unhindered a continuous approach may be looked for to 'that church, eternally uniting all men, which constitutes the visible representation of an invisible kingdom of God on earth'.[31] It will be possible if two principles, at any rate, are maintained: first, that a reasonable modesty is shown in all discussion of what is deemed to be revelation; and second, that scripture is always expounded in the interest of morality, since its function is to illustrate but not originate moral maxims. As Kant untiringly iterates: 'It must be inculcated painstakingly and repeatedly that true religion is to consist not in the knowing or considering what God does or has done for our salvation but in what we must do to become worthy of it.'[32] That again is why it is reprehensible for government authority to attempt to uphold highly disputable ecclesiastical doctrines with the offer or denial of civil advantages otherwise available to all.

Kant ends by affirming his conviction that although the coming of the true religion may be tardy its arrival is to be confidently expected, and he translates the symbolic language of the Christian apocalyptic hope in terms of the kind of development he looks for. But although the 'Teacher of the Gospel' revealed to his disciples the kingdom of God on earth 'in its glorious, soul-elevating moral aspect' – citizenship in a divine state – he also warned them to be prepared for tribulations and sacrifices. Nevertheless they could rejoice and be exceeding glad, for their reward in heaven would be great. Men would, that is to say, be ultimately triumphant, 'crowned with happiness while still here on earth, after all obstacles have been overcome'. However, this splendid ideal of the 'moral world-epoch' achieved by the advent of true universal religion cannot properly be imagined by us in empirical form, but only anticipated in the sense of being assiduously prepared for. Indeed, so far as we regard ourselves as intellectually and morally citizens of such a kingdom it is present here and now. 'Behold, the kingdom of God is within you.'

RELIGIOUS MYSTERIES: THE TRINITY

The appended section of Book Three, dealing like its equivalents for the first two Books with a *parergon* of religion, is of particular interest, as its theme is the place of 'mystery' in religion. There are, Kant reminds us, mysteries (*Geheimnisse*) or hidden things in nature (*arcana*), as there are also secrets (*secreta*) in political affairs; but although these may be described as mysterious, in not being generally known, they are not, Kant says, in principle obscure, since they rest on empirical causes. But when we look into religious faiths we invariably, at some point, encounter mystery in the form of some especially sacred matter which cannot be universally known. Being holy it must be moral and hence an object of reason, and also sufficiently capable of apprehension as to be of practical account; notwithstanding, it is beyond *theoretical* comprehension. Whether or not there actually are such mysteries is not, Kant thinks, to be settled *a priori* and objectively; we have, rather, to scrutinize our moral attitudes to see if anything at all like it is to be found within us. Certainly the grounds of morality, although inscrutable to us, are not to be listed among such mysteries as these, because whatever the ultimate origin of morality may be it is necessarily a matter of universal concern. The same is true of our sense of the will's freedom; again, its ground is inscrutable, but being experienced by everybody it is in no proper sense mysterious. Yet the idea of the highest good, something bound up with pure moral sentiment, cannot be realized by the individual alone, nor even by the help of others, but only through the co-operation of a 'moral Ruler of the world'. This indeed is a mystery, for we do not know, and have no means of knowing, what God can do in this respect, or even whether he is able to do anything. All that we can manage is to render ourselves worthy of such divine aid if and when it is made available to us.

The whole idea, then, of a moral governor of the world is a matter for the practical reason. What counts for us is not the knowledge of what God is in himself but what he signifies for us as moral beings. However, some belief as to what God himself is like is relevant to the discharge of the divine will on our part, and the religious beliefs conformable with this requirement are:

1. that God is the omnipotent creator of heaven and earth, and a morally holy legislator;
2. that he is the preserver of mankind, its benevolent ruler and moral guardian; and
3. that he is the administrator of his own law, a righteous judge.

These assertions really contain no mystery, in Kant's opinion, because they do no more than indicate the moral relation in which

God stands to the human race; and also, he holds, being such as to occur spontaneously to men's minds everywhere, they are to be met with in the religions of most civilized peoples. For something much resembling them – or so he imagines – is to be found in the ancient religion of Egypt, in Zoroastrianism, in Hinduism and in the old Gothic mythology.[33] Even Judaism in its later form, Kant suggests, seems to have entertained the idea, in that the Pharisees did not object to the notion of God having a son, but to Jesus' express claim to be identifiable with him. Kant's 'trinity', then, is not – to use the formal language of theology – an 'essential' trinity, which would imply a knowledge of God's inner nature, but only one of manifestation, an 'economic' trinity. What he is arguing is that the idea of God is intelligible to us only as it is expressive of our moral understanding, for what it asserts is a religious belief corresponding to something already familiar to us, namely the legislative, executive and judicial functions of the civil state. The supreme lawgiver is one who commands neither with undue forbearance nor despotically, but through laws addressed to man's holiness; as likewise with a beneficence that takes account of man's moral achievement before making good his moral deficiency, and with a justice which recognizes the inevitable limitations upon his attempts to measure up to its righteous requirements. 'In a word, God wills to be served under three specifically different moral aspects. The naming of the different . . . persons of one and the same Being expresses this not ineptly.'[34] In a figurative manner it gives utterance to the whole of 'pure moral religion'. Were it, however, to be regarded not merely as a symbolical idea but objectively, as purporting to describe what God is in himself, it would be a mystery transcending all human ideas, and hence 'a mystery of revelation unsuited to man's powers of comprehension'. So understood it would be ethically useless. But as a genuine because morally intelligible 'mystery' it does not elude reason, and indeed may be thought of as a revelation of reason. What it tells us may be characterized as follows.

First, there is the mystery of the *divine call* of men to an ethical state. This is mysterious because vocation implies freedom, whilst at the same time we have to see ourselves as God's creatures, 'and it is absolutely incomprehensible to our reason how beings can be *created* to a free use of their powers'.[35] Yet morally we have no doubt of our freedom and of our obligation to use it responsibly. Secondly, there is the mystery of *atonement*. Because of man's corrupted nature God's call to him to become a citizen of the kingdom of heaven is incapable of receiving a fully satisfactory response, but where man falls short God out of the fullness of his own righteousness supplements his lack. But this contradicts the essentially moral condition which demands that good is not to be supplied by another and must come from the individual himself if it is rightly to be credited to him. The moral acceptability of vicarious satisfaction thus remains for reason wholly unaccountable. Thirdly, there is the mystery of *election*. Even if vicarious atonement be admitted as a possibility, a disposition of moral faith is needed for its acceptance; yet man's natural depravity gravely impedes this and can be surmounted only by the power of grace. But why such heavenly aid should be bestowed upon one man and not – as is evident – upon another is inexplicable apart from an unconditioned divine decree. Why, then, some among mankind should be destined for salvation but others for reprobation is a question not to be answered in terms of divine justice but must be referred only to a 'wisdom whose rule for us is a mystery'.[36] Thus although we concede the place of the mysterious in the moral life we fail to understand how it has come to be there. We recognize the facts, but their cause is hidden from us. However, all that is necessary in regard to the objective regulation of our conduct is revealed through reason and scripture in a manner comprehensible to all men.

In closing his discussion of the *parergon* of mystery Kant again adverts to the doctrine of the trinity, and this time he adopts the familiar language of Christian dogma. Previously he had confined himself to listing the general properties or aspects of the divine will along the lines of natural theology rather than specifically Christian teaching,[37] and then relating these to the triple form of political power as categorized by Montesquieu in his *Esprit des lois*.[38] The highest ideal of moral perfection to which man can aspire, even though in practice he never attains it, is, says Kant, 'love of law'. To express this idea in religious terms is, he thinks, to affirm that 'God is love', which he construes as meaning that the *Father* is the 'Loving One' whose love shows itself in moral approval of man's efforts to fulfil the holy law; that the *Son* is he who reveals the Father 'in his all-inclusive idea', so becoming the archetype of humanity; and thirdly, that the *Holy Spirit* is he who reveals the divine love as resting upon wisdom: God, that is, makes his approval of men depend upon their own assent to the condition on which the same approving love is expended.³⁹ As regards this last aspect of deity, however, we may note that the function of judging devolves less upon the Son, as stated in the Christian creeds, than upon the Spirit. At any rate, as the Son judges in love and goodness, distinguishing the worthy from the unworthy and choosing as his own those to whom merit can in some degree be accredited, so the Spirit judges in righteousness, pronouncing the verdict either of guilty or not guilty, of condemnation or acquittal. Kant evidently considers that he has scriptural warrant for this by appealing (as against the clear statements of 2 Timothy 4.1 and John 3.7) to John 3.17: 'God sent not his Son into the world to judge the world, but that the world through him might be saved', and to John 3.18: 'He that believeth not in the Son is already judged' – i.e. by the Spirit, of whom it is said that 'He will judge the world because of sin and righteousness'.⁴⁰

Finally, Kant does not omit to point out that God should not actually be invoked in terms of his various 'personalities', as this would suggest a multiplicity of beings instead of the unity which his being essentially is, although it is permissible to do so in the name of him whom God loves and esteems above all else, and with whom moral union is not only our desire but our duty.

9
Institutionalism in Religion

WHAT IS THE TRUE SERVICE OF GOD?

The final Book of *Religion within the Limits of Reason Alone* is headed 'Concerning Service and Pseudo-Service [i.e. of God] under the Sovereignty of the Good Principle, or Concerning Religion and Clericalism'. This last term translates Kant's *Pfaffenthum*, which has a decidedly pejorative sense; it could be rendered by 'priestcraft'. The dominion of the good principle commences, Kant states, as soon as the basic marks of its constitution first become public, i.e. visibly manifested in a church: 'The kingdom of God, it could then be said, is at hand.' Its actual founding, however, is a work beyond the powers of humanity and must be brought about by God himself; nevertheless the setting up of a church is a task which men can and should accomplish through religion. In other words, although the divine action will in itself always be inscrutable for us, we are under moral obligation to become citizens and subjects of this kingdom and therefore have the capability of doing so at least to the extent of organizing it, even though God alone is its ultimate author. As an institution it will comprise the relatively few responsible for its administration as the church's servants, as well as the many, the congregation, who constitute a co-partnership subject to the administration's rules. True religion indeed, and the invisible church in which this finds realization, will have no place for 'ecclesiastical service' or for church officials to direct it, since the 'pure religion of reason' will have as its servants none else but the body of 'right-thinking' persons. Yet because an organized church and the statutory religion on which it rests, can still approximate to the true church in so far as it embodies a rational faith instead of an historical or 'ecclesiastical' one, the laws and the ministry of the visible church may be thought of as rendering true service to God if they have the right goal in view. Those on the other hand who do not, and who remain wholly committed to statutory religion as the way of salvation, only promote a pseudo-service (*cultus spurius*, *Afterdienst*), depending on the notion that 'one can be served by deeds which in fact frustrate the very ends of him who is being served'.[1]

With these introductory reflections Kant moves on to consider what in general is meant by the service of God in religion, repeating yet again his characteristic definition of religion as, subjectively, the recognition of all moral duties as divine commands. This, he points out, asserts nothing in the way of speculative knowledge, not even the proposition that God exists: it merely makes use of the *idea* of God; while secondly, it obviates the doctrine that religion consists of special duties directed to God alone – 'courtly obligations' (*Hofdienste*), Kant dubs them – over and above the moral obligations owed by one man to another; and therewith the possibility of exploitation in the interests of clerical ambition. He then proceeds to distinguish revealed religion from natural by saying that whereas in the one a duty is recognized as such because it is taken to be a divine command, in the other it presents itself as a divine command only because it is first recognized as a human obligation. But he further distinguishes between a man who sees natural religion as alone morally necessary and whom he terms a *rationalist* – although if the latter also denies the reality of all supernatural revelation he must be classed as a *naturalist* – and one who, while admitting a revelation to be possible, denies that knowledge of it is in any respect necessary to religion; for he would properly be described as a *pure rationalist*, although were he to hold the opposite view – that belief in revelation *is* necessary to universal religion – he would have to be classed, in matters of faith, as a *pure supernaturalist*.

Should a religion be such that it is capable of being shared widely with others it may be classified according to one or other of two kinds: as *natural*, if its appeal is to reason alone, or as *learned*, if it has to be taught. But it may also be regarded as both, for although it may be so constituted that its principles could and should have been discovered simply by the exercise of reason – in which case it is properly to be described as natural – these principles still may not have been discovered as soon or as widely as was needful. Hence an historical revelation would prove itself of advantage to men in disclosing beforehand something the truth of which would eventually become evident to them from reason alone. Such a religion, that is, would objectively be natural, but subjectively be revealed. Were the actual circumstances of that revelation to be forgotten nothing would have been lost because its truth would be seen not to have been dependent on them. However, in the case of a religion depending wholly on revelation its authority would turn upon the reliability of its traditions, although, as Kant has remarked, every religion must contain certain principles of natural religion if it is to have any purchase on the rational understanding. As an example of a religion which can be regarded as both natural and learned Kant looks to Christianity; and what Christianity is may be ascertained with complete sufficiency from the scriptures of the New Testament.

First, Kant considers it in its aspect as a natural religion. As such its constituent elements will be morality along with – since issuing therefrom – the ideas of God and immortality. Thus it will have the prime essential of the true church in possessing the character of universality; but to become a world religion it will need agents (a *ministerium*) through whose activity it will establish itself as a visible entity, membership of which is subject to certain statutory requirements imposed by authority. These of course will not constitute an end in themselves but simply the means of securing a unified and durable society. But that Christianity is basically a natural religion on account of its inherently moral character is evidenced by the recorded teachings of Jesus – teachings that are 'no other than those of pure reason' and thus bearing their own proof. For example, Kant cites St Matthew 5.20–48, from the Sermon on the Mount, to show that only the pure moral disposition of the heart can make a man well-pleasing to God, for the Jewish Law is here re-interpreted (and therefore justified) in accordance not with mere scholarship but with the pure religion of reason. The 'straight gate' and the 'narrow way' plainly indicate that what is demanded is moral duty, the pursuit of a good life, in contrast with church membership and 'churchly duty'. Kant sums up Jesus' teaching in two clear rules, the one universal: 'Perform your duty for no motive other than unconditional esteem for duty itself' – which may be construed as 'Love God above all else'; the other particular, concerning man's external relations with other men as universal duty: 'Love everyone as yourself' – which means, again, 'Further his welfare from goodwill that is immediate and not derived from motives of self-advantage'.[2]

As a 'learned' religion Christianity sustains dogmas which reason itself cannot pronounce to be necessary but which nonetheless must be delivered uncorrupted down the ages as a sacred trust. The guardianship of this trust is committed to the 'learned', upon whom devolves 'the written, authoritative, and unchanging instruction to posterity'. Acceptance of a religion's fundamental principles is the action of faith (*fides sacra*); and the Christian faith is from one angle rational, but from another revealed (*fides statuaria*). The former is a faith to which anyone can freely assent (*fides elicita*), the latter belief that is commanded (*fides imperata*); the one is a matter purely of rational conviction, but the other is imposed, in that it covers historical doctrines acceptance of which is regarded by the church as a duty:

> In the Christian church neither of these can be separated from the other as adequate in itself; the second is indispensable to the first because the Christian faith is a religious faith, and the first is indispensable to the second because it is a learned faith.[3]

However, as Kant points out, the believer cannot start with a wholly *unconditional* assent to Christianity's revealed doctrines, the 'learning' being supplied afterwards for the sole purpose of defending such assent, as this would amount to no more than a 'servile' faith. Rather must historical faith be taught as *fides historica elicita*; in other words, the learning should come first, provided by the work of the biblical scholars, because it is by them that the laity, including the civil rulers – another knock at the official censorship – must be instructed; which only goes to prove once more that in the end it is the universal human reason, 'the supremely commanding principle in a natural religion', by which an historical faith is made comprehensible.[4] Alone by acknowledging this priority – that the means be no longer mistaken for the end – will a church 'under the dominion of the good principle' be able to offer true service instead of a pseudo-service, for then no one would be expected to believe that a Christian 'must be a Jew whose Messiah has come'. For Christianity had the great advantage over Judaism in that it appeared at its inception as a moral and not a statutory religion; something, Kant supposes, which made possible its acceptance 'at all times and among all peoples with the greatest trustworthiness'. However, it became in its early stages – as was inevitable – entwined with the history of Judaism, and this Jewish element has since been transmitted as part of Christianity's legacy to the future. Unfortunately what at first were merely adventitious means of communication have been incorporated into the essential articles of Christian faith, then multiplied and reinterpreted until they have become integral to the religion's very structure, with all the legal force conferred upon them by the authoritative decrees of church councils.

'AFTERDIENST'

So, in the second part of this last Book, Kant has to face the problem of *Afterdienst*, 'pseudo-service', or the false worship of God, which is to be found in all the historical forms of religion. Statutory faith is always, Kant argues, restricted to a single people and cannot develop into a universal religion. Hence to imagine it necessary to the proper service of God is an illusion (*Wahn*), its illusory character consisting in 'the deception of regarding the mere representation of a thing as equivalent to the thing itself'.[5] The general 'subjective ground' of the religious illusion is to be seen in man's propensity to anthropomorphism, or the creating of a God for himself in a shape which he thinks will afford him, man, the readiest advantage and so preclude the constant and wearisome effort of working on his own inner moral disposition. The anthropomorphic urge is in itself natural enough and harmless, so long as it does not detract in any way from moral religion as Kant has defined it. Nor is it improper to speak of man as 'creating' his God, because in a sense this is what religious symbolism, which cannot in fact be dispensed with, always does; it is a means of honouring the Creator. But the symbol must ever be tested by our apprehension of the rational and moral ideal that is symbolized. Otherwise we fall into idolatry, the worship of a false divinity. And we cannot avoid the charge of idolatry by insisting that outward acts of devotion – penances, self-chastisements, pilgrimages and the like – at any rate testify the goodwill of those who perform them, but who are too weak – as they may think themselves – to obey the moral law. Public worship of any kind – for to private prayer Kant can attach no significance whatever – is no more than a means of acquiring a right disposition in the sight of God. But to entertain the idea that this means can ever be a substitute for the strictly moral end which alone is its justification is to foster the religious illusion a truly ethical judgment must reprehend. This inveterate tendency to replace true worship of God by the false is, one might say, the church's original sin, its radical evil.

The moral principle of religion has, then, to be firmly opposed to everything that is illusory. Kant's restatement here of his so often expressed conviction is emphatic: 'Whatever, over and above good life-conduct, man fancies he can do to become well-pleasing to God is mere religious illusion and pseudo-service of God.'[6] We need not doubt that God can and will do something beyond our own achievement to render us pleasing in his sight, but exactly what this will be, and how it will be brought about, is a mystery which we cannot fathom, and any claim on the church's part to possess such knowledge, or demand that it be believed as an essential of faith, is perilously misleading. For a man to be required to make a solemn declaration of whose truth he is not inwardly assured would be to do violence to his conscience. Far better is it that he should attempt whatever he can and trust in God to make good his failure than that he should pretend to certainty about what specific observances of his will earn the favour of heaven apart from the sustained effort to lead a good life. As the history of religion shows, men will at times go to the most extreme lengths of self-mortification on the supposition that acts of that kind are what God desires over and above a right moral disposition. And although resort to various religious practices, from a pilgrimage to the Holy Land to the twirling of a Tibetan prayer-wheel, have often enough been substituted for the moral service of God, superstition such as this, contemptible though it may be, is less dangerous than the fanaticism (*Schwärmerei*) which presumes to set grace and nature in opposition to each other or to detail exactly where the resources of the one end and the powers of the other begin.

The section which follows is concerned with 'clericalism as a government in the pseudo-service of the good principle'. Kant himself, in a footnote, explains that the word *Pfaffenthum*, although signifying no more than spiritual father ($\pi\grave{\alpha}\pi\pi\alpha$), carries with it the idea of 'spiritual despotism to be found in all forms of ecclesiasticism, as the term 'priest-craft' well suggests. Always the intention is 'to manage to their own advantage the invisible Power which presides over the destiny of men'.[7] Differences arise only about the methods of doing so, but the supposition behind them is that there is an art by which a supernatural effect can be secured by wholly natural means, and the word Kant thinks most apt to describe this is fetishism, although he admits it has other connections. There is nothing much amiss with one's employing certain formal observances if one's purpose is to make himself worthy of supernatural aid in pursuing a strictly moral end – supplementing, that is, what he realizes to be his own inadequacy; but merely to imagine that actions which in themselves have no moral worth will not only serve as a means to but are actually the condition of the satisfaction of his desires directly by God, plainly is to be the victim of illusion. When a church is so constituted that fetish-worship of this sort comes to dominate it we have 'clericalism'. Some types of church may be so impregnated with it as to exclude the ethical altogether, but even when present on a limited scale it is the same principle which obtains: submission to non-moral precepts as a compulsory service. It is the principle that sustains the hierarchical government of a church, whether monarchical, aristocratic or democratic; for in the end it is the clergy who rule as the supposed 'uniquely authorized guardian and interpreter of the will of the invisible Legislator', in defiance, it may be, of reason and scripture alike.

Indeed Kant goes on to warn his readers against the very notion of *godliness*. It tends, he argues, to make us think of God anthropomorphically, in a way that can be harmful to our basic moral principles. The concept of *virtue*, therefore, should be established first, the idea of God not being grounded in the speculative reason but only in its relation to our independent determination of duty. The doctrine of godliness cannot of itself constitute the final goal of moral endeavour, it merely serves as 'a means to strengthening that which in itself goes to make a better man, to wit, the virtuous disposition'. The doctrine of virtue, on the other hand, pertains to the soul of man. 'He is already in possession of it, undeveloped, no doubt, but not needing, like the religious concept, to be rationalized into being by means of logistics.'[8] False religious beliefs, Kant thinks, seem to engender certain characteristics in the peoples who hold them which later are assumed to be a universal human trait. Thus Judaism is seen as misanthropic, Mohammedanism as arrogantly proud, Hinduism as pusillanimous, and Christianity itself as based on a misconceived humility that quickly degenerates into the servile.

CONSCIENCE AND BELIEF

Apart from a final 'General Observation' the concluding section of Kant's treatise discusses 'the guide [or clue] of conscience in matters of faith'. The point he at once makes is that the conscience needs no guide other than itself. The question, therefore, is how it can serve as a guide in reaching decisions on complex moral issues. Certainly it is a fundamental moral principle, itself wanting no proof, that one ought not to risk doing anything that is arguably wrong (*quod dubitas, non feceris*); for, says Kant, in all strictness it is the understanding, not conscience, which judges whether an action is right or not. However, in deciding that a proposed action is right one has first to be *sure* that it really is so. Hence the doctrine of *probabilism*, familiar in the casuistry developed in the sixteenth and seventeenth centuries by the Jesuits, namely the principle that because an act *may* be right its performance is morally justified, must be firmly dismissed. Conscience might in fact be defined as 'the moral faculty of judgment, passing judgment upon itself',[9] provided it is realized that judgment is essentially a work of reason. As an instance of what he means Kant takes religious persecution. It might, on the strength of Luke 14.23, 'Compel them to come in' (*compellite intrare*), which St Augustine cited in justification of coercive measures against heretics and schismatics, that this is permissible, if not actually a duty. But the basic moral conviction, that to deprive a man of his life – as coercion may eventually mean – because of his religious belief is certainly wrong, must be upheld unless the contrary can be *known* to be in accord with the divine will. Yet are we sure that this ever could be so? If the claim that it is divinely willed is to be asserted only on the ground of historical documentation its certainty will be much less than apodictically established. For the point of weakness in all historically-based faith is that the possibility of error in the tradition can never be eliminated. Further, the saying that it is better to believe too much than too little Kant also rejects as an encouragement to religious dishonesty; for if I accept as a condition of salvation something that rests on revelation alone unauthenticated by the pure reason, although at the same time not contradicted by morality, I would be wrong either to profess it as a certainty or to deny it as indubitably false. Nevertheless, before any man accepts church dogma as divinely revealed let him ask himself whether he rightly can do so 'in the sight of Him who knows the heart'. At any rate one should query whether the method of religious education which requires only a good memory in answering questions relating to such doctrines is not in the end more likely, by fostering religious insincerity, to produce nothing but hypocrites. That Kant, while doubtless correct in insisting on the need for complete intellectual honesty, has scarcely come to grips here with the problem of receiving as true beliefs that are part of the traditions in which one has been nurtured and which may seem to him therefore not seriously to be questioned. Indeed the psychology of belief, as explored, let us say, by John Henry Newman in his *Grammar of Assent*, is something which Kant evidently did not envisage. He is content to view the matter as one purely of the decisions *in abstracto* of the individual conscience.

THE MEANS OF GRACE

In his 'General Observation' at the end of this chapter Kant turns to the last of the four *parerga* of religion as considered 'within the limits of reason alone': the meaning of *grace* (*Gnadenmittel*). The concept, he again states, of 'a supernatural accession to our moral, though deficient, capacity and even to our not purified and certainly weak disposition to perform our entire duty, is a transcendent concept, and is a bare idea, of whose reality no experience can assure us'.[10] It also is a hazardous idea, since the only true means of grace is a morally good life. For what is meant by moral obedience reason itself is enough to inform us, but as to supernatural aid we can know nothing. In general we may *assume* that grace will effect what nature alone cannot achieve – on condition we have done the very best within our power – but the notion remains one of which we can make no positive use. To talk therefore about 'means' of grace, with the implication that the divine assistance can in some way be manipulated, is an all too common form of self-deception, detrimental to true religion. However, although the true service of God is invisible, being 'a service of the heart' in spirit and in truth, man is such that the invisible for him calls for representation through the visible. It could be thought of as a 'picturing' to ourselves of our duty in God's service, risky though the attempt may be.

This 'outward' service Kant sees as expressible in four observances of duty, with four corresponding rites. All are based on the intention of promoting moral good. They are:

1. Private prayer, as a means of stimulating personal moral feeling – the only use Kant can think of it as fulfilling;

2. Church-going, as the occasion and means of the public dissemination of goodness;
3. Baptism, as a way of propagating goodness in the coming generation by receiving new members into the fellowship of faith and later instructing them in such goodness; and
4. Sacramental communion, as a means of maintaining this ethical fellowship through a repeated public formality.

Even so, Kant is unable to forbear yet again from pointing out the danger of this symbolism, in that it easily degenerates into 'fetishism', or the notion that what cannot be produced by either natural or moral laws is yet capable, by itself, of bringing about what is desired if only we screw ourselves up to believing that it will do so. Kant strengthens his warning by referring to 'the Mohammedan type of belief', with its 'five great commands': washing, praying, fasting, almsgiving and the pilgrimage to Mecca. None of these, he judges, has or can have any moral value except almsgiving: although in fact this too is without it, since it can 'well go hand in hand with the extortion from others of what, as a sacrifice, is offered to God in the person of the poor'.[11] In the case of Christianity illusory faith finds utterance in three ways, the first two of which have already been discussed, namely belief in miracles – the affecting to know through experience what rationally we recognize to be impossible – and faith in mysteries – the supposing that to be necessary to our moral interest of which reason can form no concept. The third, the means of grace – to be distinguished from *works* of grace, also discussed earlier – derives from the idea that divine influence can be brought to bear directly upon our moral life by merely natural agencies.

These supposed means of grace Kant now considers in turn. Prayer he sees as no more than a stated wish addressed to a Being who has no need to be informed of the inner disposition of him who offers it. Nothing therefore is achieved by it, and it discharges none of the duties which, although understood as divine commands, already impose themselves on us as morally obligatory. The 'Spirit of prayer', as a hearty desire to be well-pleasing to God, we ought always indeed to have; in possessing it, however, a man should expect only to affect himself, creating within himself a right disposition of mind by means of the idea of God. He is not to believe that his wishes, deep-seated though they may be, can possibly change the divine will. In the one case prayer may be offered with full sincerity even without the presumption that God exists; in the second, it is as if a man actually supposes the Supreme Being to be personally present and that his solicitations will gain him favour – an attitude which Kant can only deprecate.[12] The philosopher is confident also that petitioning for such divine favour was not enjoined by the 'Teacher of the Gospel', whose words express 'nothing but the resolution to good life-conduct, which, taken with the consciousness of our frailty, carries with it the persistent desire to be a worthy member of the kingdom of God'.[13] No specific request is countenanced for something which God in his wisdom might well refuse, and when the spirit of prayer is quickened within us the letter of it will in the end fall away.

Unlike private prayer, church-going is regarded as a public duty; it is not simply a means to the edification of the individual, although that purpose it may assuredly serve, but a duty obligating the worshippers as a group – as 'citizens of a divine state which is to appear here on earth' – so long as anything that might lead to idolatry is avoided. But to imagine that public worship as formal ritual could of itself be a means of grace, as if God were directly served by it and in return minded to bestow special benefits on those celebrating it, is, again, wholly illusory. It in no way enhances citizenship of the kingdom of God, but rather debases it, leading as always to self-deception and hypocrisy.

Baptism, as the once-for-all ceremony of admission to the church-community, Kant admits to having great significance, laying a serious obligation upon the initiate if in a position to make personal confession of his faith, or else upon the sponsors who solemnly undertake to educate him in due course in that faith. The aim here is indirectly the nurture of a man as a citizen of a divine state, but in itself the rite is not holy nor productive of holiness, and thus is not a means of grace, for all the esteem in which it has been held in the church. So too with communion, the regularly repeated ceremony by which the church renews and promotes among its members a sense of their fellowship. As such, Kant thinks, 'it contains within itself something great, expanding the narrow, selfish and unsociable cast of mind among men ... toward the idea of a cosmopolitan moral community', as well as a means of kindling brotherly love. But it is not a thing which merely by the act of its celebration can guarantee special divine favour. Once more there is nothing here that can be regarded as a *means* of grace. Unfortunately it is of the very essence *Pfaffenthum* to encourage the belief that the clergy, simply by virtue of their professional office, have such means at their exclusive disposal.

So Kant ends his long and searching inquiry into the meaning of religion, and more particularly of the Christian religion. His conclusion is that of the three divine moral attributes – holiness, mercy and justice – men's wont is to turn directly to the second in order to avoid the burdensome condition of complying with the demands of the first. 'It is tedious to be a good *servant* . . . for ever hearing only about one's duties; man would therefore rather be a *favourite*, where much is overlooked or else, when duty has been too grossly violated, everything is atoned for through the agency of some one or other favoured in the highest degree, man meanwhile remaining the servile knave he ever was.'[14] In fine, religion is good moral conduct, and nothing more – supernatural faith, devotion, prayer, worship or sacrament – besides.

10
Last Thoughts on Philosophy of Religion

THE 'OPUS POSTUMUM'

Allusion has already been made to Kant's *Der Streit der Facultäten*,[1] in which he discussed, in regard to university teaching in Germany, the relations of philosophy, studied only in the 'lower' faculties, to the subjects of the three 'higher' – or as we might say today 'vocational' – faculties of theology, law and medicine; and it will be recalled that, as touching the first of these, he entered a protest against the prevailing tendency for theologians, on the ground of the allegedly presiding authority of scripture, to dominate the whole field of religious thought to the virtual exclusion of the philosophers. Accordingly, in order to lend substance to his objection, he recapitulated the views already expressed in *Religion within the Limits of Reason Alone*, i.e. on what constitutes true religion when the presiding role of ethics has been acknowledged, and on how Christian doctrines are, in the light of this, properly to be understood and assessed. There is therefore no need to rehearse them as they reappear here, in merely summary form, although Kant also refers to objections that had been raised concerning his interpretation of Christianity and he seeks to answer them. But the work as a whole, though not without touches of ironic humour, makes dry reading and adds nothing of significance to what had been more fully said before. We may, then, pass on to consider the so-called *Opus Postumum*, edited with an elaborate analytical commentary by Erich Adickes of Tübingen and published in 1920.[2]

During the last ten years of his life Kant was engaged in the composition of what he evidently planned as a major philosophical enterprise.[3] Its original title was to be 'Transition from Metaphysical Foundations of Natural Science to Physics' and was designed to advance the process, initiated with its author's

157

'Metaphysical Foundations of Natural Science', of providing an *a priori* basis for physics. Briefly, he sought to replace the largely formal structure which he earlier devised with a scheme of thought purporting to show how some at least of the fundamental laws of nature could be formulated in advance of experience. Moreover, these speculations opened up for him the prospect of wider considerations in the realm of epistemology. However, the design was not to be carried through to completion, and what Kant actually left behind him was no more than a vast collection of notes, not a systematic treatise. Inevitably there is much repetition, although in many respects the thought remains inchoate, obscure, or even self-contradictory. Hence it is far from easy to see how the work would eventually have shaped itself, even if its author had been able to command the physical and mental resources to carry it through to a conclusion. Yet as Kemp Smith points out, this repetitiveness and lack of co-ordination in the preparation of Kant's longer enterprises 'represent his usual method of composition; and the most that can be said is that with the passage of the years Kant came more and more to depend, for the development of his thoughts, upon the processes of actual writing – passing, almost momentary conjectures finding their way to paper, as well as those formulations to which he could give his more deliberate approval'.[4] Thus there can be no certainty as to the further development of his views, still less as to how he would finally have presented them. An interesting surmise would be the extent of Fichte's influence, in spite of his decided coolness towards the latter's *Wissenschaftslehre*.

THE IDEA OF GOD ONCE MORE

A main topic of discussion in the *Opus Postumum* is the doctrine of *noumena*, or things-in-themselves, their existence and nature, which had become a focus of criticism; and in this connection the idea of God is of course brought under review. The question that arises whether Kant now sees his former mode of proving divine existence to be unsatisfactory and advocates something less theoretical – for all the supposedly 'practical' character of its former statement – and more directly and consistently moral. This would have meant reconsidering what faith in God implies and how best it can be grounded. Adickes indeed thought – and his view has been shared by other commentators on Kant – that 'the whole teaching of the highest good, together with the proofs based thereon of God and immortality, has now . . . practically disappeared'.[5] The passages dealing with the idea of God occur in the section dating from the years 1800 to 1803 and indicate the effect upon his thinking of a work by the physicist G. C. Lichtenberg (1742–99) – the second volume of whose *Vermischtes Schriften* had appeared in 1801. Lichtenberg was an admirer both of Kant's philosophy and Spinoza's – at the time there was in Germany a notable revival of interest in the seventeenth-century thinker – believing it possible as well as desirable to reconcile the two, and it seems likely that Kant, after reading Lichtenberg's book, was rather more disposed to look on Spinoza in a favourable light than he had once done.[6] Lichtenberg's view was that a 'purified' Christianity would best serve for the unphilosophically-minded in default of a pure religion of reason, and in this he would have secured Kant's agreement. But for Lichtenberg this pure religion of reason was already to be identified with Spinozism. That Kant himself, however, was in any wise ready to adjust his own philosophical attitude to Spinoza's there is no evidence apart from a measure of attention – or so it has been claimed – to the concept of divine immanence not apparent before. Thus he can say that 'God is the morally practical self-legislating Reason (*die moralisch praktische sich selbst gesetzgebende Vernunft*)'[7] where the implication would seem to be that God is to be spoken of as directly present in our moral experience.

Before returning to the question of *whether* God exists Kant rightly asks what the vocable 'God' should be taken to mean, i.e. what attributes the idea of God may be said to include. Pantheism, or anything approaching it, he rules out. Nor is God the 'World-Soul' (*Weltseele*),[8] since to describe him as such would be to posit him as a hypothetical entity introduced to account for empirical facts.[9] On the contrary, Kant states the theistic view that the concept of God is that of a Being who is the supreme cause of what exists in the world (*Weltwesen*), and who is a person. As the sovereign Being, intelligent and good – *ens summum*, *ens intelligentia*, *summum bonum* – he also is personal as possessing rights, since for Kant a person is by definition a rational being with rights – a man if he has duties as well, but if without duties, God. Further, God is 'a being for whom all human duties are at the same time his commands'.[10] The tendency here, then, is, as Webb remarks, 'to define *Person* and *Persönlichkeit* in a fashion which makes them specially applicable to the divine as distinguished from the human spirit',[11] although Kant seems now to have moved to a position in which the human spirit, when at its fullest development towards rational freedom, can be equated with the divine. Man is wont to think of God as possessing the very attributes which determine humanity in the noumenal order – except that when applied to the idea of God these must be conceived as realized in perfection, or absolutely. It is, for example, an attribute of man to be free, but he is not so without qualification; his freedom is not perfect because it has limitations imposed on it by man's receptivity, whereas God's freedom is utterly spontaneous and without limit. Man, that is, is a finite being belonging to two distinct worlds, the noumenal and the phenomenal. God, on the other hand, is infinite and wholly noumenal. The world is to be thought of as the sum total of all sensible reality, but subject to the creative power, intelligent purposiveness and holy will of God. The world and God are not therefore co-ordinate, as Kant's young contemporary, Schleiermacher, had apparently contended in his *Speeches on Religion* published in 1799; the world is subordinate to God, in a relation of dependency (*non coordinata sed subordinata*).[12]

Such is the 'Idea' of God as presented in theistic terms; but the *Opus Postumum* contains a number of statements which leave the reader in some considerable doubt whether he is to look beyond the concept itself to any real Being to which it corresponds. But because the former is necessary as an ideal of pure reason its reference is actually to *ein Gedankding*, a 'thought-thing' or *ens rationis*.[13] 'The concept of God', we read, 'is not that of a substance, i.e. of a thing which exists independently of my thinking, but the Idea (*Selbstgeschöpf*) of a Reason that was itself an object of thought and which propounds synthetic *a priori* propositions in accordance with the principles of transcendental philosophy, and an Ideal in respect of which there is no question of whether such an object exists, in that the concept of it is transcendent.'[14] Deity, it would seem, is the product of our reason, the 'ideal' of a substance which we make ourselves. In a word, God is simply a projection of the human mind, 'the morally practical reason giving laws to itself'. 'It is absurd to ask whether God exists.'[15] Yet remarks like these cannot fairly be considered in isolation, since elsewhere in the *Opus Postumum* as well as in the works published in his lifetime Kant makes it clear that the existence of God is not to be doubted. The question is whether here he is in search of an argument for believing in it more direct and immediate than that set out in the *Critique of Practical Reason*, in which Kant's critics at least perceive an element of hedonism otherwise very uncharacteristic of him. The expression, 'the recognition of all human duties as divine commands', is not, however, to be discarded; the individual is to do only what is good because it is good; he is to act, that is, without regard to any external ends whatever, either in this life or the next, but with complete autonomy, conformably with and solely on account of the categorical command of his practical reason. It is only that, as a religious person, he recognizes at one and the same time that the ideals and ends which he has himself chosen, and the laws which he has himself imposed, are those also of God, and thereby his motives for good are decidedly strengthened.[16] There is no evidence anywhere in the *Opus Postumum* that Kant seeks to qualify this position.

But if Kant holds that God is to be thought of as existing in reality then the idea of God must be shown to have a transcendent reference. As we have said, the mass of notes which make up the *Opus Postumum* do not constitute an ordered and self-coherent treatise, and statements which appear to be contradictory would presumably have been brought into some kind of harmony if the work had been finished. Nevertheless it has to be admitted that as they stand it is not easy to reconcile assertions like those quoted with belief in a Being whose real existence is capable of rational affirmation. But it is not difficult to locate similar statements in the *Critiques*, and we must assume that they were not meant to compromise the author's attempt to advance a reasoned justification for believing in God. It is simply that in the rather inchoate unpublished work the juxtaposition of apparently conflicting statements is more striking.

In trying to understand Kant's position the fact we have to weigh is that for him the idea of God, as a deliverance of the pure reason, is a 'transcendental ideal'. This means that we have no direct intuition of God – certainly we cannot know what he is in himself – nor can his real existence be deduced from this ideal, as the ontological 'proof' claims to do. 'We see him as in a mirror, never face to face.'[17] God for Kant is indeed infinite substance, but not *a* substance outside the knowing subject, since to attempt to think of him thus would be to subject him to those very categories of the understanding which infinite being must by definition transcend. In this sense it would be improper, even meaningless, to ask whether God *exists*. For deity does not exist as an entity outside of me exists. Hence he has to be 'my own thought'. To this extent Kant does not here take us beyond the arguments already used in the *Critique of Pure Reason*. God's existence, that is, can be established only 'practically', after the fashion worked out in the *Critique of Practical Reason*. 'The realism' (*das Realism*)', he says, 'of the idea of God can be proved only through the duty-imperative.'[18] And again: 'The imperative of duty proves to men their freedom, and at the same time conducts them to the idea of God.'[19] But whereas in the second *Critique* it is reflection on the requirements of the moral law which leads to the postulate of a Being who brings about the union of virtue with happiness, in this last phase of his thinking, it has been contended, Kant would dispense with any such roundabout argumentation, as he now finds the idea of God *in* the categorical imperative itself. There *is* a God, he forthrightly says, because there is a categorical imperative of duty, 'before which all knees bow, whether they be in heaven or in the earth or under the earth, and whose nature is holy, without one having to suppose a substance which represents this being to our senses'.[20] And he further notes: 'To see all things in God' – which he takes to be a reference to Spinoza.[21] 'The categorical imperative. The knowledge of my duties as divine commands, declared through the categorical imperative.'[22] Hence 'the concept of God is the concept of a self-obligating subject outside myself'.[23] Is, then, the conclusion to be drawn from this that the moral imperative addresses us *as* the voice of God? Is God somehow directly *revealed* in the moral consciousness through the moral law? As Kant himself puts it: 'There is a Being in me, distinguishable from myself as the cause of an effect worked upon me which freely ... judges me within, justifying or condemning me.'[24] However, he at once adds: 'I as a man am myself this Being, and it is not a substance external to me, its causality being no natural necessity but 'a free self-determining act on my part' (*eine Bestimmung zur Tat in Freiheit*).[25] And of course in no respect does Kant think it a qualification of his principle that the moral imperative has intrinsic force of its own which is not enhanced by describing the moral law as a divine command.[26] But if the categorical imperative is no proof whatever of a Being 'outside' me, although that same moral demand comes to me as 'the voice of God', is not God simply to be equated with the moral law, as many of Kant's critics have averred? That the existence of a divine Being as *a* substance is something which the principles of the critical philosophy inhibit us from envisaging has to be accepted. There can be for Kant no going back on this, any more than he can admit the thought that the moral law is more holy or more binding because we choose to see it as enjoined by God. This however is not to say that the categorical imperative *is* God. Kant continues to stand by the argument of the second *Critique* that the only manner in which we can be certain of God's existence, the only way indeed that we can know him, is through the moral consciousness. Whatever our final assessment may be of the success with which he sustains his belief argumentatively, we have to see that for him God does exist, but that no theoretical demonstration thereof can be adduced. If God is to be found at all it is solely through the sense of the absoluteness of moral obligation. Or as he laconically puts it in the *Opus Postumum*: 'Freedom; duties as divine commands. There is a God.'[27]

Is God, then, 'given in' the moral imperative directly? 'The consciousness of moral freedom', he declares, 'is the feeling of the presence of the Godhead in man.' But does this also mean that we can pass immediately from the divine 'idea' to the divine existent, so endorsing the ontological argument after all? There are, assuredly, some puzzling statements in this work of the philosopher's old age which seem to be saying just that. 'The mere Idea of God is at the same time (*zugleich*) a proof (*Beweis*) of his existence. To think him and believe in him is an identical act.'[28] 'The thought (*Gedanke*) of him is at the same time belief in him and in his personality.'[29] The impression might appear to be confirmed that Kant, despite his well-known refutation of the ontological argument, has now actually summoned it to his aid is further reinforced when we read also that 'a necessary being is one the concept of which is at the same time (*zugleich*) a sufficient (*hinreichender*) proof of its existence'.[30] But once more we have to recognize the essential distinction Kant makes between a theoretical proof – one, that is, which may be seen to have strict logical rigour – and the sort of 'proof' which is enough to convince the moral understanding. So, he maintains, once we admit our freedom and the moral obligation which freedom entails, we are in effect confronted by God; for what we have is 'practical' certainty to a degree to which the use of the word 'proof' is not unwarrantably applicable.[31] Or to put it somewhat differently, we do not first frame the notion of God and from it proceed to infer the fact of his existence. Rather is it that in the moral imperative we apprehend God as addressing us directly; we do not discover him as it were *behind* our consciousness of moral obligation, as in a relation of cause and effect; we encounter him in the very force of the imperative itself. It is not that any empirical concept, any metaphysic, constrains us; it is the moral law itself which 'conducts' us to the idea of God.[32] To apprehend God in that law is simultaneously to believe in him, for 'in recognizing the Law we find ourselves in God's presence'.[33] He is, we might say, morally *immanent*. He is 'within' us, although only as a deliverance of our consciousness of the uncircumscribed command of duty.

But moral 'immanence' – however we are to conceive it – could not for Kant involve ontological or naturalistic immanence as well, not least because of its deterministic implications, amounting, as he would have thought, to a non-moral fatalism. Nor would he have countenanced any doctrine of the indwelling Spirit, which in his opinion too easily led to the absurdities of *Schwärmerei*, fanaticism. What he offers indeed is the assurance that when we are fully aware of the strength of the moral imperative within us we are conscious not only of the law itself but of the 'voice' of him who imposes it. And to recognize this 'voice' is to believe in God. Obviously Kant's asseverations are insufficient to amount to an argument, although as we have suggested it may readily call to mind the procedure of the ontological argument. For were we to insist that the moral law may bind the conscience without its necessarily inducing belief in God there is nothing, it would appear, that a defender of Kant's position could say to meet the objection. The statements in the *Opus Postumum*, however, are enough to show that Kant's own reverence for the moral law was so profound – one is almost disposed to say so mystical – that when he contemplates it he is as one who in very truth feels himself in the presence of God, so that his language takes on something at least of religious fervour. Not surprisingly, many readers are likely to be more impressed by such statements than ever they were by the circuitous reasoning of the second *Critique*.

But does this mean that Kant himself had by now repudiated his earlier view? Such was the opinion of Kant's editor Erich Adickes, quoted above.[34] The 'new' proof of God's existence, he claimed, expresses 'only a subjective experience of the transcendent God in the categorical imperative, hence a pure personal faith'.[35] This, however, would have constituted a quite radical change in Kant's outlook. All his life he had believed in God; the difficulty, he realized well enough, lay in according that belief the force of theoretical reason. Basically it was a matter of faith; not blind or merely emotional faith but one which could at any rate be supported rationally (*Vernunftglaube*), presenting divine existence as a postulate of the practical reason, an implicate of our recognition of absolute moral obligation. Adickes's case is that this argumentation ceased eventually to satisfy Kant, as failing to convey that sense of the immediacy of the divine with which the moral law, in Kant's own judgment, must imbue the human consciousness. It is not improbable that contemporary interest in Spinoza, and the 'immanentist' type of thinking which this encouraged among some younger man, had moved him to adopt a phraseology he had not hitherto used. It is clear also that his religious concern had been stimulated by a knowledge of Zoroaster derived from his reading of a German translation on the ancient Iranian prophet that had appeared a few years before in French.[36] Indeed, he had even considered introducing Zoroaster's name in the title of his projected book.[37] Doubtless Zoroastrian teaching on the opposing principles of Good and Evil would have impressed him, in view of what he himself had to say on the subject in *Religion*. Thus he could bring himself to describe God not only as a Power commanding men through the categorical imperative but more specifically as a real Person, even though not perceptible as an object of the senses. But to argue, on the strength of jottings made by Kant in the very terminal years of his life, that he had decided to drop the 'moral proof' altogether because his manuscript contains no restatement of it, that he had indeed come to deny that any proof at all of divine existence could be devised, and that instead he finally had turned to a direct revelation of God in the categorical imperative, tantamount presumably to an immediate personal intuition affording a full subjective faith, is not enough to carry conviction that the aged thinker had undergone a fundamental change of mind. The first point has no positive weight, being a mere appeal to silence; the second asserts only what Kant had always contended – that no theoretical proof of God's existence can be sustained – while the third fails because the concept of God, like that of freedom, cannot rest upon direct knowledge but depends on a necessary mediating principle. That there can be no valid theology purporting to be grounded in anything other than the moral law addressing the rational consciousness was an assurance he never questioned.[38]

11
Conclusion

RETROSPECT

Kant's attack on the whole notion of speculative metaphysics meant that for him a 'natural' or rational theology could no longer be sustained. 'I maintain', he wrote in the *Critique of Pure Reason*, 'that all attempts to make a purely speculative use of reason in reference to theology are essentially fruitless and of their inner nature null and void; that the principles of its employment in the study of nature do not lead to any theology whatever; consequently that there can be no theology of reason at all unless one takes moral laws as its basis, or uses them as a clue.'[1] Theology, that is, could no longer present itself as a 'factual' science, providing knowledge of the supraphenomenal order. This, however, was not a mere confession of scepticism. As we have said, not only did Kant believe in God, he believed also that God's existence could be affirmed as a matter of reasoned faith. But divine being could not be demonstrated in the way that entities within the phenomenal world may be shown to exist, nor could it be proved from the bare concept of God itself. The difficulty that confronted him therefore was to explain what, in these circumstances, the idea of God could mean. The theologian uses language about God that purports to have determinate significance, and indeed as a rule such language is quite explicit. But if also theological language is derived, as it clearly is, from the world of experience, how can it properly be applied to a being who is altogether beyond that world? In which case can anything meaningful at all be said of God? Even to speak of him as 'first cause' is not legitimate, while the attempt to found the concept of deity on the basis of the assumed teleology of nature is at least equally vain. Only on the ground of morality can the statement that God exists be made rationally intelligible. We cannot discover God as a being anywhere in the world known to us through sense, nor yet beyond it. If we are to affirm him we must look to the moral consciousness and nowhere else. In a word, it is not the theoretical but the practical reason – the object of which is action – that renders theology intelligible. Theological assertions do nothing whatever to enlarge our knowledge of what is, but they are instructive of what we ought to do. Kant's theology, then, is to be described as moral, not speculative; although being moral it nonetheless is, he urged, rational, since it is the part of reason not only to ascertain facts but to determine values. Apart from values we cannot 'cognize' God, but at the same time God is not 'proved' by values in the way, or with the universal certainty, that the reality of an object is proved by the evidence of the senses. Further, Kant's point is that moral action is not less an area for the exercize of reason than is that of sense-experience. Indeed it is an autonomous area, in no respect dependent on extraneous sanction.

The justification of this argument would divert us into the realm of Kantian ethics, and today Kant's assurances look far more questionable than they probably did in his time. Our concern in this book has been to examine its bearing on his attitude to religion, and in particular his understanding of Christianity. *Religion within the Limits of Reason Alone* is undoubtedly a landmark in the history of philosophical theology, yet its view of religion, for most readers, would appear sharply restrictive. For if religion is neither more nor less than the recognition of all our duties as divine commands then morality can scarcely be seen as other than *constitutive* of religion, so that whatever in religious belief and practice cannot be assessed in strictly moral terms is an irrelevance or worse. Theology does not arise from intellectual curiosity about the supersensible world, nor on the other hand is information concerning such a world gratuitously imparted 'from on high'. Its content, Kant insists, is exclusively moral, and must be so if religion is to be universally significant, since man himself is indefeasibly moral.

Nevertheless he does distinguish religion from morality. If the scope of all philosophy is indicated by the three questions: What can I know? What ought I to do? and What may I hope for?, then the third pertains to the religious sphere. Morality of course is wholly autonomous, as resting upon reason alone, without authorization from either speculative metaphysics or religious doctrine. However, it is proper for rational man to question himself as to the ultimate *meaning* of his moral actions, and in seeing his duties as divine commands he does not subject them to heteronomy, but rather interprets them by reference to a moral Author of nature who, as such, is capable of reconciling human freedom with the causal determination of the natural world and of bringing about the coincidence of morality and happiness to realize the highest good. This *Vernunftglaube* has logical consistency to the extent at least that it includes nothing which the first *Critique* would rule out as impossible, and it also is moral in that it is wholly disinterested as deriving from neither fear nor desire. Hence 'rational faith' may be taken to be responding to the legitimate hopes of ethical man whose right it is as a rational being to affirm that, despite the difficulties and disappointments of life and all its unanswered problems, his existence in this world is not an idle dream. That is why Kant can speak of morality as leading necessarily to religion, since acceptance of moral obligation, he holds, must entail belief in what it implies for our understanding of human life as a whole. Moral faith may fall short of theoretical knowledge, but its content is more than simply practical, even though the only path to sound religious belief is by way of ethics.

Yet when Kant looks at religion more closely he leaves mere abstractions behind him, and the reader is soon treated to a searching discussion of the characteristic doctrines of historical Christianity: original sin, conversion, salvation, Christ, the church. Does this then mean that Kant can find a place for 'revelation' after all? In light of what he has to say in *Religion* it is plain that it is not so. But he so far departs from the standpoint of Enlightenment deism – although in this regard he was following in the steps of Lessing – in recognizing that the quest of true moral faith will set aside any attempt to devise a religion of reason on purely theoretical grounds and instead take account of religion as it actually exists, in the shape of a positive creed and cult. Such an approach would have been risible to the French *philosophes*, who looked on traditional Christianity as an 'infamy' to be crushed. But Kant views Lutheran Protestantism seriously, using it as the proper framework on which to construct his own scheme of rational faith. Thus his starting-point is the – to him – undeniable fact of the 'radical evil' in man, with the biblical story of the fall of Adam as a symbol of the moral condition of each one of us. His assessment of this evil as something total (in the individual), ineradicable – incapable, that is, of being explained in non-moral terms – inexpiable because an evil action can never be effaced, and finally, universal, as affecting all men through their moral freedom. A belief like this was one which the generally complacent optimism of most eighteenth-century thinking about humanity found incomprehensible except as an invention of priests eager to exploit it in the interest of their own power. Certainly it brings Kant nearer to the classical Protestantism of the Reformation – harking back, as this did, to Augustine – which so far as human nature and its destiny are concerned when unsalvaged by grace, was pessimistic. But unlike the Reformers Kant could not look on the moral will as itself impaired.[2] Men's evil decisions are their own, with the will allowing itself to be perverted. Frailty of nature and impurity of motive are only conditions, as it were, under which moral volition operates; as Kant says, there is nothing morally evil but that which is our own *act*. It also is of interest to note how Kant seems to discover the very heart of evil in the *lie*, which he condemns as unpardonable because it counterfeits the truth, so destroying its value. The really corrosive effect of evil is to be seen even more in the man who is satisfied with his own virtue – the pharisee – than in the mere criminal.

On Kant's understanding of the origin of moral evil it has to be said that his notion of an intelligible act 'outside time' is far-fetched and obscure. An act cannot be timeless, for we are unable to think of it except as occurring in time. It would seem that Kant's mind on this was predetermined by the narrative character of the biblical account of the fall, so that he is impelled to use language that describes temporal sequence even though what he rightly is looking for is the *Vernunft-ursprung* of evil, an explanation of how it is inseparably connected with the human will, not how a rational being may be observed to pass from a state of innocence to one of sinfulness. Indeed, how this transition is in fact to be accounted for was the subject of an essay of Kant's dating from 1786 entitled *Muthmasslicher Anfang der Menschengeschichte* ('Probable Beginnings of Human History').[3] In it the loss of innocence is traced in the change from a merely animal condition to that of rational humanity. From the point of view of the race this was a clear advance, but from that of individual existence by no means necessarily so. Previous to the emergence of reason – how? – there could be neither positive command nor prohibition, and hence no transgression. Moral evil arises when rationality and animality clash. 'Natural' history, as the work of God, begins with good, but human history, the story of man's freedom, begins with evil, which is of man's own choosing. It is through the power of rational freedom that mankind progresses, even though the individual life has to bear the moral cost involved. For if it is rational man who is the only possible object of the divine decree then the 'fall' into rationality – along with personal moral evil – must be judged a necessary stage in the process, a view which Kant's successor Hegel was to take up and elaborate.[4] But one discerns also that transgression, or at least consciousness of evil, and free moral choice are inextricably connected. Wrongdoing can occur only when moral responsibility is recognized. In *Religion within the Limits of Reason Alone*, however, the point which Kant is concerned to make is that evil is implicit in the moral consciousness. An original act of evil, therefore, would have to presuppose such consciousness – a paradox not easily to be explained. What we have to grasp is that moral evil is a matter always of responsible decision, so that man's state of radical evil, however come by, cannot be divorced from the freedom of the rational will. Hence time does not, in principle, enter into it.

The same difficulty recurs with Kant's idea of moral conversion. Man can free himself from radical evil only by a change of heart no less radical. This too requires a decisive act of freewill which, like the original 'fall', takes place 'outside time', even though it manifests itself in time by continuous moral progress. In other words, there has to be a complete revolution in man's moral disposition, whereby he instantaneously adopts a totally new attitude of mind affecting his entire future life. But again one has to ask how it is that a perverted will can suddenly change itself purely on its own strength. Kant himself admits this to be beyond explanation, for how can an evil tree bring forth good fruit? His own answer is simply to repeat the familiar maxim that obligation implies ability. Conversion is possible because at any single moment of our waking, rational life we are morally obliged to effect it.

Superficially this position resembles that of Luther's *peccator in re, justus autem in spe*. But the philosopher resolves it quite differently. Conversion is not brought about by divine grace, since grace itself has to be earned, and in contrast with the theologian he argues that there is a sufficient 'seed of goodness' (*Keim des Guten*) in every man, for all the evil that he does, as something which reason itself testifies. This it is which enables us 'to fulfil the law's demand' and thus become pleasing to God. The argument plainly shows, however, that Kant is not thinking in terms of human psychology any more than in those of the theology of grace, but only of abstract moral principle. Not surprisingly the modern reader finds it hard to be convinced.

Kant's treatment of religion is wholly consistent with his ethical position and suffers from the same limitations. The concept of God is central, but it is a concept little removed from that of deism, in spite of Kant's obviously greater sympathy with the actual beliefs of Christianity than had the deists. According to it God has no direct relations with man, nor does he reveal himself in any specific acts. Yet he is referred to as exercizing 'will' and as having 'created' the world and the finite intelligence within it. But the meaning of creation is not explained, nor is the manner of creation indicated. Kant, though, unlike the deists, does not attempt to account for God as First Cause, and indeed the deistic 'natural theology' is expressly precluded. But if divine existence is not to be thought of as 'substantial' how is it to be distinguished from a mere idea in the mind? What Kant's postulate of such existence in the second *Critique* seems really to be telling us is that it is not the *being* of God which is demanded by the moral consciousness but only the *concept* of him as requisite to complete a pattern of thought.

This essentially anthropocentric moralism is extended to each of the main Christian doctrines. The 'Son of God' is a moral ideal; Christ, in so far as he represents that ideal in realized form, is the archetype of humanity in its moral self-fulfilment. The phrase 'came down from heaven' is to be construed in the sense only that as sinners men could never of themselves have devised such an ideal – albeit that this could be interpreted as a concession to the transcendence claimed by religion. Christ's death on the cross betokens the passing-away of the 'old man' and the coming, not without much suffering, of the 'new', although the suffering may itself be understood as subjectively expiatory and redemptive. The resurrection and ascension signify the soul's immortality and ultimate moral destiny. But it is to be noted that Kant clearly distinguishes the eternal or 'archetypal' Christ from the historical Jesus of Nazareth, a man pre-eminent for his moral example and the 'divine' quality of his teaching as 'a great and wise moral legislator'. Speculative questions about Christ's metaphysical status are of course vain, as well as being destitute of any moral value, whilst simply to deify Jesus is an obvious error because he then ceases to be for us a credible moral example. Nevertheless the doctrine of the trinity is important as signifying the three 'powers' in the Godhead which in human terms may be designated as supreme Lawgiver, beneficent Ruler and just Judge. Finally, the Holy Spirit represents the Comforter, the Paraclete, who in spite of all that the principle of evil can accomplish, witnesses to the truth that we have within us the resources for fundamental moral renewal, the positive capability of doing what the moral imperative bids us do.

If Christ himself is symbolical of the struggle between the two great antithetic moral principles and the eventual victory of the good – although the mediatorial role assigned to him in orthodox Christianity is by-passed – the church which bears his name is to be seen as ideally the 'universal ethical commonwealth' whose support and aid are necessary if the morally regenerate individual is not to succumb to the corruption of unregenerate society. Putting it otherwise, if the principle of the good is to triumph in society it must be given determinate social embodiment, 'the people of God obedient to the moral laws'. Such a society will moreover differ in essence from civil society or the state, the concern of which is the legality of human acts more than their morality. Yet it is no less necessary to insist, according to Kant, that the true ethical commonwealth is invisible, for no man can read the heart of another, nor do we know 'what God may do directly to translate into actuality the idea of his kingdom'. The discrepancy between the ideal kingdom and any attempt to embody it institutionally is revealed by the many and radical defects by which the latter has always been marred.

For when Kant discusses what he calls 'statutory religion', he includes under it both scripture in its literal interpretation and the traditional theological dogmas, whether formally defined or as presupposed in liturgical practice. And it is clear also from everything he says about *Pfaffenthum* that it is not only Catholic sacerdotalism that he is objecting to but something much nearer home, the Lutheran doctrine of justification by faith, which for the dogmatic theologians had increasingly turned itself into correct theological assent and for the pietists justification by *feelings* – the *Schwärmerei* he so greatly despises. Indeed he goes so far as to suggest that Protestant orthodoxy enslaves men's intelligences more surely than do forms of religion which lay the stress on externals, for the latter call only for meaningless gestures whereas the former, in demanding belief without moral conviction or the endorsement of reason, ensnare the conscience itself. In contrast to many contemporary critics of religion his real case against statutory faith was not so much that it is intellectually contemptible as that it is morally baneful. But as we have had more than one occasion to remark, he concedes the need for religious doctrine and ritual in a visible society if its members are to be held together and the continuity of its corporate life preserved. Dogmas and sacraments, that is, are not of themselves an inevitable danger to faith, but only when superstitiously credited with an authority, or with powers, capable of placing them above that righteous will which is the *sine qua non* of true religion. *Aberglaube* is for Kant the ever-recurrent folly and deception of historical religion. No doubt as a man of his century he took a simplistic view of what constitutes superstition, but the value of his contribution to theological thought is to be found not least in the separation of the substance of religion from its forms in a way that was to give the liberal Protestantism of the nineteenth century both inspiration and direction. His conviction that religion without ethics, or with an inadequate emphasis on its necessary moral commitment as judged by conscience, reaffirmed biblical teaching at its deepest level.

But the obvious weakness of Kant's interpretation of Christianity is his lack of historical sense, and with this his deficient understanding of religion as a social phenomenon. These were limitations of sympathy which were of course not merely his own; he shared them with Enlightenment pundits generally. But they were also characteristic of the man himself, springing from temperament and personal experience. For all his wide-ranging intellectual curiosity he possessed little historical imagination; his early interests, it will be recalled, were predominantly scientific. Men and events in all ages were simply to be seen and judged according to standards of reason and morality regarded as universal and unalterable. Any sense of development in the historical process is similarly absent. Historical occurrences add to our knowledge and understanding only in so far as they illustrate principles and norms of human behaviour, not because they themselves have a significance that may lead us to modify our view of such norms and principles by the factual light it sheds. Thus it is that Kant has no philosophy of history in which historical events as such are accorded a determinative role. The superficiality of his own attitude to history is quite evident when one compares it with that, only two or three decades later, of

Hegel, or even of Herder, whose *Ideas for a Philosophical History of Mankind* had appeared in 1784.[5] The Kantian view is the very antithesis of the historicist. Kant's respect for the Bible, or at any rate the New Testament, is manifest. But he seems to have had no interest in the then newly-emerging discipline of historical and literary criticism, which he was prone to dismiss as antiquarianism and therefore largely irrelevant to the only sort of biblical exegesis that mattered. With the publications of Semler, who had replied to the opinions of Reimarus set out in Lessing's *Fragments* in 1779, he was evidently unacquainted.

Kant's idea of the 'ethical community' likewise shows scant recognition of the social character of religion in any of its historical forms. He appreciates well enough how the supremacy of the good principle in the life of the individual can be secured only when it has already been established in the life of the society of which he is a member. But this community is to be founded, not on the laws of civil society but upon those of personal virtue, of whose operation only the 'Searcher of all hearts' can have true knowledge. Unfortunately, for Kant the Christian church as an historic institution falls so far short of this ideal as to constitute at least as much of a hindrance to its attainment as a means thereto. At the same time he appears not to understand the essentially corporate nature of the Christian life, while of the church as a 'mystical' body sustained by supernatural grace he can of course entertain no idea. For prayer as a formal act of devotion he has no use; only its subjective ethical effect in making for a right moral disposition in the individual is worthy of consideration. With his well-known personal distaste for liturgical worship he totally failed to appreciate its place in the life of religious believers. As for the sacraments, he allows them an incidental utility for ethical ends – moral sentiments can be stimulated by external observances – but of their psychological effectiveness outside the sphere of rational moral choice he perceives nothing. Religious symbolism has no other function or power than what is capable of rational articulation such as would eventually render the symbols unnecessary. Imaginative and emotional overtones are disregarded.

In dealing with the Christian doctrines Kant's fault is to treat them only as so many separate items each capable of its own 'rational' explanation. For him, that is, there is no unifying principle either behind or within them, whether theological (as with Calvin), or metaphysical (as with Hegel), or psychological (as with

Schleiermacher). But the signal weakness in his account of religion is its simplistic individualism, even if in this respect he was typical of his age. He seems to assume that the moral consciousness is one and the same thing for all men, irrespective of racial inheritance, social environment or personal temperament. Yet something at any rate of this limitation of vision may be attributed to Kant's own temperament and circumstances. It is these, one suspects, which for him turned the moralistic rationalism so widely professed in his day into a matter of profound conviction. His Protestantism, taken not in a doctrinal sense but as an attitude to life, he never threw off. There was absolutely nothing of the hedonist in his nature, any more than there was of the inconoclast. His early years, even when not oppressed by sheer poverty, afforded him little in the way of material comforts, and with his independent, self-reliant nature this meant a strict discipline of living. Above all, there was his intellectual and moral integrity, which could brook no easy compromises or accommodation with mere worldly advantage. Life for Kant, morally and emotionally, was a straight and narrow path, the pursuit of which determined his character permanently. His guides through the years were his reason and his conscience, and responsibility, either professional or personal, could not be passed on to another. Thus always cognisant of their demands, he saw himself as a man perhaps necessarily walking alone. Not that he shunned the company of his fellows, by any means, for he was markedly sociable. But his sense of vocation alike as philosophical teacher and moral man imposed standards upon him which he saw as, in principle, of universal application.

The criticism most commonly directed against Kant's religious position is that he had no real understanding of or sympathy with what most men in fact look on as religion. In his view at any rate no distinction is to be drawn between a specifically religious consciousness and the moral; whence his inability to countenance the notion of any sort of 'faith' that is not an expression of moral volition. Was he then devoid of a sense of the *holy*, of what Rudolf Otto called 'the numinous'?[6] Here one can only speculate. Kant was representative of his time in his dislike of 'mystery' in religion, as of anything that appeared to inhibit reasoned inquiry. The word 'holy' to him meant no more, if no less, than 'saintly' in the ethical sense, as to most persons it probably still does; although saintliness itself – discounting its pietistic unction –

could not be held to mean anything like a total fulfilment of an individual's moral obligations, inasmuch as ethical achievement in this world can never be more than an approximation to the ultimate goal. The nearest Kant comes to a feeling for the holy in the numinous sense of the word is in his heart-felt respect for the 'practical reason' itself, the supremacy of which even in the order of cognition he always stressed. The inexplicable presence of the moral law within us he held to be something which forbids self-conceit (*Eigendünkel*), while at the same time imbuing us with a proper awareness of human worth and dignity – a sentiment which Kant designates by the word *Achtung*.

But if Kant's interpretation of religion is through and through ethical, his residual pietism is so deep-seated that it is no less true to say that this ethical conviction carries with it a quality which can be fairly described as religious fervour. Kant's emphasis upon the rootedness of human sin and the need for moral conversion is more characteristic of the eighteenth-century evangelical revival in England or the 'great Awakening' in America than the rationalism of the *Aufklärung*, for all his claim that he is only stating truths that are native to reason itself; although the orthodox believer may well press the question how such sin is to be overcome and conversion realized if not by a 'grace' over and above man's inherent moral resources.

KANT AND MODERN THEOLOGY

In the history of modern philosophy Immanuel Kant is a Janus-figure. One face looks back across the century which produced him, while the other is turned toward that which succeeded it, of which his doctrines are in important ways the herald. The social and evolutionary aspects of the rational and moral life of man, to which the nineteenth century was to devote so much attention, he scarcely glimpses. Hence, as we have seen, the significance of history as a necessary dimension of man's self-understanding is something he really does not grasp. In these respects he remained typical of his age and thus can only appear to us today increasingly remote. Yet his work provides the immediate philosophical background of the idealist movement of Fichte, Schelling and above all Hegel, who regarded themselves as his true spiritual heirs and successors, even though the starting-point of their own thinking was a reaction against his. Certainly the general effect of Kant's achievement was to determine the paths in philosophy to be trodden through the decades that followed his death. The fact of this divided intellectual 'personality' of his would seem to imply, furthermore, that his thought is composed of elements which in the end do not present a consistent whole, so that what his work offers is less than a systematic unity. A dualism is latent in it – of nature and mind, of the theoretical and the practical reason, of science and ethics, of the individual and society – the disparate sides of which have made it virtually impossible to accept Kantianism as its creator left it. Doubtless it is from this very condition that much of the abiding interest of his teaching comes. He raises questions which, unanswered or answered unsatisfactorily by himself, were to lead subsequent thinkers, among them some of the most influential of modern times, into courses of their own, and the fertility of his suggestions is by no means exhausted even now. For in its many-sidedness Kant's philosophy is like Plato's, in both of which seekers after truth have continued to discover pointers to their goal precisely of the kind of which they have felt themselves to be most in need. Other systems have, to a greater or less degree, been built upon Kant's, but not in such completeness as to deprive the foundation itself of its intrinsic interest and value.

What is true of Kant's philosophy in general clearly applies to his contribution to religious philosophy in particular. In this regard Paul Tillich did not exaggerate when he described it as 'decisive for the theology of the nineteenth century'.[7] However, his long-term influence stemmed from the contents of the great *Critiques* rather than from the treatise he expressly devoted to the interpretation and evaluation of religion, which students of Kant have tended to neglect. To its first readers, as its very title was enough to indicate, it must have seemed to possess much in character with the rationalist and deist attitudes, in spite of its bold reassertion of what could have appeared only as a doctrine of original sin. In fact, *Religion within the Limits of Reason Alone* marked the end of an era rather than the beginning of one, and within a few years interest in the religious question had taken an altogether new turn, concerned with the development of religion in history and the nature of the religious, and particularly the Christian, consciousness as such. To close Kant's book and open Schleiermacher's *Speeches on Religion*, which made its appearance only six years later, is to enter a new world of thought.[8] But Kant had some immediate followers whose views bore the impress of his teaching more or less plainly. In certain instances it was the 'agnostic' side of this philosophy that proved especially influential, in others the ethical. Thus the orthodox might avail themselves of the arguments set out in the first *Critique* as a defence against the negations of rationalism, behind which they could continue to maintain their historical dogmatism founded on divine revelation. Others were willing to accept his moralism, albeit in a less rigorous form, while at the same time adjusting it more readily than did Kant himself to the standpoint of traditional belief. Both, in fact, were prepared to use Kant's distinction between phenomena and noumena to point the difference between the respective spheres of knowledge and faith. Scientific reason might be absolute in its own realm, but its authority did not extend to revelation, which dealt only with the supersensible and addressed man at the 'higher' level of his moral personality.

A fair example of a Kantian theologian is Heinrich Tieftrunk (1759–1837) of Halle.[9] Like Kant he found the sole basis of a universal religion in man's autonomous moral freedom, the endowment whereby he belongs essentially to the spiritual realm, above that of sense, and the attribute which renders him truly godlike, since in the order of spirit there is difference only of degree, not of kind. The moral qualities which, ideally, distinguish humanity are those precisely that exist in their total perfection in God – qualities which man could not exhibit were not his own will and the law to which it is subject those of God himself. What separates man from God is, on the other hand, his sensible nature which is the constant obstacle to his spiritual self-realization. The law, that is to say, which is the principle of our moral being, is continuously thwarted by both our own sensual inclinations and the impediments created by the external world. Were it possible for us to overcome these we should actually be self-sufficient spiritually and obedience to the moral law would be the end and object of our lives. Even God would be unnecessary. Such not being the case, however, we are in fact dependent on him for resolving the contradictions in which our very existence as finite creatures ensnares us. This God effects by subordinating the natural world to our purposes as moral beings, so vindicating our intrinsic ethical sovereignty. Thus we achieve the happiness we merit.

The similarity of this argument to that of Kant is obvious. Again God becomes a postulate which the fulfilment of our inherently rational and moral existence requires if the world of sense is not render the attainment of its ends impossible. At the same time Tieftrunk's view of the relation of God and humanity in the moral order is obscure; for does not man appear in principle at least to be morally self-sufficing? And it is also difficult to see what *religious* function the idea of God may serve. Man's ethical vocation is enough in itself to afford him all the satisfaction he needs, provided the conditions under which it is pursued offer no final hindrance to it. And as with Kant immortality likewise is a necessary postulate if moral progress is to be indefinitely sustained. In theology Tieftrunk follows Kant's exposition of the Trinity, with God as at once Creator – though how? – and Lawgiver, Ruler and Judge. But freedom and the moral law alone furnish the basis of true and universal religion, to which religious sentiment and theological doctrine are entirely secondary. Nevertheless Tieftrunk did not exclude the forms of historical religion as of little account. There is, he judged, good reason to expect a divine revelation when the state of morality is in decline; and if such revelation may occur one could expect it to be accompanied by supernatural evidence. The substance of revelation is contained in scripture, the essential teachings of which are, however, inherently rational and moral.

A striking example in England of the use of Kantian 'agnosticism' in defence of biblical orthodoxy is provided by Henry Longueville Mansel (1826–71), who held professorships at Oxford before his appointment, shortly before his death, to the deanery of St Paul's cathedral, London, and whose Bampton lectures of 1858 caused a considerable stir in the contemporary academic and ecclesiastical world.[10] Mansel, who was conversant with German idealist philosophy, was far from persuaded by what he saw as its pretentious rationalism. Philosophically he has a disciple of the Scottish thinker Sir William Hamilton, professor of logic and metaphysics at Edinburgh from 1836 to 1856, who in his *Discussions on Philosophy and Literature* (1852) had urged that all knowledge is relative.[11] For Mansel as for Hamilton such conceptions as the Absolute, the Infinite or the First Cause involved inescapable contradictions, and theologians who have had recourse to them for a metaphysical defence of Christian faith have, in attempting to explain the being of God and his relation to the world, only entangled themselves in the same difficulties. 'What', he asked, 'does theology gain by the employment of a weapon [i.e. speculative metaphysics] which may at any moment be turned against her? . . . Her most precious truths are cut from the anchor which held them firm, and cast upon the waters of philosophical speculation, to float hither and thither with the ever-shifting waves of thought.'[12] Indeed no effort at constructing a rational theology could be made without a prior examination of the nature and scope of reason itself. And this would quickly reveal reason's limitations. The Infinite, it would be discovered, is not a positive concept but merely a negation of thought – 'a name for the absence of those conditions under which thought is possible'. God cannot be found by the searchings of the finite human mind. Not that Kant, for whom Mansel had the profoundest respect, was wholly to be excused for giving his idealist successors their cue. He may have shown the complete insecurity of any metaphysical theology, but at the same time he had allowed reason in its practical or moral capacity a purchase on ultimate reality which he denied to its theoretical. In short, we can no more subject the idea of God to dependence on moral certainties than on metaphysical ones. The divine is, in itself, above human reason, and if we are to speak of God at all it is only in the terms which he himself has afforded us in his scriptural self-revelation, terms which allow us a *regulative* idea of the divine sufficient to guide our practice, although not to satisfy the inquiring intellect.[13] This use of his criticism of metaphysics would not, it need scarcely be said, have approved itself to Kant, and Mansel's book was attacked, from widely differing standpoints, by both J. S. Mill, who found it 'loathsome', and F. D. Maurice, who felt driven to make a full-scale reply to it. But is significant of the way in which Kant's philosophy might be called in aid – for had he not himself denied knowledge in order to secure a place for faith? – by those who sought to shield faith altogether from the probings of reason.

But a theological reversion to Kantianism much more in the spirit of Kant's own philosophy is to be seen in the work of Albrecht Ritschl (1822–89). At first, as a follower of F. C. Baur at Tübingen, he was a convinced Hegelian, but in 1856 he broke with the Tübingen master, and on his acceptance of a professorship at Göttingen settled down to the composition of his *Justification and Reconciliation*, one of the most influential theological works of the century.[14] It would be too much to describe Ritschl himself as a professed Kantian, but his philosophical mentor at Göttingen was Hermann Lotze, whose combination of idealism and empiricism and concern with the idea of value had marked Kantian affinities.[15] The Kantian note is clearly audible in Ritschl's definition of religious activity as an 'interpretation of man's relation to God and the world, guided by the thought of the sublime power of God to realize the end of man's blessedness'.[16] Ritschl, like Kant, could not regard religious doctrine as theoretical knowledge, religion being a practical matter, pertaining to the moral will. Its special function and power were to deliver man in his spiritual capacity both from the determinism of his physical environment and the enslaving impulses of his own sensible nature. For in his physical existence man is part of the order of nature, ever subject to external forces, whereas as spirit his vocation is to maintain his independence of them. As Ritschl puts it: 'In this juncture, religion springs up as faith in superhuman spiritual powers, by whose help the power which man possesses of himself is in some way supplemented and elevated into a unity of its own kind, which is a match for the pressure of the natural world.'[17] Religion thus has nothing to do with purported knowledge of the Absolute or the Infinite, but it serves a necessary purpose in human life in countering the deterministic assumptions of natural science. If Kant introduced the idea of God in response to man's legitimate desire for happiness, Ritschl sees it as a *Hilfsvorstellung* to the attainment of properly human ends in this world. The parallelism of their thinking is obvious, though the rational grounds for Ritschl's argument are hardly more cogent than they are for Kant's. But Ritschl's may be held to have psychological value, as indicating the real nature of the religious consciousness and the need which it embodies – the deep-seated belief in man that he is more than a product merely of material forces.

Ritschl's treatment of religious doctrines again resembles Kant's, in that for him also they are not statements of 'supernatural' facts but 'value-judgments' (*Werthurtheile*), determined by man's attitude to the world around him and directly relating to his spiritual needs; whether, that is, he 'either enjoys the dominion over the world vouchsafed him by God, or feels grievously the lack of God's help to that end'.[18] It is not that Ritschl held that value-judgments are no more than personal, subjective preferences having no necessary correspondence with reality, but it does mean that 'the knowledge of God' is an expression without significance apart from the thought of him as the agent of man's spiritual deliverance. Metaphysical knowledge, if such it can be called, is of no account.[19] Natural theology therefore provides no basis for Christian belief, which is concerned only with spiritual regeneration, the context of which is the church, 'the community of believers'. To see truth in terms of value is simply and rightly to relate it to practical ends.[20]

Ritschl differs radically from Kant, however, in his attitude to history, a difference to be explained by the fact that he was living in the nineteenth century, for which the historical had become an all-important dimension of human experience. Indeed to the history of religious thought Ritschl was himself a notable contributor, despite his partisanship, especially when dealing with matters with which he had little personal sympathy.[21] The true knowledge of God, he insisted, rests on man's understanding of God's unique self-disclosure in the historic Christ as portrayed in the gospels, in whose inner life we have our authoritative example and norm – a principle which subsequent New Testament criticism has rendered less secure than seemed to Ritschl himself. The historical person, whose life-work was the establishment of the universal ethical fellowship of mankind,[22] is at once both moral example and the substance of religious faith.

It would be less than fair to Ritschl to accuse him of reducing religion to ethics, for like Kant he seeks to draw a distinction between them. But for him the religious had always to be interpreted in relation to the ethical, and he sees Christianity as the 'specifically moral religion'.[23] Hence to present it in metaphysical guise, as in the church's traditional dogma, is an error which a new Reformation would have to correct. But this means that Ritschl side-stepped the ontological question, relying for such philosophical support as he deemed necessary upon the epistemological ideas of Lotze. Moreover, his dislike of mysticism was as strong as was Kant's of *Schwärmerei*. Similarly the disjunctions to be found in Kant reappear no less plainly in Ritschl: nature and spirit, knowledge and faith, fact and value, the theoretical and the practical are juxtaposed rather than correlated.

Although it is far wide of the mark to describe Kant as the philosopher of Protestantism in its classical forms, the designation could well hold as regards its modern liberal manifestations, which to a considerable extent stem from Ritschl. Thus if the main challenge to religious faith in the nineteenth century came from the growth of natural science and the outlook on life which the scientific attitude has fostered then Kant's bold attempt to limit the province of science to the phenomenal world would seem to provide the religious believer with firm standing-ground. Mind is not to be explained by matter, and thought is no mere mechanism. Experience in space-time is not to be accounted for, and does not even have coherence, unless it is dependent on the constitutive action of rational self-consciousness. The methods of science, it could now be argued in the way anticipated by Kant, have no absolute validity, and not, certainly, outside the sphere in which they are in practice found applicable. The materialist standpoint cannot therefore be philosophically upheld and as against deterministic 'scientism' theology may urge the ultimate freedom of the spirit. A 'nature' isolated from consciousness is simply a methodological abstraction, not a palpable fact. Phenomena can be rationally related and subsumed under principles of natural law, but final questions of origin and end cannot be answered in terms descriptive only of the phenomenal order. Again, Kant's distinction between the causal and the teleological was reflected in the views of the liberal theologians on nature and human history respectively. Nature, they agreed, cannot properly be interpreted in the language of teleology, but in any realm where human purposiveness operates an *immanent* teleology may well be a constitutive element. Indeed it was this idea, whether in the form of an articulated philosophy of history or simply as an underlying assumption that the natural process has direction or even a goal, which characterized much nineteenth-century thinking in general. In theology it took shape in a belief in something like the Kantian 'ethical commonwealth' or 'kingdom of God'; a time, that is, was to be envisaged when moral standards derived from the biblical tradition would win universal assent and compliance. 'Progress', one might say, was an article of the creed of later nineteenth-century theological liberalism.

Another mark of Kantian influence was the emphasis on faith as essentially *praxis*. If knowledge rightly so called belongs only to the scientific sphere metaphysics is an illegitimate enterprise claiming to know what in the nature of things cannot be known. This conviction was reinforced by the disillusionment with absolute idealism which in Germany overtook both philosophy and theology – in so far as the latter was affected by it – in the second half of the century. The cry raised, accordingly, was 'Back to

Kant', although to a Kantianism obliged now to take cognizance of history as the context except by reference to which no human belief or institution could be fruitfully assessed. Faith may truly give 'the assurance of things hoped for', especially when, despite intellectual reservations, the hope in question can be represented as dependent on the moral will. It affords entry to premises which neither the natural scientist nor the metaphysician as such has a right to forbid. Faith, in short, is its own justification to the extent that its terrain is identical with the ethical.

However, for the liberals belief in God did not rest, as with Kant himself, on the supposedly direct implications of the moral imperative, but rather on morality as an autonomous field of human experience which finds natural and appropriate expression in religion. Thus for liberal Protestantism the problem of God can be assigned an answer only in terms of *value*. For if the idea of God is to have valid content one must look into the moral consciousness: for example, divinity is not to be ascribed to Jesus Christ because of some special ontological status enjoyed by him but for the divine 'worth' he has for us.[24] This view was widely adopted by nineteenth-century theological liberals, who maintained that faith deriving from a sense of freedom and moral obligation demands belief in God, but no longer with the help of metaphysics to support it. Hence the question inevitably arises whether words like 'faith' and 'value' can be shown to have any transcendental reference at all, but signify only subjective aspirations and hopes. Unless faith and value can be united in a way that amounts to something more than an expression of personal conviction it is difficult to see what place, in the end, is left to rational judgment in affirming religious belief. Ritschl's disciple, Julius Kaftan, was no doubt sincere in holding that according to a right interpretation of his master's teaching 'the truth of the propositions of faith means nothing else, and can mean nothing else, than that they are objectively true'.[25] He further states: 'Nowhere have I affirmed that the religious judgments *are* value-judgments, but I hold this expression itself to be at least open to misunderstanding; nay, value-judgments are their basis, but they themselves are theoretical propositions.[26] Nevertheless 'theoretical' propositions based on value-judgments are to be distinguished from the theoretical judgments of science or philosophy. They arise in a different manner in that the conviction of their truth is founded *subjectively*. The reasons for maintaining their *objective* ground are not made clear, so that the problem posed by Kant's own moral theology recurs.

The liberal Protestant attitude to traditional dogmas has varied from the relatively conservative, as with Kaftan, to the radically reductive, as with Adolf von Harnack (1851–1930), famous as a New Testament scholar and church historian, who distilled the 'essence' of Christianity purely from the teaching of Jesus as recorded in the gospels. It could, he thought, be summed up under two heads: God as Father and the human soul so ennobled that it can and does unite with him.[27] The entire scheme of the received dogma could thus be jettisoned as an alien accretion – *Aberglaube*. Others, taking the line of Kant himself, chose rather to construe doctrine symbolically. The French liberal Protestants August Sabatier (1839–1901) and Eugène Ménégoz, for instance, devised a theory of religious symbolism – *symbolo-fidéisme* – based on the principle that all religious ideas are symbolical, as being inadequate to their object, mere approximations thereto more or less unsatisfactory in view of the materials on which they perforce must draw. But, when recognized simply as symbols they have expressive force and can at least point to the truth.[28] Knowledge is one, but faith can carry us beyond knowledge. Hence the fideist formula that 'salvation is by faith, independently of beliefs'[29] – belief being equated with intellectual assent in contrast to faith, which connotes a 'change of heart', a conversion – or in Kantian language, the adoption of a new maxim. Tillich, more recently, has argued that religious language cannot be anything other than symbolic, and that apart from the basic assertion that God is being itself whatever we say about the divine can be said only in the form of symbols.

The Kantian attempt to understand religious belief solely in an ethical sense has had its signal counterpart in the present century, and unsurprisingly this has tended more and more to take the shape of social ethics. An early example was the 'social gospel' of the American theologian Walter Rauschenbusch, professor at Rochester Theological Seminary, New York, from 1897 until 1918, who quite explicitly identified the Christian mission in the modern world with the advance of socialism, to the extent even of a revolutionary transformation of the social order. In other words, the 'kingdom of God', in the circumstances of today, means a total reconstitution of human social relations. Such, he judged, was the fundamental purpose of the church's existence, and political action would be seen to be necessary to achieve it. Nevertheless Rauschenbusch, who in other respects was an old-fashioned evangelical, did not deny the ultimately supernatural character of the kingdom, which he believed to be 'divine in its origin, progress and consummation . . . miraculous all the way'.[30] But since the second world war, and with the dissemination of the ideas of Dietrich Bonhoeffer about 'religionless Christianity', the social gospel has assumed a markedly 'this-worldly' tone and at times is scarcely to be distinguished from secular humanism, or from ideologies to a greater or less degree Marxist-inspired. Latin American 'liberation theology', largely politicized in content, offers a case in point.

But whatever the particular areas in which one may trace Kant's influence, direct or indirect, on modern theological thought, the general effect of his philosophy on theology is unmistakable and ubiquitous, and lies in his stress on *personality*. The importance of the self-conscious, purposive subject in his epistemology needs no further underlining: man's ordered experience depends immediately upon its synthetic activity; while in his ethical theory the key-principle is the autonomy of the moral will: man, that is to say, is by nature self-determining, his volition, in the end, not subject to the mechanistic determinism of the natural world. But as exercizing the true causality of reason and possessing the power of moral initiative he is entitled to be regarded as an 'objective end' subordinate to no other. Kant's thinking is thus imbued throughout with a sense of the supreme worth of human existence. For man is himself the legislator whose law it is his own paramount obligation to obey. Where then the Kantian influence has made itself felt most strongly any tendency towards a depersonalizing pantheism or mysticism or naturalistic evolutionism has been arrested. That there is much in religion he failed to appreciate has often of course been said. But no view of religion claiming to be biblical can ever without self-betrayal fall into the error of minimizing the demand it makes upon the moral will or its estimate of the status and destiny of the spiritual personality. Immanuel Kant understood this profoundly, and his doing so is the measure of his importance for religious thought from his day to ours.

References and Notes

INTRODUCTION: THE YOUNG KANT – PIETISM AND RATIONALISM

1. A similar claim might, however, be made on behalf of Heinrich Müller (1631–75), a prolific devotional writer and popular preacher for whom theological orthodoxy did not exclude an emotionally charged personal faith. His *Der himmlische Liebeskuss* ('The Heavenly Kiss of Love') was published in 1659.
   Albrecht Ritschl's *Geschichte des Pietismus* (3 vols, Bonn, 1880–86) remains the chief work on the subject, despite its author's evident lack of sympathy with pietism. Recent studies include: F. E. Stoeffler, *The Rise of Evangelical Pietism* (Leiden, 1965) and J. Wallmann, *Philipp Jakob Spener und die Anfänge des Pietimus* (Tübingen, 1970).
2. See E. Beyreuther, *August Hermann Francke 1663–1727: Zeuge des lebendigen Gottes* (Marburg, 1956).
3. Count Niklaus Ludwig von Zinzendorf (1700–60) was the founder of the Herrnhuter Brethren. Born at Dresden and educated at Francke's Adelpädagogium, he was first employed in the Saxon government service, but from 1727 onwards he dedicated his life to evangelization, placing the religious settlement at Herrnhut under his personal care. He travelled widely, both in Europe and in America, especially after 1737, in which he was consecrated a bishop in the Moravian church, and numerous Moravian communities were established by him on both sides of the Atlantic, the Moravian Episcopal Church ('Unitas Fratrum') in England being recognized by an act of parliament in 1749. As with Spener and Francke, his theological orthodoxy was impugned, but charges of heresy brought against him were not sustained. The type of Christocentric religion he taught was fervently emotional. John Wesley was profoundly touched by it, and the latter's conversion-experience of 24 May 1738 occurred at a Moravian place of worship.
4. Ed. P. Steudel, Stuttgart, 1891.
5. cf. Emil Brunner, *The Divine-Human Encounter* (E.T. London, 1944) p. 34.
6. William Chillingworth (1602–44) is best known for his *The Religion of Protestants* (1637), in which he argued that the basis of belief is scripture, the truth of which could be ascertained by sound reasoning and personal judgment. 'Unity of opinion', he thought, could thus be reached on essentials. John Tillotson (1630–94), who towards the end of his life became archbishop of Canterbury, also combined supernaturalism with rationalism. He considered faith to be 'a

persuasion of the mind concerning anything', i.e. an assessment of its probability, and as such conducive to virtue, with the prospect hereafter of due reward (or, in the case of failure, of punishment). This expectation is for him 'the great motive and argument of a holy life'. Tillotson upheld the necessity of divine revelation while maintaining that it required to be tested both by its accordance with the principles of natural religion and by the evidence of prophecy and miracle; especially the latter, by which he understood a supernatural effect 'evident and wonderful to sense'. Yet not even miracle, he stresses, can truthfully attest a claim that is inherently 'unreasonable and absurd . . . unworthy of God, and . . . contrary to the natural notions which men have of him' (Works, 1857 edn, iii, pp. 493ff.). The use of religion is to provide sanctions for morality. Tillotson sums up his position thus: 'We do not found our belief of Christianity upon any one argument taken by itself; but upon the whole evidence which is proper and reasonable to prove any religion to be from God.' To intuition or 'feeling' he makes no appeal. On Anglicanism generally in the later seventeenth century see G. R. Cragg, *From Puritanism to the Age of Reason: a Study of Changes in Religious Thought within the Church of England, 1660–1700* (Cambridge, 1950).

7. Lord Herbert's *De veritate* appeared in 1624, although his *De religione gentilium*, containing a fuller expression of his views, was not published until 1663. Herbert makes universal consent the prime test of religious truth. Such consent, he argues, shows five principles to be fundamental to all religions: that (1) there is a supreme deity, who (2) ought to be worshipped, virtue and piety (3) forming the main element of that worship; that (4) our sins must be repented of and expiated, and that (5) after this life we receive reward or punishment according to our deserts. But Herbert might better be described as the founder of the 'natural religion' beloved of the eighteenth century. There is an English translation of the *De veritate*, with introduction, by M. H. Cane (Bristol, 1937). See also W. R. Sorley, 'The Philosophy of Herbert of Cherbury' in *Mind*, N.S. iii (1894) pp. 491–508.

8. The book's full title is: *Christianity not Mysterious; or, a Treatise Showing that There Is Nothing in the Gospel Contrary to Reason, nor above It; and that no Christian Doctrine Can Properly Be Called a Mystery*. A second edition was brought out in 1702.

9. Cf. B. Erdmann, *Martin Knutzen und seine Zeit* (Berlin, 1878), pp. 116, 45, 119.

10. Deism is a term which in the early eighteenth century was used with only a loose connotation, rather as is the epithet 'radical' today, and ranging as it did from Locke and Toland to Collins and Tindal it could cover almost any deviation from the orthodoxy of the Prayer Book and the Thirty-Nine Articles. John Toland (1670–1722) went beyond Locke, according to whom some accepted religious doctrines may, as 'mysteries', be 'above' reason, by arguing that what are commonly considered such are simply things intrinsically rational, whether teachings or alleged events, which have not been directly

verified but rest only on the testimony of others. All sound religious doctrine must be seen to be in accord with reason. Locke himself discovered the essentials of Christianity to be but two, viz. the belief that Jesus is the Messiah and the obligation to lead a righteous life. To him these were 'the indispensable condition of the new covenant to be performed by all those who would obtain eternal life' (*The Reasonableness of Christianity*, edited and abridged by I. T. Ramsey [London, 1958] pp. 44–5). For most of the deist writers revelation served no other purpose than to reinforce the truths of natural reason. Matthew Tindal's *Christianity as Old as the Creation*, published in 1730, is typical in this respect. It is wrong, he argues, to look to religion for beliefs and practices that are morally indifferent. True religion is 'natural' religion, which has always existed as 'a perfect thing' and to which revelation can add nothing. 'If', he asks (ch. vi), 'revelation itself be not arbitrary, must it not be founded upon the reason of things? And consequently be a republication or restoration of the Religion of Nature?' The whole purpose of religions is the promotion of morality, which differ from each other only in so far as the latter acts 'according to the reason of things considered in themselves', whereas the former acts 'according to the same reason of things considered as the will of God' – a clear anticipation of Kant's teaching. He would also have agreed with Kant that miracles have no evidential value. 'Duties neither need nor can receive any stronger proof from miracles than what they have already from the evidence of right reason.' God is wholly benevolent. 'To imagine He can command anything inconsistent with His universal benevolence is highly to dishonour Him.' 'The same light of nature which shows us there is such a good Being, shows us also what such goodness expects.'

On English deism generally see: G. V. Lechler, *Geschichte der englischen Deismus* (Stuttgart, 1841); L. Stephen, *A History of English Religious Thought in the Eighteenth Century* (London, 1876), i, pp. 74–277 (including bibliography, pp. 276f), which is still the best comprehensive review, despite the author's bias. Also Cragg, op. cit.

11. Particularly to be noted among these German-language works is *Vernünftige Gedanken von Gott, der Welt, und der Seele, auch aller Dingen überhaupt* ('Rational Ideas of God, the World, and the Soul of Man'), 1719.

12. An English translation, *The Real Happiness of a People under a Philosophical King demonstrated*, was published in London in 1750.

13. *Philosophia prima, sive ontologia*, Frankfurt, 1729. Critical edn by J. Ecole, Hildersheim, 1962.

14. If Wolff could be said to have had an English counterpart Samuel Clarke (1675–1729), a theologian to whose intellectual powers Voltaire paid tribute, would seem to fit the role. His Boyle lectures of 1704–5 were published under the title *Demonstration of the Being and Attributes of God*. Clarke was however accused of Arianism by his critics.

15. The most satisfactory general study of Wolff's thought is M. Campo, *Christiano Wolff e il razionalismo precritico* (2 vols, Milan, 1939).
16. The matters discussed in the *Fragments* were: 1. Toleration of the deists; 2. The decrying of reason from the pulpit; The impossibility of a revelation which all men should have grounds for believing; 4. The passage of the Israelites through the Red Sea; 5. The Old Testament does not offer a revealed religion; 6. The Resurrection story; and 7. The aims of Jesus and his disciples.

    Lessing secured permission to publish them only on the condition, imposed by Reimarus' family, that their actual authorship were not divulged. Cf. B. Brandl, *Die Überlieferung der Schutzschrift des Hermann Samuel Reimarus* (Pilsen, 1907). On the *Fragments* generally see Albert Schweitzer, *The Quest of the Historical Jesus: a Critical Study of its Progress from Reimarus to Wrede* (translated by W. Montgomery, London, 1906. New edn, with introduction by James M. Robinson, New York, 1968).
17. Cf. Karl Barth, *Protestant Theology in the Nineteenth Century* (translated by B. Cozens and J. Bowden, London, 1972) pp. 169–71.
18. See H. E. Allison, *Lessing and the Enlightenment* (Ann Arbor, Michigan, 1966).
19. This is the view which has usually been held, and it is a conclusion difficult to resist when Lessing's own statements are broadly assessed. See H. Chadwick (ed.), *Lessing's Theological Writings* (London, 1956), Introduction; also Barth, op. cit., pp. 234–65. Barth puts the question: 'Is it not a fact that Lessing's man is self-sufficient, and has no need of God in any event?' (p. 264). Yet Helmut Thielicke, in *Offenbarung, Vernunft, und Existenz: Studien zur Religionsphilosophie Lessings* (Gütersloh, 1957) sees him as a definite theist, and Otto Mann, in Lessing, *Sein und Leistung* (2nd edn, Hamburg, 1961), takes him for a believing Christian. Neither of these opinions is very easy to sustain.
20. *Über der Beweis des Geistes und der Kraft* ('Concerning the Demonstration of the Spirit and Power') (1777).
21. An English translation by F. W. Robertson was published in 1858.
22. Founded by Albert, Duke of Prussia, in 1544.
23. Knutzen was professor of logic and metaphysics at Königsberg, though he taught mathematics as well. His *Elements philosophiae rationalis* was published in 1747. See B. Erdmann, op. cit.
24. 'Of the teachers at the university of Königsberg, Knutzen alone represented the European concept of universal science' (Ernst Cassirer, *Kant's Life and Thought* (translated by J. Haden, with introduction by S. Körner) (New Haven and London, 1981) p. 25. He it was who introduced Kant to the works of Newton, and indeed it was Knutzen's breadth of intellectual outlook which influenced the pupil who was to revolutionize philosophical thinking.
25. Our main sources for the knowledge of Kant's childhood and youth are L. E. von Borowski, *Darstellung des Lebens und Charakter Immanuel Kants* (Königsberg, 1804) and R. B. Jachmann, *Immanuel Kant geschildert in Briefen an einer Freund* (Konigsberg, 1804).

26. Author of *Ansichten aus Immanuel Kants Leben* (Königsberg, 1805).
27. Quoted by F. Paulsen, *Immanuel Kant: his Life and Doctrine* (English translation, London, 1902) p. 28.
28. Cassirer, *Kant's Life and Thought*, p. 30.

CHAPTER 1: THE PRE-CRITICAL PERIOD

1. In 1764 Kant had been offered the chair of poetry in the university, but he declined it, as he did a like offer from Jena in 1769.
2. Throughout this book references to Kant's original text will be to the *Gesammelte Schriften*, edited by the Berlin Academy of Sciences, 1910–83. The *Allgemeine Naturgeschichte* is printed in vol. 1, pp. 215–368. Further references to the Berlin edition will appear as *GS*, with the appropriate volume and page numbers. For an English translation of the *Allgemeine Naturgeschichte* see W. Hastie, *Kant's Cosmogony* (Glasgow, 1900).
3. *GS*, 1, p. 306.
4. *GS*, 1, pp. 222f.; Hastie, op. cit., pp. 19f.
5. *GS*, 1, pp. 225f.; Hastie, pp. 23.
6. *GS*, 1, p. 228; Hastie, p. 26.
7. *GS*, 1, pp. 229f.: Hastie, pp. 28f.
8. *GS*, 2, pp. 63–163.
9. *GS*, 2, p. 163.
10. *GS*, 2, ibid.
11. *GS*, 2, p. 78.
12. Moses Mendelssohn (1729–86), with whom Kant was on very friendly terms, was a philosopher of the Leibniz–Wolff school whose main interests lay in the fields of aesthetics, psychology and religion. He was widely influential in the Germany of his day.
13. *GS*, 2, pp. 273–301.
14. *GS*, 2, p. 286.
15. *GS*, 2, p. 283.
16. *GS*, 2, pp. 299f.
17. Swedenborg (1688–1772), the original form of whose name was Swedberg, was a scientist as well as a mystical thinker. His 'spiritual' experiences began after 1743, and in this area of his thought his *Arcana coelestia* (in 8 vols) is his most important work. See C. O. Sigstedt, *The Swedenborg Epic: the Life and Works of Emanuel Swedenborg* (New York, 1952).
18. *GS*, 2, pp. 315–73. For further light on Kant's reaction to Swedenborg's assertions see his letter to Charlotte von Knoblock (1763) *GS*, 10, p. 40.
19. *GS*, 2, p. 329.
20. *GS*, 2, p. 342.
21. Sulzer's translation of Hume's *Enquiry concerning Human Understanding* appeared in 1755, and in the following year Kant was recom-

mending it to his classes. Presumably he had not read it in the English original.
22. *GS*, 2, pp. 315f.
23. *GS*, 10, p. 66.
24. *GS*, 2, pp. 385–419. An English translation is given in G. B. Kerferd and D. E. Walford (eds.), *Kant: Selected Pre-Critical Writings and Correspondence with Beck* (Manchester, 1968).
25. Geneva, 1768.
26. *GS*, 2, p. 400.
27. *GS*, 2, p. 403.
28. *GS*, 2, p. 392.
29. *GS*, 2, p. 396.
30. *GS*, 2, p. 395.
31. *GS*, 2, p. 411.

CHAPTER 2: THE SO-CALLED PROOFS OF DIVINE EXISTENCE

1. Printed at Halle, its publisher was Hartnoch of Riga.
2. E.g. that in the *Gelehrte Anzeiger of* Göttingen, 19 Jan. 1782, by Garve of Breslau (abbreviated and modified by J. G. Feder).
3. Kant himself was by no means unaware of the impression the book might create. 'The method of my discourse', he observes in a diary note, 'has a prejudicial countenance; it appears scholastic, hence pettifogging and arid, indeed crabbed and a far cry from the note of genius' (quoted Cassirer, op. cit., p. 140).
4. It is contained in vol. 4 of *GS*. There is an English version by P. Carus, revised by L. W. Beck (New York, 1950).
5. This second edition differs in some notable respects from the first. Thus the section on the 'Deduction of the Categories' was rearranged and re-written, a considerable part of the discussion on the 'Soul' was omitted, and the doctrine of substance and reality underwent modification. The first edition is usually referred to as *A*, the second as *B*. The former is printed in vol. 4 of *GS*, and latter in vol. 3. The English translation most commonly used is by Norman Kemp Smith (2nd edn, London, 1933), although that by J. M. D. Meiklejohn, with an introduction by A. D. Lindsay, in the Everyman Library (London: J. M. Dent) is also serviceable.
6. *A*, VIII.
7. *B*, XV.
8. *A*, XII.
9. *A*, XII (*GS*, 4,
10. By 'Transcendental Dialectic' Kant means, briefly, a criticism of understanding and reason as touching their claims to arrive at a knowledge of things in themselves (*Dingen-an-sich*) and supersensible reality. Cf. *B*, 88: *A*, 63–4.
11. *B*, 454–5, 462–3, 472–3, 480–1.
12. Kant's use of the term 'metaphysics' is not unambiguous, in that he

does not reserve it for speculative metaphysical thinking alone. It may also refer to the general body of philosophical knowledge attainable by the pure reason, and in this case the 'critical' philosophy, the aim of which is to investigate the capacities of reason in respect of *a priori* cognition, is essentially preliminary to metaphysics. On the other hand, the critical philosophy will itself form part of metaphysics in so far as the word is applied to all non-empirical philosophical knowledge. Moreover, although speculative metaphysics as an attempt to reach scientific knowledge of supersensible realities, is inadmissible on the principles of the critical philosophy Kant distinguishes what he can only regard as a mere pseudo-science and what he recognizes to be man's natural impulse towards metaphysical thinking, which in itself is not at all to be deplored. This spontaneous metaphysical curiosity has however to be met by other means than those of the theoretical reason.

13. *Méditations métaphysiques*, V.
14. B, 623.
15. It may be remarked that for Kant the very notion of 'an absolutely necessary yet unconditioned Being' is self-contradictory, inasmuch as the idea of necessity is inseparable from that of conditions, for without the latter there could be no necessity.
16. B, 626. GS, 3, p. 401.
17. B, 627. GS, 3, ibid.
18. We are not here concerned with estimating the force of Kant's objections to the ontological argument. Some would say that these are less telling when brought against the form of it adopted by St Anselm in his *Proslogion* (ch. ii). Indeed the argument continues to fascinate modern philosophers. Cf. J. Hick and A. C. M. McGill (eds.), *The Many-Faced Argument: Recent Studies in the Ontological Argument for the Existence of God* (London, 1967).
19. B, 632–3. GS, 3, p. 404.
20. B, 633.
21. B, 647.
22. B, 651. GS, 3, p. 415. The argument receives much fuller treatment in the *Critique of Judgment*.
23. B, 649–50. GS, 3, p. 414.
24. B, 655.
25. B, 657.
26. On Kant's *Vorlesungen über die Religionslehre* see below, ch. V, section 1.
27. B, 662.
28. B, 664.
29. B, XXX. GS, 3, p. 18.
30. B, 667.
31. *Prolegomena zu einer jeden künftigen Metaphysik*, GS, 4, pp. 350f.

CHAPTER 3: THE MORAL ARGUMENT

1. 'The ground of moral obligation', Kant tells us, 'must not be sought in the nature of man or in the circumstances in which he is placed but sought *a priori* solely in the concepts of pure reason' (*Grundlegung*, Preface (trans. Beck; see n. 2 below), p. 52; *GS*, 4, p. 389). Kant does not mean, of course, that an entire code of moral principles is to be deduced from the pure concept of moral obligation. He considered that to be impossible.
2. It is printed in vol. 4 of the *Gesammelte Schriften*. There are English translations by T. K. Abbott in *Kant's Critique of Practical Reason and Other Works on the Theory of Ethics* (London, 1873; 6th ed. (1909) reprinted photographically 1948); by J. H. Paton, *The Moral Law, or Kant's Groundwork of the Metaphysic of Morals* (London, 1948); and by L. W. Beck, in *The Critique of Practical Reason and Other Writings in Moral Philosophy* (Chicago, 1949).
3. Beck, op. cit., p. 54; *GS*, 4, p. 392.
4. Beck, p. 61; *GS*, 4, p. 400.
5. Beck, p. 62; *GS*, 4, p. 401.
6. Beck, p. 63; *GS*, 4, p. 402.
7. Beck, p. 97; *GS*, 4, p. 440.
8. See, e.g., H. B. Acton, *Kant's Moral Philosophy* (London, 1970), or B. Aune, *Kant's Theory of Morals* (Princeton, 1971).
9. See W. H. Walsh, *Hegelian Ethics* (London, 1969).
10. The passage occurs in the 'Conclusion' to the *Critique of Practical Reason*. 'Two things', Kant says, 'fill the mind with ever new and increasing admiration and awe, the oftener and more steadily they are reflected on: the starry heavens above me and the moral law within me. I do not merely conjecture them and seek them as though obscured in darkness or in the transcendent region beyond my horizon: I see them before me, and associate them directly with the consciousness of my own existence' (Beck, op. cit., p. 258; *GS*, 5, p. 161).
11. Beck, p. 225; *GS*, 5, p. 121.
12. Beck, p. 55; *GS*, 4, p. 393.
13. See below, p. 101.
14. We have here one of those points of resemblance between Kant and Luther which have been frequently remarked on. Kant's idea seems to parallel the Reformer's distinction between a believer's condition as both *justus in spe* and *peccator in re*.
15. The *Kritik der praktischen Vernunft* is contained in vol. 5 of the *Gesammelte Schriften*. For English translations see those of Abbott and Beck (note 2 above).
16. Kant defines happiness as 'the satisfaction of all our inclinations (*Neigungen*): extensively, as regards their multiplicity; intensively, as regards their degree; and progressively, as regards their duration' (*B*, 834).
17. Beck, p. 215; *GS*, 5, p. 110.

18. Kant is emphatic on this. 'All attempts', he states, 'to construct a theology through purely speculative reason, by means of a transcendental procedure, are without result'; also: 'Through concepts alone it is quite impossible to advance to the discovery of new objects and supernatural beings; and it is useless to appeal to experience, which in all cases yields only appearances' (*A*, 638; *B*, 666).
19. *B*, 670.
20. Beck, p. 103; *GS*, 4, p. 448.
21. Beck, p. 226; *GS*, 5, p. 122.
22. Beck, p. 228; *GS*, 5, p. 125.
23. Such, for example, was Schopenhauer's objection, made with his usual asperity: 'This in the last resort is nothing but morality aiming at happiness and therefore based on selfishness; this is the eudaemonism which Kant, with much fuss, has thrown out of the front door of his system, as being heteronomous, and which now sneaks back again through the back door under the name of the highest good' (*Grundlage der Moral*, ed. A. Hübscher [Leipzig 1938], p. 124.
24. *B*, xxix.
25. *A*, 811; *B*, 839.
26. Cf., e.g., J. H. Newman, *An Essay in Aid of a Grammar of Assent* (London, 1870) and A. E. Taylor, *The Faith of a Moralist* (London, 1930). See also H. P. Owen, *The Moral Argument for Christian Theism* (London, 1965).
27. Something very like Kant's argument, if given this latter interpretation, was propounded by R. B. Braithwaite in his Arthur Stanley Eddington Memorial Lecture at Cambridge in 1955. Thus he says: 'Just as the meaning of a moral assertion is given by its use in expressing the asserter's intention to act, so far as in him lies, in accordance with the moral principle involved, so the meaning of a religious assertion is given by its use in expressing the asserter's intention to follow a specified form of behaviour' (*An Empiricist's View of the Nature of Religious Belief* [Cambridge, 1955]), pp. 15f.
28. Beck, pp. 229f.; *GS*, 5, pp. 126f.
29. Beck, p. 231; *GS*, 5, p. 128.
30. Beck, p. 245; *GS*, 5, p. 143.
31. Beck, p. 226; *GS*, 5, p. 12, 2.
32. Beck, pp. 226f.; *GS*, pp. 122f.
33. Cf. C. D. Broad, *Five Types of Ethical Theory* (London, 1930) p. 140.
34. See n. 23 above.

CHAPTER 4: TELEOLOGY

1. It is printed in vol. 5 of the Berlin Academy edition. There are English translations by J. H. Bernard (London, 1931; re-printed New York, 1951 and 1974) and J. C. Meredith (Oxford, 1921). Citations here are from the latter.

References and Notes to pp. 69–81   197

2. Meredith, First Part ('Critique of Aesthetic Judgment'), p. 14; GS, 5, p. 205.
3. Meredith, p. 18; GS, 5, p. 207.
4. Meredith, pp. 50f.; GS, 5, p. 211.
5. Meredith, Second Part ('Critique of Teleological Judgment'), pp. 22f.; GS, 5, pp. 374f.
6. Meredith, p. 38; GS, 5, p. 388.
7. GS, 8, p. 169.
8. Meredith, p. 100; GS, 5, p. 436.
9. Meredith, p. 52; GS, 5, p. 399.
10. Meredith, p. 53; GS, 5, pp. 399f.

CHAPTER 5: RATIONAL THEOLOGY REVIEWED, AND THE QUESTION OF THEODICY

1 See K. Vorländer, *Immanuel Kants Leben* (Leipzig, 1911) p. 212. On Kant's earlier theological lectures cf. the same author's *Immanuel Kant: der Mann und das Werk* (Leipzig, 1924) 2, pp. 10–15.
2. Vol. 28, 2:2.
3. There is an English translation of the lectures by Allen W. Wood and Gertrude M. Clark (Ithaca, 1970). See also Wood's *Kant's Rational Theology* (Ithaca, 1975).
4. R. B. Jachmann, *Immanuel Kant* (Königsberg, 1804) pp. 29f.
5. The idea of the *ens perfectissimum* is equivalent to that of the *ens realissimum*, a being not to be thought of, however, as the mere juxtaposition of *specific* – and often mutually incompatible – perfections. It is rightly conceived of as the unity of unlimited, pure perfections in one simple and supreme Being. This at any rate Kant portrays as the transcendental Ideal of pure reason.
6. Wood and Clark, *Kant's Lectures on Philosophical Theology* (Ithaca) p. 39; GS, 28:2,2, p. 1010.
7. Wood and Clark, p. 30; GS, 28:2,2, p. 1002.
8. Wood and Clark, p. 79; GS, 28:2,2, p. 1046.
9. Wood and Clark, p. 80; GS, 28:2,2, p. 1046. Cf. Wood and Clark, pp. 90f.
10. Wood and Clark, p. 123; GS, 28:2,2, pp. 1083f.
11. *Biographia Literaria* (ed. Shawcross) (London, 1907) i, pp. 135f.
12. As evidently is done by Allen W. Wood in *Kant's Rational Theology*, who goes so far as to claim that the argument is 'entirely compatible with the principles of the critical philosophy, and accomplishes an important part of Kant's task in the Dialectic of the *Critique of Pure Reason*' (p. 149). On the contrary, Kant's essential notion of belief in God must be so understood as to exclude the possibility that our cognition of things divine is theoretical.
13. The text may be found in vol. 8 of the *Gesammelte Schriften*, pp. 253–71.
14. GS, 8, pp. 255f.
15. GS, 8, pp. 265f.

16. See the 'Vorrede' to *Der Streit der Facult*äten, *GS*, 7, p. 316.
17. The first edition had been reprinted at Frankfurt and Leipzig, as too was the second.

CHAPTER 6: THE RADICAL EVIL IN HUMAN NATURE

1. *A*, 805; *B*, 833.
2. *GS*, 11, p. 429.
3. Meredith, p. 7; *GS*, 5, p. 170.
4. *Religion within the Limits of Reason Alone*, by Immanuel Kant, translated, with introduction and notes, by Theodore M. Greene and Hoyt H. Hudson (Illinois, 1934), Harper Torchbook (New York) reprint, 1960, p. 11 (*GS*, 6, p. 12). In references to it this translation will be cited as GH.
5. Cf. *Reflexionen*, nos 4291 (*GS*, 17, p. 498), 4865 (*GS*, 18, p. 14), 4887 (*GS*, 18, p. 20) and 5675 (*GS*, 18, p. 325).
6. Kant is not concerned with religion as a universal phenomenon of human cultural life, and such a work as Hume's *Natural History of Religion* has very little in common with his, which suggests on the part of its author a purpose very different from that of his German contemporary. In his 'Introduction' Hume states that in regard to religion there are 'two questions in particular which challenge our attention, to wit, that concerning its foundation in reason, and that concerning its origin in human nature'. The first question, he thinks, is easily answered. 'No rational enquirer', he informs us, 'can, after serious reflection, suspend his belief a moment with regard to the primary principles of genuine Theism and Religion'. The other however, which is the subject of Hume's little treatise, is more difficult to investigate. But the answer he gives in his ensuing pages – that it is largely from the emotions of hope and fear that religion takes its rise – does little to strengthen the reader's confidence in the philosopher's assurance, that 'the whole frame of nature bespeaks an intelligent author. See *David Hume, The Natural History of Religion*, edited with an introduction by H. E. Root (London, 1956) p. 21.
7. *GH*, pp. 4f.; *GS*, 6, p. 5.
8. *GH*, p. 9; *GS*, 6, p. 10.
9. C. C. J. Webb, *Kant's Philosophy of Religion* (Oxford, 1926) p. 92.
10. I John 5:19.
11. From his *First Principles of Government* (1768), cited by J. B. Bury, *The Idea of Progress* (London, 1920) p. 221.
12. See pp. 99f below.
13. *Protestant Theology in the Nineteenth Century* (English trans., London, 1972) p. 292.
14. See his *Idea of a Universal History in a Cosmopolitan Interest* (1784) and *Towards Perpetual Peace* (1795).
15. *GS*, 8, p. 18.
16. Quoted Webb, op. cit., p. 96.

17. Beck, op. cit., p. 347.
18. *GH*, p. 16; *GS*, 6, p. 20.
19. Were man wholly evil his nature would be not human but devilish, incapable of choosing the good. Rather is he *perverted* away from the good which was his in his original state or disposition. Thus Kant speaks of man's *Bösartigkeit*, his wickedness, more than his *Bosheit*, by which he would seem to have understood an essential malignancy of nature. Man's wickedness is in his corruption (*Verderbtheit*) or perversion of heart (*Verkehrheit des Herzens*).
20. *GH*, p. 24; *GS*, 6, p. 29.
21. *GH*, p. 35; *GS*, 6, p. 40.
22. *GH*, p. 38; *GS*, 6, p. 43.
23. *GH*, p. 37: *GS*, 6, p. 42.
24. Horace, *Satires*, I, 1.
25. Kant quotes the Latin version: *in quo omnes peccaverunt*, not the original Greek, which yields a somewhat different meaning.
26. Beck, p. 103.
27. *Goethes Briefe* (Hamburg ed, 1964) 2, pp. 165f.
28. *Sämmtliche Werke* (ed. B. Suphan, Berlin, 1880) 20, p. 130; also pp. 220 and 222.
29. *Schillers Briefe* (ed. F. Jonas, Berlin, 1893) 3, p. 289 (Letter to Gottfried Körner, 28 Feb. 1793).
30. *GH*, p. 40; *GS*, 6, p. 45.
31. *GH*, pp. 42f; *GS*, 6, p. 47.
32. *GH*, p. 44; *GS*, 6, p. 49.
33. Cf., for example, Romans 6:1–6; Galatians 3:1–10; Colossians 3:1.
34. *GH*, p. 42; *GS*, 6, p. 46. 'The restoration of the original incentive to good in us', says Kant, 'is not the acquiring of a lost incentive for good, for the incentive which consists in respect for the moral law we have never been able to lose, and were such a thing possible, we could never get it again' (ibid.).
35. Cf. *Reflexionen*, no. 7312 (*GS*, 19, p. 309).
36. *Reflexionen*, no. 4842 (*GS*, 17, p. 744).
37. *GH*, p. 43; *GS*, 6, pp. 47f.
38. *GH*, p. 62; *GS*, 6, p. 68.
39. *GH*, p. 62: *GS*, 6, pp. 68f.
40. Weimar ed., 56, p. 269.
41. *GH*, p. 40; *GS*, 6, p. 44.
42. *GH*, p. 47; *GS*, 6, p. 52.
43. Printed in vol. 7 of the *Gesammelte Schriften*, pp. 1–116.
44. *GS*, 7, p. 36.
45. *GS*, 7, pp. 40f.
46. *GS*, 7, p. 52.
47. *GS*, 7, p. 43.
48. Beck, op. cit., p. 231.

CHAPTER 7: GOOD AND EVIL IN CONFLICT

1. *GH*, pp. 52f; *GS*, 6, pp. 59f.
2. John 1.3.
3. *GH*, pp. 55; *GS*, 6, p. 61.
4. Although Kant uses the term *incarnation* what he means by it is a good deal less than what the Christian dogma connotes. Rather is it that the 'Son of God' illustrates an ideal which primarily has to be sought not elsewhere than within ourselves, in human hearts and consciences. The living embodiment of the ideal, that is, is not itself the ideal; he simply exemplifies it in his teaching and good works. Hence Kant's account of Christ leans either to docetism – that the divine ideal was not really made flesh – or to Arianism – that its human embodiment was not really the ideal in its divine fulness.
5. John 8.46.
6. *GH*, p. 62; *GS*, 6, p. 68.
7. *GH*, p. 65; *GS*, 6, pp. 70f.
8. St Anselm (c. 1033–1109), archbishop of Canterbury, propounded in his *Cur Deus Homo* a view of the atonement which interpreted the doctrine as meaning that sin, being an infinite offence against God, required a satisfaction likewise infinite, and inasmuch as no finite being, human or angelic, could offer such satisfaction, it was necessary that an infinite being – God himself, no less – should take man's place and by his death render the complete satisfaction demanded by divine justice. By making the death of Christ signify a debt paid to God it superseded the older theory of its being a ransom paid to the devil.
9. *GH*, pp. 68f.; *GS*, 6, pp. 74f.
10. *GH*, p. 71; *GS*, 6, p. 76.
11. In an amusing footnote Kant refers to the story of a French Jesuit missionary to the Iroquois Indians of Canada, Père Charlevoix (1682–1761), of whom he had read in a book of travel. The worthy priest was teaching from the catechism about all the evil that the wicked spirit had brought into the world, which at the first had been good, and how thereafter he persistently sought to frustrate the best of God's designs, when his pupil quite understandably asked why God had not struck the devil dead there and then. The learned Jesuit had candidly to admit that, for the moment, he was lost for an answer. (*GH*, p. 73; *GS*, 6, p. 79).
12. *GH*, p. 74; *GS*, 6, p. 80.
13. John 14.30.
14. *GH*, p. 77; *GS*, 6, p. 82.
15. John 1.11–12.
16. Titus 2. 14.
17. *GH*, p. 78; *GS*, 6, p. 83.
18. Ibid.
19. *GH*, p. 81; *GS*, 6, p. 86.
20. Hume's definition (*An Enquiry concerning Human Understanding,*

Section X, 'Of Miracles'), that 'a miracle is a violation of the laws of nature', is decidedly more negative; but he adds in a note that 'accurately defined', it is 'a transgression of a law of nature by a particular volition of the Deity, or by the interposition of some invisible agent'. Hume's aim is clearly polemical. As the laws of nature have been established, he says, by 'a firm and unalterable experience', 'the proof against a miracle, from the very nature of the fact, is as entire as any argument from experience can possibly be imagined' (l. A. Selby-Bigge, *Hume's Enquiries* (2nd edn, Oxford, 1902, pp. 114f.).
21. *GH*, p. 81; *GS*, 6, pp. 86f.
22. *GS*, 19, pp. 617–23.
23. *GS*, 18, pp. 320–22.
24. Stäudlin actually suggested that he and Kant should collaborate in a theological work on Kantian lines, a proposal that Kant declined, although he did dedicate his *Streit der Facultäten* to him. Reuss, a professor at Göttingen, was both a Catholic and a convinced Kantian (see a letter of 1 Apr. 1796. *GS*, 12, pp. 68f.), who sought to pass on his own enthusiasm to philosophically-minded fellow-Catholics.

CHAPTER 8: THE VICTORY OF GOOD OVER EVIL

1. *GH*, p. 85; *GS*, 6, p. 94.
2. It is only here, in the third Book of *Religion within the Limits of Reason Alone*, that Kant first presents his idea of an 'ethical commonwealth', but the concept had already been anticipated in his theory of history – notably in his essay *Idee zu einer allgemeinen Geschichte in weltbürgerlicher Absicht* ('Idea towards a Universal History in a Cosmopolitan Interest') (*GS*, 8, pp. 15–31), published in 1784 – and in his moral philosophy. In the former he shows himself, whilst dubious of individual moral capability, cautiously optimistic as to the future of society, despite his pessimism in regard to the influence its members have on each other. Indeed, if advance at the empirical level is to be secured it will be on the part of the race, not the individual. But he considers that progress, if by no means inevitable, is reasonably to be expected, the goal of human development being for him, not happiness, as with so many Enlightenment thinkers, but perfect obedience to the moral law. Thus towards the end of the *Critique of Pure Reason*, in the section called 'The Canon of Reason', he states that the idea of a moral world has objective reality 'as a *corpus mysticum* of the rational beings in it, so far as the free will of each being is, under moral laws, in complete systematic unity with itself and with the freedom of every other' (*B*, 836), while in the *Fundamental Principles of the Metaphysic of Morals* he defines a 'kingdom' of ends' as 'the union of different rational beings in a system of common laws', and in the *Critique of Practical Reason* says that Christian morality represents a world 'wherein reasonable beings single-mindedly devote themselves to the moral law', a 'kingdom of

God, in which nature and morality come into a harmony, which is foreign to each as such, through a holy Author of the world, who makes possible the highest derived good'.
3. GH, p. 87; GS, 6, p. 96.
4. Near the end of his life Kant is said, in conversation, to have declared that 'there is nothing good in men. Each of them all but hates his neighbour, seeks to set himself above those who surround him, and is full of envy, ill-will and other devilish vices. *Homo hominis nicht deus, sondern diabolus*' (J. G. Hasse, *Letzte Aüsserungen Kants von einem Tischgenossen*, Königsberg, 1804, p. 28; quoted J.-L. Bruch, *La philosophie religieuse de Kant* [Paris, 1968] p. 159.
5. GH, p. 88; GS, 6, p. 96.
6. It is fair to point out that Hobbes himself observes that 'the Nature of War consisteth not in actual fighting but in the known disposition thereto during all the Time there is no Assurance to the contrary' (Leviathan, 1, ch. 3).
7. GH, p. 89; GS, 6, p. 97.
8. GH, p. 91; GS, 6, p. 99.
9. Titus 2.14.
10. Acts 5.29.
11. The sixteenth-century Reformers were in the main concerned to distinguish firmly in principle between the church visible and the church invisible. The latter, in Luther's view, was the company of all who possess the gift of faith, and he held that this 'true Church' of faith, 'without spot or wrinkle', could not receive visible and tangible embodiment: *abscondita est ecclesia, latent sancti* – 'the Church is concealed, the saints hidden'. For Calvin the true church was *universus numerus electorum* – 'the entire number of the elect' (*Institutes*, IV, 7); but he in no way minimized the importance of the visible institution, stressing it indeed in a manner that Luther did not.
12. The characteristic marks (*notae*) of the church are those first listed in the so-called Nicene Creed in the fifth century, namely, one, holy catholic and apostolic. As a topic of theological discussion, however, they did not figure prominently until the Reformation era, when Roman Catholic theologians appealed to them in their disputes with the Reformers as to how the true church – as distinct from bodies spuriously claiming ecclesial status – was to be recognized. See G. Thils, *Les Notes de l'Eglise dans l'apologétique catholique depuis la Réforme* (Gembloux, 1937). For the Lutherans the essential marks of a church were the preaching of the gospel and due administration of the sacraments of baptism and the Lord's Supper. Cf. Article XIX of the Church of England's Thirty-Nine Articles.
13. GH, p. 93; GS, 6, p. 103.
14. GH, p. 94; GS, 6, p. 103.
15. GH, p. 95; GS, 6, p. 104.
16. Mt. 7.21.
17. GH, p. 96; GS, 6, p. 106.
18. GH, p. 98; GS, 6, p. 107.
19. GH, pp. 985ff.; GS, 6, pp. 107ff.

20. *GH*, p. 102; *GS*, 6, p. 111.
21. Cf. John 7.17.
22. *GH*, p. 105; *GS*, 6, p. 115.
23. *GH*, p. 110; *GS*, 6, p. 119.
24. *GH*, p. 112; *GS*, 6, p. 122.
25. Mt. 12.28.
26. *GH*, p. 113; *GS*, 6, p. 122.
27. *GH*, p. 116; *GS*, 6, p. 125.
28. *GH*, p. 119; *GS*, 6, p. 128.
29. *GH*, p. 121; *GS*, 6, p. 130.
30. *GH*, pp. 121f.; *GS*, 6, pp. 130f. The quotation is from Lucretius, *De rerum naturae*, I, 101: 'Such evil could religion give rise to!'.
31. *GH*, p. 122; *GS*, pp. 131ff.
32. *GH*, p. 123; *GS*, 6, p. 133.
33. Hegel also entertained the same idea. cf. *Philosophy of Religion*, trans. E. B. Speirs and J. B. Saunders (London, 1875), ii, pp. 14f.
34. *GH*, p. 132; *GS*, 6, p. 141.
35. *GH*, p. 133; *GS*, 6, p. 142.
36. *GH*, p. 134; *GS*, 6, p. 143.
37. These Kant took from the Wolffian philosopher J. A. Eberhard's *Vorbereitung zur natürlicher Theologie*, published at Halle in 1781, in which the will of God is represented as active in a threefold manner, corresponding to his goodness, his holiness and his justice. See *GS*, 18, pp. 491f.
38. Livre xi, ch. 6.
39. *Reflexion* no. 6307 comprises a further statement of Kant's understanding of the trinity. It runs as follows: 'Of God as first cause of the world. The ideal of humanity in its entire perfection in his first-born Son, the reflection (*Abglanz*) of his Lordship in whom and through whom all things were made. That is why the Son is called the originating Word (the Ground of becoming). It is in him alone that God loves the world, and it is in relation to him alone that the creator of the world is also called the Father of men, in his Son as his ectype. In order to bring man into full accord with this ideal of the Son, the Holy Spirit is from all eternity in him. In order to approximate the defective creature to the deal of the Son, he unites him with the most holy Will in making good the defect from his own righteousness. He is the judge in us, who brings before us the holy law; he judges in accordance with it, but he also supplements the deficiency of our righteousness by the ideal of humanity as soon as we have begun to bring ourselves nearer to him. And he draws us nearer to himself and to his blessedness in an uninterrupted and infinite progress' (*GS*, 18, pp. 598f.).

It may be remarked that Kant's interpretation of the trinitarian doctrine on the analogy of the diverse powers of the civil government tends itself to the anthropomorphism which he rightly deprecates. In Christian theology the divine functions and powers are united in a single Being, not dispersed among the 'Persons'. That Kant was himself aware of this is clear from a comment of his

elsewhere (*Reflexion* no. 7971 [*GS*, 19, p. 567]: 'The three persons can be united only in the divinity, inasmuch as the latter contains at once all perfections within itself.' cf. *Reflexionen* nos. 6092 and 6094 (*GS*, 18, pp. 449, 450).
40. The Greek is not κρινεῖ, but ἐλέγξει, which Luther translated not by *richten* but by *strafen*.

CHAPTER 9: INSTITUTIONALISM IN RELIGION

1. *GH*, p. 141; *GS*, 6, p. 153.
2. *GH*, p. 148; *GS*, 6, p. 160.
3. *GH*, p. 152; *GS*, 6, p. 164.
4. *GH*, p. 153; *GS*, 6, p. 166.
5. *GH*, p. 156; *GS*, 6, p. 168.
6. *GH*, p. 158; *GS*, 6, p. 170.
7. *GH*, p. 164; *GS*, 6, p. 176.
8. *GH*, p. 171; *GS*, 6. p. 183.
9. *GH*, p. 174; *GS*, 6, p. 186.
10. *GH*, p. 179; *GS*, 6, p. 191.
11. *GH*, p. 182; *GS*, 6, p. 194.
12. It is at this point that Kant makes his well-known observation about a good man who, being taken unawares while praying aloud, or at least acting in a manner indicative of prayer, could be expected to be seized with confusion and embarrassment as though discovered in a situation of which he should be ashamed – likely, that is, to be suspected of 'a slight attack of madness' (*GH*, p. 183; *GS*, 6, p. 195).
13. *GH*, p. 183; *GS*, 6, p. 195.
14. *GH*, p. 188; *GS*, 6, p. 200.

CHAPTER 10: LAST THOUGHTS ON PHILOSOPHY OF RELIGION

1. See above, p. 00.
2. By Reutter & Reichard of Berlin, under the title: *Kants Opus Postumum, dargestellt und beurleitelt*, although sections of it had been printed nearly forty years earlier in the *Altpreussische Monatsschrift* (1882–84). The work itself comprises volumes 21 (1936) and 22 (1938) of the Berlin Academy edition (edn by A. Buchenau and G. Lehmann). For a short account of the *Opus Postumum* see N. Kemp Smith, *A Commentary on Kant's 'Critique of Pure Reason'* (2nd edn, London, 1923) Appendix C.

   In June 1794 Kant published an article in the *Berliner Monatsschrift* entitled *Das Ende aller Dinge* ('The End of All Things') dealing with the subject of the last judgment and the life everlasting (*GS*, 8 (1923), pp. 325–39). The purpose of the essay is to draw attention to the conceptual difficulties involved in the idea of eternal life, starting with the consideration that eternity is not to be thought of as simply a continuation of time but as its complete transcendence. Human life has perforce to be conceived of under the form and conditions of time, which cannot be transposed into the eternal order. The idea is then taken up that a certain quality of life here and now may be described as 'eternal', since virtue, which pertains to the 'noumenal' man, is unaltered either in time or in eternity. However, this notion is a purely speculative or transcendental one which reason cannot demonstrate, any more than it can prove the truth of other beliefs about the life after death which may be cited from religious teachings current in all ages and among many different peoples. Some of these Kant refers to here, as also to a number of passages in the Apocalypse, for which he offers his own rationalizing interpretation. But given the doctrine that there will eventually be an end of all things the question occurs whether the world is likely in the meantime to deteriorate morally or whether progress may be hoped for. Kant's response is, not uncharacteristically, pessimistic, since faith in the power of virtue as a force for good appears to be less potent than fear of the conditions which the 'end' would bring about. The article concludes with some reflections on what contribution Christianity might make to future betterment. Here the author shows a greater confidence, believing that the Christian religion has the power not only to strengthen the motives of duty but further to enhance them by those of love. Love cannot indeed ever be a substitute for duty, although men being what they are it can bring to them an added incentive for good. But love, it must be understood, is never to be constrained, and were the Christian church to try to impose it by the exercize of coercive authority it would act in denial of its own true nature and cast aside its greatest asset – an observation prompted, we may suspect, by Kant's own recent brush with the censorship. The essay concludes by saying that if this were to come to pass the religion which was designed to become universal would then no longer be thus favoured by destiny. Rather would we witness from the moral point of view a preposterous (*verkehrte*) 'end of all things' (GS, 8, p. 339).

3. Adickes dates the twelve main sections of it as having been begun not later than 1797. Work on it continued until 1803.
4. Adickes, op. cit., p. 609.
5. Op. Cit., p. 846.
6. Kant had received an advance copy, possibly in the previous year, which still survives and bears his marginal notes.
7. Adickes, op. cit., p. 819.
8. GS, 21, p. 19.
9. Cf. Adickes, pp. 775, 776.
10. GS, 21, p. 17.
11. *Kant's Philosophy of Religion*, p. 183.
12. GS, 22, p. 62.
13. GS, 21, pp. 32f.

14. *GS*, 21, pp. 27.
15. Adickes, op. cit., p. 798.
16. Adickes, op. cit., p. 847.
17. 'Wir schauen Ihn an gleich als in einem Spiegel: nie vom Angesicht zu Angesicht' (*GS*, 21, p. 33).
18. Cf. Adickes, p. 802.
19. Adickes, p. 808.
20. Adickes, p. 820.
21. The phrase, 'To see all things in God', is in fact used, not by Spinoza, but by his Catholic contemporary Nicolas Malebranche (1638–1715), a disciple of Descartes and author of *Recherche de la vérité* (1674). According to his philosophy, known as ontologism, God is the immediate cause of all knowledge and the 'place of our ideas'. Thus 'to see all things in God' implies a particular theory of sense-perception, which is not what Kant had in mind. As Adickes points out (p. 762), the latter was probably recollecting Spinoza's *res sub aeternitatis specie contemplari*.
22. *GS*, 21, p. 15.
23. Ibid., p. 15.
24. Adickes, p. 824.
25. Adickes, pp. 824f.
26. Cf. *GS*, 22, p. 64.
27. *GS*, 22, p. 104. Cf. Adickes, p. 826.
28. *GS*, 22, p. 109.
29. *GS*, 22, p. 62.
30. *GS*, 22, p. 113.
31. Cf. *GS*, 22, p. 111.
32. Cf. Adickes, p. 808.
33. Webb, op. cit., p. 192.
34. See p. 00.
35. Adickes, p. 846.
36. The German translation by J. F. Kreutker of Anquetil du Perron's version (with comments) of the Zend-Avesta, published in 1771, had appeared in 1776 (2nd edn, 1786) under the title *Zend-Avesta, Zoroaster's lebendige Wort*.
37. One title he envisaged was: *Zoroaster, das Ideal der physisch und zugleich moralisch praktischen Vernunft in Einem Sinnen-Objekt vereinigt*.
38. The case against Adickes's interpretation was cogently put by G. Schrader, 'Kant's Presumed Repudiation of the "Moral Argument" in the *Opus Postumum*', in *Philosophy*, 26 (1951) pp. 228–41. As Schrader says, 'to assume that in the last three or four years of his life Kant had lost his distaste for subjectivity and was willing to base religion upon subjective experience', while not impossible, is highly improbable. To maintain the contrary is an unnecessary construction on anything the *Opus Postumum* actually states.

CHAPTER 11: CONCLUSION

1. *B*, 664; *A*, 636 (Kemp Smith's trans.).
2. To speak of Kant as 'the philosopher of Protestantism' is mistaken. His outlook had but little in common with Luther's, and much more closely resembled that of Erasmus. To the orthodox Protestant 'our willing acknowledgment of the right and its claim upon us really does not convince us that by this very fact we are one with God; on the contrary, it convicts us of a deep inward antagonism to God, and our complete inability, as of ourselves, to keep His "law"' (H. R. Mackintosh, *Types of Modern Theology*, London, 1937, p. 24).
3. *GS*, 8, pp. 107–23.
4. Cf. *The Philosophy of Religion*, trans. E. B. Speirs and J. B. Sanderson (London, 1895) 1, pp. 175ff.
5. The spirit of Kant's own approach to history is plain enough from the introductory section of his 'Idea of a Universal History from a Cosmopolitan Point of View'. One cannot avoid', he says, 'a certain feeling of disgust when one observes the actions of man displayed on the great stage of the world. Wisdom is manifested by individuals here and there; but the web of human history as a whole appears to be woven from folly and childish vanity; often, too, from puerile wickedness and love of destruction; with the result that at the end one is puzzled to know what idea to form of our species which prides itself so much on its advantages' (*GS*, 8, pp. 17f.).
6. Otto's *Das Heilige* was first published in 1917. An English translation, *The Idea of the Holy*, appeared in 1923. The book emphasizes the part played by the 'numinous' – a word coined by the author – to denote factors of a non-rational and non-moral kind – sheer awe and self-abasement, for example, as well as fascinated wonder (*mysterium tremendum et fascinans*) – in what is expressed in religion as 'holy'.
7. *Perspectives on 19th and 20th Century Protestant Theology* (London, 1967), p. 64.
8. F. D. E. Schleiermacher's *Über die Religion. Reden an die Gebildeten unter ihren Verächten* (*Speeches on Religion, to the Cultured among its Despisers*) was first published in 1799. A second, revised edition came out in 1806. The essence of religion, its author maintained, is to be sought neither in dogma nor in ethics, but in man's deepest feeling (*Gefühl*) or intuition. 'True religion', he declared, 'is sense and taste for the infinite.' In his *The Christian Faith* (1821–22) he states that religious doctrines are but attempts to express in words the content of religious feeling. Their basis is 'the immediate description of the religious dispositions themselves'.

    J. G. Herder's *Von Religion und Lehrmeinungen* appeared two years before Schleiermacher's *Reden* and did something to prepare the way for it.
9. Author of, among other works, *Zensur des christliche protestantische Lehrbegriffs* (3 vols, 1791–95) and *Die Religion der Mündiger* (2 vols, 1799–1800).

10. *The Limits of Religious Thought Examined* (1859).
11. Hamilton was much influenced by the teaching of Thomas Reid, but also by Kant's, although it is questionable how far he was personally familiar with Kant's writings. His *Lectures on Metaphysics and Logic* were published posthumously (1859–61).
12. *The Limits of Religious Thought Examined*, p. 10.
13. Op. cit., pp. xivf.
14. *Rechtfertigung und Versöhnung* (1870–74). An English trans. of the third volume was brought out in 1900.
15. Leonhard Staehlin, in *Kant, Lotze and Rischl* (E. T. and D. W. Simon, Edinburgh, 1889), contended that because Ritschl's theory of knowledge was essentially Kantian his theology was incompatible with orthodoxy, which in his view required a metaphysical basis (cf. p. 284). Otto Pfleiderer, *The Development of Theology in Germany since Kant and its Progress in Great Britain since 1825* (London, 1890) describes Ritschl's epistemology as 'eclectically derived' from Kant and Lotze, and dismisses it as 'a dilettante confusion' convincing only to amateurs (p. 183). The Scottish theologian James Orr (*The Ritschlian Theology and the Evangelical Faith* [London, 1897] denied that Ritschl really got his epistemology from Lotze, arguing that it was in fact purely Kantian (p. 237).
16. *Justification and Reconciliation*, p. 194.
17. Op. cit., p. 199.
18. Op. cit., p. 205.
19. See *Theologie und Metaphysik* (1881), a polemical essay in which Ritschl attempts to clarify his philosophical opinions. There is an English trans. by Philip Hefner in *Albrecht Ritschl: Three Essays* (Philadelphia, 1972, pp. 151–212). Ritschl was convinced that theology needs an epistemology. 'Each theologian is under necessity as a scientific man to proceed according to a definite theory of knowledge, of which he must be conscious and the legitimacy of which he must prove' (*Theologie und Metaphysik*, 2nd edn, 1887, p. 60).
20. An explanation of Ritschl's views on this subject was provided by his son Otto in the latter's *Über Werthurtheile* (1895), pp. 9–12).

    The Danish philosopher Harold Höffding (1843–1931), who was also concerned with the concept of value, maintained that a distinction must be made, in the order of knowledge, between *explanation* and *evaluation*. It is the part of science to explain particular events in the natural process, although the point of finality in its so doing is never actually reached. Religion therefore cannot offer a 'causal' explanation of its own that would in any way complete or supplement the function of science. However, the purpose of religion, so Höffding contends, is to evaluate life, and he declares that 'the conservation of value is the characteristic axiom of religion' (*The Philosophy of Religion* [E.T. by B. E. Meyer, London, 1931] p. 10).
21. This is particularly evident in his *Geschichte des Pietismus* (1880–86). Ritschl, like Kant, had little regard for the place of emotion in religion and had no appreciation of mysticism.
22. *Justification and Reconciliation*, p. 443.

23. Op. cit., p. 527.
24. Another Scottish theologian, James Denney, put the matter succinctly when he remarked of the Ritschlian Christology: 'Though Jesus has for the Christian consciousness the common real value of man, He is in truth and reality, to the neutral consideration of science, mere man like any other; it is only in the *Werthurtheil*, the subjective estimate of the pious character, that gives him the nature of God' (*Studies in Theology* [London, 1894], p. 14).
25. *Das Wesen der christlichen Religion* (1881) p. 102. Kaftan became professor of the philosophy of religion at Berlin in 1883. He died in 1926.
26. Op. cit., p. 49.
27. See *Das Wesen des Christentums* (1900). E.T. by T. B. Saunders, *What is Christianity?* 1901).
28. See Sabatier's *Esquisse d'une Philosophie de religion* (Paris, 1897).
29. Ménégoz, *Publications diverses sur le fidéisme et son application* (Paris, 1900) 1, p. 251.
30. *A Theology for the Social Gospel* (New York, 1917) p. 139.

Select Bibliography

Acton, H. B., *Kant's Moral Philosophy* (London, 1970).
Barth, Karl, *Protestant Theology in the Nineteenth Century* (E.T. by B. Cozens, J. Bowden et al., London, 1972) pp. 266–312.
Beck, L. W., *A Commentary on Kant's 'Critique of Practical Reason'* (Chicago, 1960).
Bohatec, J., *Die Religionsphilosophie Kants in der 'Religion innerhalb der Grenzen der blossen Vernunft'* (Hildersheim, 1966).
Bruch, J.-I., *La Philosophie religieuse de Kant* (Paris, 1968).
Bruford, W. H., *Germany in the Eighteenth Century* (Cambridge, 1933).
Cassirer, Ernst, *Kant's Life and Thought* (E.T. by J. Holden, Yale, 1981).
Copleston, F., *Wolff to Kant* (*A History of Philosophy*), 7 (London, 1960).
England, F. E., *Kant's Conception of God* (London, 1929).
Fackenheim, E. L., 'Immanuel Kant', in *Nineteenth Century Religious Thought in the West* (ed. N. Smart and others, Cambridge, England, 1985), 1, pp. 17–40.
Körner, S., *Kant* (Harmondsworth, London, 1955).
Michalson, G. E., *The Historical Dimensions of a Rational Faith: the Role of History in Kant's Religious Thought* (Washington, 1977).
Millar, M. E., *The Moral Law and the Highest Good* (Melbourne, 1928).
Paton, H. J., *The Categorical Imperative: a Study of Kant's Moral Philosophy* (London, 1946).
Raschke, C. A., *Moral Action, God and History in the Thought of Immanuel Kant* (Montana: American Academy of Religion, 1975).
Schweitzer, Albert, *Die Religionsphilosophie Kants in der Kritik der reinen Vernunft bis zum Religion innerhalb der Grenzen der blossen Vernunft* (Freiburg, 1899).
Smith, N. Kemp, *A Commentary on Kant's 'Critique of Pure Reason'* (2nd edn, London, 1923; repr. 1979).
Thom, M. (ed.), *Kants Schriften zur Religion* (Union VLG, Berlin, 1981).
Vorländer, Karl (ed.), *Kant: Die Religion innerhalb der Grenzen der blossen Vernunft* (with introduction by H. Noack) (Hamburg, 1966).
—, *Kant's Criticism of Metaphysics* (Edinburgh, 1975).
Walsh, W. H., 'Kant's Moral Theology' (*Proceedings of the British Academy*, 49 (1963) pp. 263–2.
Webb, C. C. J., *Kant's Philosophy of Religion* (Oxford, 1926).
Wood, A. W., *Kant's Moral Religion* (Ithaca, 1970).
—, *Kant's Rational Theology* (Ithaca, 1978).
Wundt, M., *Kant als Metaphysiker* (Stuttgart, 1924).
Zeldin, M. B., 'The *summum bonum*, the moral law, and the existence of God', *Kantstudien*, 62 (1971) pp. 43–54.

Index

Adickes, E., 157, 164, 205
aesthetic judgment, 70
Afterdienst ('pseudo-service' of God), 146, 149–51
Anselm, St, 31, 194, 200
anthropomorphism, 149, 157
antinomies, 42
art, 70f.
atonement, the, 115f, 135–7, 142f, 172, 200
Aufklärung, 1, 4, 8, 14; see also Enlightenment
Augustine, St, 79, 152, 170
autonomy (of the will), 52, 187

Baptism, 154, 155
Barth, K., 94
Baumgarten, A. G., 13, 76, 78
Baumgarten, S. J., 9
Bengel, J. A., 8
Bonhoeffer, D., 187
bonum perfectissimum, 54
Braithwaite, R. B., 196

Calvinism, 96, 175, 202
categorical imperative, 52, 55, 58f, 161, 162, 185
categories (of the understanding), 42
Charlevoix, Père, 200
Chillingworth, W., 8, 188
Christ, *see* incarnation
Christianity, historic, Kant's attitude towards, 90f, 139, 147–9
church, the, 126–8, 129–32, 140, 145, 173, 175, 202f
as visible and invisible, 127, 131, 145
notes (or marks) of, 127, 202f
churchgoing, 154, 155
Clarke, S., 190
clericalism (*Pfaffenthum*), 145, 150, 156, 173
Coleridge, S. T., 79
collegia pietatis, 5
Collegium Fridericianum, 19
Collins, A., 9
communion, holy, 155f
conscience, 151–3
conversion, 53, 101–9, 171f

cosmological argument, 31f, 45g
D'Alembert, J., 3, 22
deism, English, 9, 13, 14, 17, 189f
Denney, J., 209
Descartes, R., 43, 62, 79, 194
Dingen-an-sich ('things-in-themselves'), 49, 61
duty (defined), 51

Election, 143
Enlightenment, principles of the, 1–4, 5, 94, 100, 120, 169, 170, 174; see also *Aufklärung*
ens perfectissimum, 43, 197
ens realissimum, 44, 45, 77, 197
ens summum, 159
Ernesti, J. A., 8
eternal life, 204f
ethical commonwealth, 123–6, 127, 137, 173, 175
ethical principles, Kant's, 49–53
ethical 'state of nature', 124
evil, as human choice, 98f, 170
in conflict with good, 110–19
not in man's animal nature as such, 111
personified in the devil, 117, 118, 119
radical (*das radicale Böse*), 88, 91f, 93–100, 105

Faith, saving, 134, 139
fall of man, the, 95, 99
fanaticism (*Schwärmerei*), 119, 127, 134, 150, 164, 173
'fetishism', 150, 154
Fichte, J. G., 158
Francke, A. H., 6f
Frederick William II, 80, 82f
Freedom, as a postulate of the practical reason, 56, 57f

Gibbon, E., 3
God, as a postulate of the practical reason, 56, 59, 61–4, 75, 165
concept of, 159–66, 172
Goethe, J. W. von, 100
grace, divine, 102, 106, 108f, 115, 153–6

Hamilton, Sir W., 180, 208
Harnack, A. von, 186
Hegel, G. W. F., 53, 171, 175
Herbert of Cherbury, Lord, 9, 189
Herder, J. G., 100, 175, 207
Hinduism, 151
history, Kant's attitude to, 174f
Hobbes, T., 125, 202
Höffding, H., 208
holiness, 58f, 65f, 109, 113, 126f, 176
Hume, D., 4, 34, 48, 51, 90, 198, 200f

Illuminism, 127, 133f
immortality, as a postulate of the practical reason, 56f, 65–7, 172
incarnation, the, 112f, 136f, 139, 172, 200

Jesus, teaching of, 147, 155, 172, 186
Judaism, 138
justification by faith, 7, 102, 103, 108

Kaftan, J., 185, 209
Kant, Immanuel
early years, 18–23
influence on religious thought, 178–87
WRITINGS
Das Ende alle Dinge ('The End of All Things') (1794), 204f
de mundi sensibilis et intelligibilis forma et principiis (1770), 35–9
Der Streit der Facultäten ('The Controversy between the Faculties'), (1798), 106f, 109, 157
Die Religion innerhalb der Grenzen der blossen Vernunft ('Religion within the Limits of Reason Alon'), (1793), 81–3, chs 6–9 *passim*, 168, 171, 178
Grundlegung zur Metaphysik der Sitten ('Fundamental Principles of the Metaphysic of Morals'), (1785–6), 51, 88, 99, 201
Idee zu einer allgemeinen Geschichte in weltbürgerlicher Absicht ('Idea towards a Universal History in a Cosmopolitan Interest'), (1784), 198, 201, 207
Kritik der praktischen Vernunft ('Critique of Practical Reason'), 54, 68, ch. 3 *passim*, 162, 163, 195, 201f

Kritik der reinen Vernunft ('Critique of Pure Reason'), (1781; 2nd edn, 1787), 40f, 68, 87, 161, 162, 167, 201
Kritik der Urteilskraft ('Critique of Judgment'), (1790), 68–75, 88
Metaphysische Anfangsgründe der Naturwissenschaft ('Metaphysical First Principles of Natural Science'), (1786), 54
Mutmasslicher Anfang der Menschengeschichte ('Probable Beginnings of Human History'), (1786), 170f
Opus Postumum, (1797–1803), 157–66, 204
Prolegomena zu einer jeden künftigen Metaphysik ('Prolegomena to any Future Metaphysic'), (1783), 40
Träume eines Geistersehers erläutert durch Träume der Metaphysik ('Dreams of a Ghost-seer explained by Dreams of Metaphysics'), (1764), 32f
Über das Misslingen aller philosophischen Versuche in der Theodicee ('On the Miscarriage of all Philosophical Attempts at Theodicy'), (1791), 79
Über den Gebrauch teleologischer Principien in der Philosophie ('On the Use of Teleological Principles in Philosophy'), (1788), 73
Vorlesungen über die Religionslehre ('Lectures on Philosophical Theology') (posthumous), 76–9, 94, 197
'Kingdom of God', 134–7, 140, 145
Knutzen, M., 17f, 29, 191
Königsberg, university of, 16f, 20, 21

Lange, J., 13
Lehmann, G., 76
Leibniz, G. W., 9, 11, 12, 35, 36, 38, 43, 79f, 90
Lessing, G. E., 13, 14–16, 169
Lichtenberg,, G. C., 159
Locke, J., 3, 9
Löscher, V. E., 13
Lotze, H., 182, 183, 208
Lutheranism, 5, 8, 53, 79, 103, 105, 169, 170, 171, 173, 202

Index

Malebranche, N., 206
Mansel, H. L., 180f
Maurice, F. D., 181
maxims, 96, 101
mechanism and teleology, antinomy of, 73f
Mencken, G., 16
Mendelssohn, M., 32, 192
Ménégoz, E., 186
metaphysics, validity of, 33–9, 41, 47, 66f, 193f
Michaelis, J. D., 8
Mil, J. S., 181
miracles, 120–2, 154, 200f
Mohammedanism, 151, 154
moral ideal as heaven-sent, 111f, 172
'moral theology', 47, 62–5, 90, 92f, 141, 167f
Müller, H., 188
'mysteries' in religion, 140f, 142f, 154, 176

Natural (or rational) theology, 42f, 47f, 76–9, 90, 146
Newman, J. H., 153
Newtonianism, 27, 28, 35

Ontological proof, 31, 32, 43–5
Orr, J., 208
Otto, R., 176, 207

Parerga of reason, 106, 107f, 120–2, 140–4, 153f
Pfaffenthum, see clericalism
Pia Desideria (Spener), 5
pietism, 4–7, 16–18, 188
Pöllitz, K. H. L., 76
postulates of the practical reason, 55–60, 153, 154f, 175
prayer, 149, 204
Priestly, J., 94
probabilism, 152
Protestantism, liberal, 174
punishment, eternal, 114

Rationalism, 8–18, 188–91
Rauschenbusch, W., 186f
reason, speculative and practical contrasted, 47f, 60f, 68f, 196
Reimarus, H. S., 13f, 191
religion and morality, 43, 168f, 176f
Reuss, M., 122, 201
revelation, 107, 129, 130, 133, 146, 152, 169

Rink, F. T., 20, 76
Ritschl, A., 181–3, 208
Rousseau, J. J., 90, 96

Sabatier, A., 186
Sacraments, see baptism; communion, holy; 'mysteries' in religion
salvation, as exclusively moral, 119
Schelling, F. W. J. von, 177
Schiller, J. C. F., 95, 100
Schleiermacher, F. D. E., 160, 176, 178, 207
Schopenhauer, A., 66, 196
Schultz, F. A., 17, 19, 20
scripture, 130, 132–4, 138, 140
Semler, J. S., 13f, 175
sin, original, 94, 98; see also evil, radical
'Son of God', see incarnation
Spener, P. J., 5f
Spinoza, B. de, 159, 165, 206
Spirit, Holy, 143f, 172
'statutory religion', 145f, 148, 149, 173f
Stäudlin, C. F., 87, 122, 201
Stoics, 110f
superstition (*Aberglaube*), 119, 127
summum bonum, *supremum bonum*, 54, 58, 62, 63, 65, 67, 92, 159, 169
Swedenborg, I., 33f, 192
symbolism in religion, 175, 186

Teleological argument, 28–30, 31f, 46f
teleology, 31, ch. 4 *passim*
Theologische Bedenken (Spener), 6
Thomasius, C., 6
Tieftrunk, H., 179f
Tillich, P., 178, 186
Tillotson, J., 8, 188f
Tindal, M., 190
Toland, J., 9, 189
'Transcendental Dialectic', 42, 193
transcendental Ideas (or regulative principles), 46, 56, 70, 72f
trinity, doctrine of, 90, 142, 143f, 172f, 203f

Understanding (*Verstand*) contrasted with judgment (*Urteilskraft*), 69f

Value-judgments, 182f, 185f, 208, 209
Virgin Birth, 118
virtue and happiness, union of, 54f, 59
Voltaire, 4, 9, 80

Wesley, J., 8, 188
Wolff, C., 9–12, 13, 43, 62
Wolfenbüttel Fragments
    (Reimarus-Lessing), 13
Wöllner, J., 80f

worship, divine, 129

Zedlitz, von, 88
Zinzendorf, N. von, 7, 188
Zoroaster, 165, 206